PLANNING IN A FAILING STATE

Reforming Spatial Governance in England

Edited by
Olivier Sykes and John Sturzaker

P

First published in Great Britain in 2024 by

Policy Press, an imprint of
Bristol University Press
University of Bristol
1–9 Old Park Hill
Bristol
BS2 8BB
UK
t: +44 (0)117 374 6645
e: bup-info@bristol.ac.uk

Details of international sales and distribution partners are available at policy.bristoluniversitypress.co.uk

© Bristol University Press 2024

British Library Cataloguing in Publication Data
A catalogue record for this book is available from the British Library

ISBN 978-1-4473-6504-4 hardcover
ISBN 978-1-4473-6506-8 ePub
ISBN 978-1-4473-6507-5 ePdf

The right of Olivier Sykes and John Sturzaker to be identified as editors of this work has been
asserted by them in accordance with the Copyright, Designs and Patents Act 1988.

Cover design: Robin Hawes
Front cover image: Alamy/Edward Moss
Bristol University Press and Policy Press use environmentally responsible print partners.
Printed and bound in Great Britain by CPI Group (UK) Ltd, Croydon, CR0 4YY

FSC
www.fsc.org
MIX
Paper | Supporting
responsible forestry
FSC® C013604

For Will Brady, who knew that planning doesn't have to fail and when it doesn't it can make all our lives better.

Contents

List of figures and tables

Figures

Tables

Notes on contributors

Chia-Lin Chen is Lecturer in the Department of Geography and Planning at the University of Liverpool, with a research interest in exploring territorial development questions through the lens of transport and mobility. Her recent publications include *Improving Interchanges: Toward Better Multimodal Railway Hubs in the People's Republic of China* (ADB, 2015), *Handbook on Transport and Urban Transformation in China* (Edward Elgar, 2020), a special issue of *Built Environment* on 'Impacts of high-speed rail: hub, linkage and development' (2020) and *High-Speed Rail Cities and Regions: Spatial Implications and Planning Criteria* (Routledge, 2021).

Richard Cowell is Professor of Environmental Planning at the School of Geography and Planning, Cardiff University. His research focuses on the relationship between land-use planning and sustainability, with particular interest in the environmental dimensions of planning reforms and the role of planning in shaping sustainable energy transitions. His work also examines how shifts in governance scale can recast the dynamics of planning/environment problems, including devolution in the British state and Brexit. Richard's recent work has begun to explore how environmental and climate-change targets intersect with planning.

Sebastian Dembski is Senior Lecturer in the Department of Geography and Planning at the University of Liverpool. His work concentrates on urban transformation processes and land policy instruments, often from a comparative perspective. Sebastian is currently working on an Economic and Social Research Council-funded project on suburban densification and has recently completed a project for the Scottish Land Commission on 'Housing land allocation, assembly and delivery: lessons from Europe'. He guest-edited a special issue of *Town Planning Review* on 'Urban densification' (2020) and coordinated a study into reurbanisation and the urban periphery in North-west Europe in *Progress in Planning* (2021).

Richard J. Dunning is Professor of Land Economy and Housing at the University of Liverpool. His research focuses on planning for housing need, affordability and development. Richard uses behavioural economics to explain human decision making in the built environment, and his work has been funded by national governments, local authorities, charities and research councils. His research has been instrumental in defining affordable housing subsidies in Scotland and land-value capture mechanisms in England. He is the joint-editor-in-chief of *Housing & Society* and was previously the vice chair of the Housing Studies Association.

Thomas B. Fischer is Professor at the University of Liverpool. He has over 30 years of experience in spatial, transport and environmental policy and planning, strategic environmental assessment, environmental impact assessment, health impact assessment and other types of impact assessment internationally. Thomas has worked in the public and private sectors, and is one of the most widely published authors on environmental and health assessments globally. He is the director of the Environmental Assessment and Management Research Centre and head of the World Health Organization Collaborating Centre on Health in Impact Assessments at Liverpool.

Urmila Jha Thakur is Senior Lecturer in the Department of Geography and Planning at the University of Liverpool. Her work focuses primarily on planning and the management of environmental sustainability, as well as exploring ways for making policies, plans, programmes and project developments more environmentally sustainable. Her research and publications have addressed environmental assessment at both project and strategic levels, exploring such issues as health, climate change, education, green infrastructure and learning. Urmila's research also looks into environmental sustainability within the business and urban context. She takes a special interest in developing and emerging economies, with strong research links with South Asia.

Alex Lord is Lever Chair of Town and Regional Planning in the Department of Geography and Planning at the University of Liverpool. He works on the economic effects of urban and environmental planning and has conducted research for a wide range of funders, including an Economic and Social Research Council 'Urban Transformations' award on the behavioural economics of real-estate markets. Alex has also conducted research for the Royal Town Planning Institute on the potential value of planning as a formal animator of development, as well as leading the consortium that completed 'Valuing planning obligations 2016/17' for the Ministry of Housing, Communities and Local Government.

Manuela Madeddu is Senior Lecturer in urban design at the University of Liverpool. She has previously worked at London South Bank University and the Politecnico di Torino, and has practised as an architect and urban designer in Italy and the UK. Her research focuses on cultures of design and regulation, bringing together perspectives from architecture, urban design and urban planning; recent projects have looked comparatively at housing quality in Italy and the UK, and explored the impacts of Feng Shui on Chinese built environments.

Tom Moore is Senior Lecturer in planning at the University of Liverpool. His research focuses on housing policy and practice, and community planning, with particular interests in forms of community-led housing and enterprise. Tom is co-editor-in-chief of the journal *Housing & Society* and has previously held editorial positions with the *International Journal of Housing Policy*.

Alexander Nurse is Senior Lecturer in urban planning at the University of Liverpool, with research and teaching interests in sub-national governance, particularly at the city and city-regional scales. He has undertaken funded research for the UK Prevention Research Partnership and Engineering and Physical Sciences Research Council. He has published widely on the topic of English city/city-regional devolution, including the Northern Powerhouse and levelling up. Along with John Sturzaker, he authored *Rescaling Urban Governance: Planning, Localism and Institutional Change* (Policy Press, 2020).

Phil O'Brien is Lecturer in real estate and housing economics at the University of Glasgow. His research is mainly concerned with the relationship between state and market in land development, encompassing land-value capture, public-goods provision and the economic role of land-use planning. Phil has undertaken research for such funding bodies as the Economic and Social Research Council, the Joseph Rowntree Foundation, the Royal Institution of Chartered Surveyors and the Royal Town Planning Institute. Phil has published on comparative investigations into alternative modes of land-use planning and land development across Europe, as well as on the use of spatial concepts in city and regional planning and economic development.

Mark Smith is a social scientist and urban planner working as a research associate in the Department of Geography and Planning at the University of Liverpool. He specialises in the integration and implementation of policies, plans and programmes, including the development and deployment of planning policy instruments, and maintains an academic interest in knowledge utilisation and transfer in public policy production processes.

John Sturzaker is Ebenezer Howard Professor of Planning at the University of Hertfordshire. He has had a varied career as a planner in both practice and research. His teaching and research interests include community planning, planning and housing, and sustainable urban development. In recent years, he has closely followed the localism agenda in the UK and its implementation, with a particular focus on neighbourhood planning. Along with Alexander Nurse, he co-authored *Rescaling Urban Governance: Planning, Localism and Institutional Change* (Policy Press, 2020).

Olivier Sykes has researched, published and taught extensively across the fields of European spatial planning, international planning studies and comparative urban policy and regeneration. He is currently the leader of the planning discipline at the University of Liverpool and has held visiting fellowships and professorships at a number of other institutions. Olivier is the editor-in-chief of the *Transactions of the Association of European Schools of Planning and Policy* and viewpoints editor of the *Town Planning Review*. He has worked on a range of research projects for the European Union, national, regional and local governments, and professional bodies.

Acknowledgements

We would like to thank all those who have directly assisted us with writing this book, including an anonymous reviewer who had the thankless task of reading the entire draft manuscript and made wholly positive and helpful comments.

We have been grateful for the help and support of many colleagues and friends who have helped and supported us over many years in the work this book draws on. These are too many to name, but we would like to specifically mention Sue Kidd, who was a valued collaborator to us all and a colleague to most of us before she retired in 2020.

Finally, and most importantly, our thanks go to our families for their enduring support.

Introduction

Olivier Sykes and John Sturzaker

Introduction

This book aims to contribute to reflection on the current state of planning on the island of Britain. More specifically, it brings together a collection of chapters from experts in different fields of planning to provide a review of the past decade or so of reforms of, and debates about, the planning system in England. The initial prompt for the book was the publication in 2020 of a White Paper, *Planning for the Future* (MHCLG, 2020). This was one of a series of governmental statements of intent and reform proposals for planning that have peppered the period since 2010. Since 2020, both the debate and governmental personnel have moved on. In 2022, the *Levelling Up White Paper* and the subsequent Levelling-up and Regeneration Bill were published as steps towards the enactment of the planning reform agenda. England has seen the departure of three secretaries of state with responsibility for planning – though one was subsequently reinstated – and the latest rebranding of the 'home' ministry for planning, which has changed from the Ministry of Housing, Communities & Local Government (MHCLG) to the Department for Levelling Up, Housing and Communities (DLUHC). Between the first draft of this book being submitted in August 2022 and its publication, the UK has also had three prime ministers. The reflections in the book and proposals for planning reform have taken place against this background of wider political churn and policy flux. As well as reflecting on planning reform and performance since 2010, the authors have therefore been asked to consider how far the planning proposals in the Levelling-up and Regeneration Bill differ from those that were floated in the Planning White Paper of 2020, and whether and to what extent, if applied, the proposals in the Levelling-up and Regeneration Bill might result in a change in current planning practices and outcomes.

The title of the book, *Planning in a Failing State*, uses the different meanings and usages of the term and noun 'state' as a means of framing its reflections on 'the state of *planning*' and 'the *state* planning is in'. The word 'state' can refer to 'a condition or way of being that exists at a particular time'.[1] This can relate not only to the physical world, where elements may be in solid, liquid or gaseous states, but also to human affairs and society, which is the sense in which it is used here. One question that the contributions to the book explore is therefore the *state* of planning, in the sense of its 'condition', in relation to the different domains of planning addressed by each chapter. In more simple language, the question might be expressed as: how is planning 'getting on' with addressing the issues and delivering sought-after policy goals in the domains of planning covered? Is it helping, for example, to deliver sufficient housing, improved environmental outcomes, adequate public involvement in planning processes, good-quality design, certainty for citizens and developers, and adequate infrastructure? Or, conversely, is it failing to deliver positive outcomes or even exacerbating the situation, and thus arguably in a condition, or 'state', of failure?

Another common definition of 'state' refers to 'a country or its government' or 'a politically organized community usually occupying a definite territory' (Allen, 2001). This kind of 'state' definition is the focus of political and public policy debates, and is explored by the work of political scientists, sociologists, planners and political geographers, among others. There is a whole body of 'state theory' that explores different state forms and how states evolve and change through history (Sturzaker and Nurse, 2020), and there is also a strong tradition in planning scholarship stretching back to the 1970s of situating planning within the political economy of different state forms. In the present book, this second connotation of 'state' is used to pose the question: what kind of state does planning in England find itself in?

The two meanings of 'state' outlined earlier have been used to frame previous reflections on state and society in Britain. Perhaps one of the most well known of these is Will Hutton's (1995) *The State We're In*, published in the 1990s on the eve of the first Blair government. This reflected on the state of Britain at the time in the sense of its 'condition' and the state/condition of the British state as a political entity charged with its governance. More recently, the veteran broadcaster Jon Snow (2023) has titled his reflection on privilege, politics and inequality in the UK *The State of Us: The Good News and the Bad News about Our Society*. The present book similarly deploys the different meanings of the word 'state' as a way of reflecting on the current condition of planning, with a particular focus on the outcomes of the planning reforms that have periodically punctuated the 'long 2010s' since the Conservative–Liberal Democrat Coalition government took power in the UK in 2010.

The book's title also hints at the fact that, over recent decades, rhetoric from across the political spectrum has often represented planning as failing and blamed it for a range of societal problems, including insufficient homes being built, the poor design of those homes that are constructed, slow economic development and bureaucratic processes that are unresponsive to public input and wishes. The book's title seeks to respond to this narrative and queries whether any shortcomings or dissatisfaction with planning might be caused less by the failures of planning and the planning profession than by ineffective and inconsistent government policies. What if the constant tinkering and attempts to 'fix' real and perceived issues with planning actually exacerbate the challenges it faces, for example, through austerity and budget cuts that strip out capacity from the planning system, a focus on minutiae and process rather than substantive issues, or measures to deregulate certain kinds of development so that it no longer comes within the purview of planning control? Alongside considering how planning is performing in the different areas they review (its 'state/condition'), authors have also therefore been asked to reflect on how this performance has been, and might be, affected by centrally (UK state) determined policy choices and extant and proposed reforms.

The rest of this chapter, first, provides an account of how a narrative of planning as 'failing to deliver' has been constructed over recent decades. Second, the chapter turns to the question of whether many of the issues that the planning system and profession have had to contend with may, in fact, reflect central state 'failings', for example, endless and accelerating cycles of reform, policy churn and tinkering by governments that have rarely allowed one set of planning reforms to bed down before new policy reforms and initiatives have been launched. Finally, the contents and structure of the rest of the book are outlined.

Constructing the narrative of planning failure

Critiques of planning and planners are not new and pre-date the rise in the scapegoating of planning for various socio-economic and environmental ills since the 1970s by neo- and social-liberal critics and concepts. Commentators and observers of the evolution of 'town and country' on the island of Britain as diverse as John Betjeman, Ian Nairn or Joe Strummer have had words to say about the role of planning and local government in either failing to prevent undesirable change in urban and rural landscapes, or actively fostering it (Tewdwr-Jones, 2011). The mass housing clearances of the post-war decades across cities and city regions in England, for example, were critiqued by progressive planners, urban sociologists, journalists, playwrights, novelists and filmmakers, who documented the effects of uprooting communities. Although the intention to alleviate urban conditions may have been good, the results were sometimes disappointing. Planners and planning academics too have long engaged in self-reflection and critique of the activity, goals and practice of planning. The latter provides a valuable intellectual heritage for the profession and contributes to planning education and iterative professional practice in the model of Schön's (1983) 'reflective practitioner'. Informed by the experience of planning in the decades of the mid-20th century, practice reforms sought to address such issues as the need to facilitate more public consultation around planning decisions, develop planning frameworks better able to manage dynamic change in built and natural environments, and strengthen the preservation of areas and buildings of architectural or historic interest.

The most trenchant critiques of the very notion, value and legitimacy of planning itself have, however, arisen since the end of the post-Second World War social-democratic consensus, usually dated to the mid-1970s. The rise and growing influence of (neo)liberal views of state and society, as well as neoclassical economics, fuelled various episodes of attempted deregulation of planning under different UK governments (Allmendinger and Haughton, 2013; Waterhout et al, 2013).

The intellectual basis of Thatcherism was rooted in texts extolling the virtues of a return to 'classical', more liberal social and economic structures, as reflected in its ambition to 'roll back the state'. As Monbiot (2016) observes, neoliberal thought 'maintains that "the market" delivers benefits that could never be achieved by planning'. Under the first Thatcher government from 1979, planning was often painted as a regulatory hindrance to entrepreneurial activity. In a statement that became famous (at least among planners), Secretary of State for the Environment Michael Heseltine (1979: 27) thus referred to 'jobs locked away in the filing trays of planning departments'. An agenda of 'streamlining' planning was pursued as part of a wider 'rolling back of the state', and in Government Circular 22/80, it was made clear that the planning system 'should play a helpful part in re-building the economy' and that 'Development control must avoid placing unjustified obstacles in the way of any development especially if it is for industry, commerce, housing or any other purpose relevant to the economic regeneration of the country' (quoted in Taylor, 1998: 138). The imperative of economic growth thus implied a 'market-supportive' role for planning.

The title of a government White Paper from 1985, *Lifting the Burden*, seemed to sum up government thinking. It demoted the role of development plans in decision making in favour of 'other material considerations', such as the need to create employment. Far from speeding up the decision-making process, however, this encouraged developers to appeal against the refusal of planning permission by local planning authorities, leading to a period of 'appeal-led' planning that placed a severe strain on the Planning Inspectorate. This provides an example of how problems in planning ('planning failure') can arise as a consequence of a – frequently ideologically inspired – centrally defined change to how the planning system operates (central 'state failure'). Another example from this time was the way in which ideologically fraught relationships between central and local levels of government impacted on planning. Partly in response to such contestation and conflict, the Local Government Act 1986 abolished Metropolitan County Councils, which brought an end to metropolitan structure planning in England (Stead and Nadin, 2014: 198), creating a strategic vacuum in planning at the 'larger than local' scale that continues to be an issue of debate to this day (see Chapters 4 and 10).

The years around the end of the 1980s and start of the 1990s also reflected the impacts of a 'tiller left, tiller right' approach to planning from central government, as a number of factors coalesced to rehabilitate planning. The end of the 1980s saw a major property recession that dealt a blow to property- and project-led urban regeneration, growing environmental concern and international commitments, the rise of the sustainability agenda, and growing anti-development pressure from the 'conservative', as opposed to 'liberal', business interests who supported the Conservative Party. Many 'traditional', small-'c' Conservative voters in rural areas, outer suburbs and smaller towns were not very keen on the excessively radical deregulation of planning if this meant development that might bring significant change to the places in which they lived and their own amenity and perceived rural 'way of life'. With the government having only a small parliamentary majority after the 1992 general election, the views of this group of Conservative voters carried greater weight, prefiguring the impacts of the shifting loyalties of this constituency of Conservative support in tempering the radicalism of the proposals for planning reform floated in 2020 (Allegretti, 2021).

Influenced by this context, the early 1990s saw a shift back towards a more 'plan-led' planning system, with the primacy of the development plan in decision making being restored through a new planning act in 1991. There was also the production of a suite of national planning policy guidance notes (PPGs), which not only underlined the importance attached by government to planning but also gave it significant centralised control over local planning decisions. The strong 'presumption in favour of development' was retained in many of these documents (for example, PPG1 on the general principles of the planning system), but there was also a growing emphasis on sustainability often driven by the influence of European Union (EU) legislation (Stead and Nadin, 2014: 201; see also Chapter 8).

The New Labour years (1997–2010) saw a generally more positive stance towards planning, but government rhetoric that the planning system needed to change to become more efficient and a more effective enabler of development continued. Key documents about 'modernising' planning (for example, the *Planning: Delivering a Fundamental Change* Green Paper [DTLR, 2001]), the process of planning reform and reflection in the 2000s, and government-commissioned reviews that supported this (notably, the 'Barker Reviews' [Barker, 2004, 2006] on housing and land-use planning) were infused with the assumption that the relationship of planning with economic development was problematic.

In introducing the Planning Green Paper of 2001, the then secretary of state for transport, local government and the regions thus claimed:

> some fifty years after it was first put in place, the planning system is showing its age. What was once an innovative emphasis on consultation has now become a set of inflexible, legalistic and bureaucratic procedures. A system that was intended to promote development now blocks it. Business complains that the speed of decision is undermining productivity and competitiveness. People feel they are not sufficiently involved in decisions that affect their lives. (Byers, 2001)[2]

When major reform of planning legislation was enacted under the Planning and Compulsory Purchase Act 2004, it drew on an evaluation and interpretation of planning that echoed critiques from the more avowedly neoliberal governments that preceded and followed the 'New Labour' era. Development plans were seen as being too lengthy and detailed, and as taking too long to produce. There was again the view from parts of the government machine that planning was acting as a brake on economic development. The 2004 act and accompanying changes to planning policy introduced a number of changes designed to address these purported issues. There were subtle shifts like the rebranding of development control as development management, as well as other changes to respond to some of the issues noted in the previous quote, such as an enhanced emphasis on community engagement in planning.

The policy documents and legislation enacted by the New Labour governments thus emphasised the need for planning and planners to adopt a more proactive 'spatial planning approach' and incorporate a consideration and coordination of different public (and private) activities with an influence on the functioning and making of places (see ODPM, 2005: 13). Planners themselves were also encouraged to embrace a 'culture change' to make the new planning system work (Stead and Nadin, 2014; Lord and Tewdwr-Jones, 2014).

In opposition between 1997 and 2010, the Conservatives continued to portray planning as bureaucratic, undemocratic and a brake on business. They notably argued that the regional planning system was unaccountable, undemocratic and 'top-down' in nature, depriving local communities of an effective say over development in their areas – ideas that were presented in a policy Green Paper for planning preceding the 2010 general election (Conservative Party, 2010). It was no surprise that the post-2010 Coalition, with the Conservatives as the senior partner, introduced an immediate shift in the emphasis of planning and placed 'streamlining' firmly back on the agenda. References to integrative spatial planning all but vanished from government documents, and regional-level planning was soon abolished, as the key message became one of localism and the decentralisation of decision making. In Greater London, the London Plan survived, but to 'replace formal regional planning' in other parts of England, the government introduced a 'duty to cooperate' between neighbouring authorities (Winter et al, 2016: 8).

Reforms to promote competitiveness spanned 'a range of policies, including improving the UK's infrastructure, cutting red tape, root and branch reform of the planning system and boosting trade and inward investment' (HM Treasury and BIS, 2013: 1). The reform process since 2010 was thus once again marked by the recurring view that planning can be a restriction on economic growth, competitiveness and wealth creation. For example, a government document published in 2011 stated: 'Planning is acting as a serious brake on growth, slowing the delivery of much needed new jobs and new business' (DCLG, 2011). Reflecting this view, the changes to planning introduced after 2010 were justified through strongly articulated criticisms of the planning system and the invocation of the narrative of planning failure, which presented a 'broken planning system' as one symptom of the 'Broken Britain' that Conservative Party rhetoric claimed was the legacy of the New Labour years. This was expressed, for example, through claims that planning was stifling economic development, responsible for very low rates of house building and operating in a centralised, top-down and bureaucratic way (the latter criticism of regional planning being heard particularly in South East England and London). There were strong echoes of the 1980s in these criticisms of planning, as well as some of the solutions proposed to improve it, such as enterprise zones, with simplified planning arrangements and more 'freedom from planning control', which would, it was claimed, 'benefit growth'.[3]

The Localism Act 2011 formalised the removal of regional spatial planning and introduced 'neighbourhood planning' at a scale below that of local planning authorities. While not all such changes were necessarily negative and, as in every wave of reform, needed time to bed down for their outcomes to be evaluated, the general narrative of planning failure was certainly on the front foot again. Surveying the contemporary planning scene in one of his final articles, Peter Hall (2014) thus noted:

> Planning has become the villain, held responsible for an accelerating housing shortage, powerless to stop bad development. It appears to have lost the capacity to plan good urban places, and is supine in the face of proposals for low-grade development backed by repeated appeals. Planning and planners have thus steadily become residualised, returning to their marginal status in 1914: we have been borne back ceaselessly into the past.

Planning in England in the 2010s therefore experienced one of its frequent episodes of rescaling and flux. Growth and competitiveness objectives associated with a critique of planning's alleged impacts on economic growth and rates of house building became leitmotifs of the arguments justifying reform. The *National Planning Policy Framework* (NPPF) (DCLG, 2012), adopted following the Localism Act, replaced all previous government planning guidance for England, providing a more concise version of national planning policy compared to the extensive collection of documents that comprised the former series of PPGs and planning policy statements (PPSs).

In the Foreword to the NPPF, then Minister for Planning Greg Clark stated that, 'In part, people have been put off from getting involved because planning policy itself has become so elaborate and forbidding – the preserve of specialists, rather than people in communities' – adding that 'This National Planning Policy Framework changes that. By replacing over a thousand pages of national policy with around fifty, written simply and clearly, we are allowing people and communities back into planning' (DCLG, 2012: i). However, to accompany the NPPF, in 2014, the government introduced a suite of additional policy guidelines titled 'Planning Practice Guidance', which provides more information and the view of the secretary of state on how the NPPF's policies should be 'used in practice' (Winter et al, 2016: 6, 15).

Following the election of a majority Conservative government in 2015, the cycle of reform continued against a background of further austerity and cuts to local government budgets. In July 2015, the government published the *Fixing the Foundations: Creating a More Prosperous Nation* report, which stated that England's 'excessively strict planning system can prevent land and other resources from being used efficiently' (HM Treasury, 2015: 43) and this was one reason why 'The UK has been incapable of building enough homes to keep up with growing demand' (HM Treasury, 2015: 11). One of the proposals floated in this document was the introduction of 'a new zonal system which will effectively give automatic permission on suitable brownfield sites' (HM Treasury, 2015: 11), an idea that was to become a theme in proposals for planning reform over the next half-decade (see Chapter 7).

In 2016, a new Housing and Planning Bill was proposed, which was presented as being necessary to stimulate rates of house building and included provisions for intervention by the secretary of state in the production of local plans where local authorities were judged to be too slow and the creation of permission in principle for housing on brownfield land (Smith, 2016: 4). Permitted development rights allowing offices to change to residential use, in some circumstances, without the need for planning permission also became permanent (Smith, 2016: 4).

The centrality of housing supply as a theme justifying planning reform continued, though the Housing White Paper of 2017 marked a subtle shift in how responsibility (or blame) was apportioned for the housing crisis. As we saw earlier, since the 1970s, in keeping with neoliberal views of state, society and economy, blame for the undersupply of housing had often been laid at the door of an overly regulatory, bureaucratic and slow land-use planning system. The argument was that too many rules and regulations were slowing down the development process and that this was limiting the supply of new homes and hindering the proper functioning of the housing market.

Yet, as researchers and planning associations constantly sought to point out, there were, in fact, far more extant 'consents' (approved planning permissions) in the system at any one time than were being 'built out' by private developers. The Housing White Paper of 2017 provided a rather belated acknowledgement of this by central government, noting how more than a third of new homes granted planning permission between 2010–11 and 2015–16 had not yet been built. In response, it advocated measures to encourage house builders to start building more quickly once planning permission is secured (to be valid for two years rather than three) and to report how soon they commence work on new projects. Elsewhere in relation to planning, the White Paper revisited well-established notions of: reusing brownfield land and surplus public land; only amending Green Belt boundaries in exceptional circumstances as an option of last resort in meeting housing requirements; and building at higher densities.

By the time the Planning White Paper of 2020 was published, however, the narrative of planning's culpability and failure to deliver desired outcomes was firmly back in place. Prime Minister Boris Johnson's Foreword to the White Paper thus argued: 'as we approach the second decade of the 21st century … [the potential of this country] is being artificially constrained by a relic from the middle of the 20th – our outdated and ineffective planning system' (MHCLG, 2020: 6). He continued with the kind of loose analogy and cloying rhetorical flourish that plays well in the debating societies of the 'elite' academic institutions he attended and at Conservative Party conferences to note that the planning system, 'Designed and built in 1947 … has, like any building of that age, been patched up here and there over the decades' (MHCLG, 2020: 6). Scarcely leaving the reader time to digest the tenuous analogy, Mr Johnson moved swiftly to regurgitate some further tropes from the now-familiar narrative of planning failure, commenting:

> Thanks to our planning system, we have nowhere near enough homes in the right places. People cannot afford to move to where their talents can be matched with opportunity. Businesses cannot afford to grow and create jobs. The whole thing is beginning to crumble and the time has come to do what too many have for too long lacked the courage to do – tear it down and start again.

That is what this paper proposes.

Radical reform unlike anything we have seen since the Second World War. Not more fiddling around the edges, not simply painting over the damp patches, but levelling the foundations and building, from the ground up, a whole new planning system for England.

The Foreword by then Secretary of State Robert Jenrick and the text of the White Paper itself adopted a more moderate tone, with the former noting that 'Our proposals seek a significantly simpler, faster and more predictable system' and promising that 'We are cutting red tape, but not standards' (MHCLG, 2020: 8). The trajectory of the debate on planning reform since 2020 and changes to the subsequent proposals in the Levelling-up and Regeneration Bill are discussed in the remainder of the book, so we will not review these further here.

State failure and planning

One of the impacts of the narrative of planning failure has been that since the 1980s, the planning system in England has faced a seemingly never-ending cycle of criticism, reform and tinkering. As Pritchard (2022: 244) notes, for example, 'if enacted', the Levelling-up and Regeneration Bill will be 'the 20th piece of legislation to amend the Town and Country Planning Act 1990'. For Lord and Tewdwr-Jones (2014: 355), planning is thus subject to an 'almost constant process of piecemeal tinkering rather than wholesale reform'.

As we saw earlier, the argument for reform has often been that there is a 'housing crisis' and that more homes need to be built, and that it is the planning system that is stopping this happening. Yet, somehow, despite the constant tinkering, the number of new homes being built has remained more or less stable: the number of new homes begun in the last quarter of 2019 was only 8 per cent higher than the number begun in the first quarter of 2010. One reaction to this might be to stress the need for 'first principles' reform, the implication being that previous changes were too timid – despite being described as 'radical' at the time. This was certainly the kind of claim being made by former Prime Minister Boris Johnson in the Foreword to the 2020 Planning White Paper quoted earlier – a man who has built a career on promising to do what has never been done and win what has never been won.

However, promising to radically change how the planning system operates is one thing, resolving purported failings and changing its performance in the face of political contradictions and weakness in government is another. An example of this is provided by the current (as of 2023) ruling Conservative Party's long-standing and intractable attempts to balance the interests of two opposing groups that provide electoral and financial support to the party but that are commonly aligned on opposing sides when it comes to proposals for development, from the national to the very local level. This non-alignment finds a flashpoint around the desire to build more houses, whether because government sees a genuine need for these or because key figures in the development industry who are also Conservative Party donors support this stance. The latter constitute a pro-development camp, which calls for deregulation of planning and echoes the narrative of planning failure heard since the 1970s. In 2020, then prime ministerial advisor Dominic Cummings provided a characteristically forthright expression of this attitude towards planning as a brake on potential and productivity when he promised to take an 'axe' to planning laws and described the planning system as 'appalling'. Commenting on the influence of this tendency on the Planning White Paper of 2020, Tim Marshall (2020: 306) stated:

> The way to deal with this White Paper is therefore, I argue, to focus on the real drive conforming with the ideology, which is about freeing up development land and development opportunities for the property sectors most closely allied with current Conservatism. Certainly opponents should point out the absence of positive impacts on the real world. But they should not be so surprised at the fact that this new system will not improve social, environmental or economic living for the great majority: this is not its primary goal.

Yet, whatever the ideological underpinnings of the deregulatory stance towards planning, government and statecraft also involve navigating practical political realities. The 'Classical Economics 101' stance towards planning of the deregulatory camp thus often runs into the reality that the places where the development industry would most like to build new homes strongly correspond with Conservative-run local authorities and Conservative constituencies, where, for many decades now, it has been obvious that substantial numbers of politicians and voters do not welcome the idea of more houses being built.

This conflict has bedevilled attempts by Conservative ministers to loosen restrictions on where new homes are built since at least the 1980s. The 'radical' proposals of 2020 soon ran into heavy weather politically too, facing opposition from Conservative MPs in Parliament, including the former Prime Minister Theresa May. Discontent from 'traditional' Conservative voters with proposed change to planning was then cited as among the causes of two by-election losses. By September 2021, under a new minister, the planning reforms were being rethought, with some of the more 'radical' elements being watered down or dropped. By 2022, the Levelling-up and Regeneration Bill had moved away from 'some of the more radical reforms proposed in the 2020 Planning White Paper' (Pritchard, 2022: 244). The latest cycle of reforms of planning has therefore already altered trajectory. It is in light of such vacillation that this book posits that a narrative of planning failure advanced by successive governments as a justification for delivering 'a fundamental change' to planning (New Labour in the 2000s) or 'radical reform' (Conservative in the 2020s) can be countered by posing the question: how far might any deficiencies in planning also stem from centrally directed proposals and changes?

The narrative of 'planning failure' is deployed by central government at will, but there is perhaps more reticence about 'looking down the other end of the telescope' to question the degree of central government/state failure to get to grips with the planning issues they ostensibly claim to wish to see resolved. The notion of 'state failure' is invoked in public debate and academic work on certain kinds of 'failed, weak and collapsed states' (Rotberg, 2003), where authority and governing capacity have been undermined, for example, by civil conflict or other challenges from the internal and external environment. As a result, there may be a breakdown in the capacity of the state to deliver public goods and services, and to guarantee the rule of law. In such a state, ensuring the effectiveness and legitimacy of planning among other aspects of public policy and governance can be challenging or, at times, impossible. As the United Nations Human Settlements Programme (UNHSP, 2018: 79) observe: 'Planning is part of the rule of law and an integral element of governance.' Therefore, where these are under pressure, weak or have failed, then this affects the potential of planning to deliver. Over recent years, it has become more common for commentators to identify aspects of weakness in specific domains of public policy and sometimes link these to the notion of state failure or things being 'broken'. The use of such terms is, of course, not neutral, and governments and their political opponents employ such emotive rhetoric to seek to gain political advantage. In 2021, for example, former Labour Party Prime Minister Gordon Brown warned that the UK was in danger of becoming a failed state without deep reforms in the way it is governed (Gayle, 2021). Earlier, when Brown was prime minister, during the 2010 general election, the Conservative Party promoted a narrative trope around the notion of 'Broken Britain'. This found its planning expression in the party's *Open Source Planning Green Paper*'s reference to plans to 'fix our broken planning system' (Conservative Party, 2010). If Brown's Britain was deemed to be 'broken' in 2010 by the Conservatives, one might reasonably ask how it looks now after nearly 13 years when they have had their hands on the wheel of the ship of state. It is beyond the scope of this book to comprehensively review how such processes as the 'hollowing out' of the state through austerity, deregulation, disregard for previously accepted standards of behaviour in public life and the rule of law, or the UK's chaotic retreat from the EU have weakened the capacity of the UK state to deliver 'political goods' at an aggregate level. However, the contributions in this book do highlight whether, as regards the aspects of planning they address, central/state policy and actions have fostered or failed to promote the delivery of the positive planning outcomes that post-2010 governments have claimed they wish to see delivered.

Conclusion

The terms in which the proposed reforms of planning set out in the 2020 Planning White Paper were couched clearly reflected a reactivation of the narratives of planning failure summarised in this chapter and seemed to powerfully reflect the wider agenda of radical state reform that the regime in power in the UK at that time sought to pursue. Informed by this context, the contributions in this book offer a robust, evidence-informed analysis of what has occurred over the last decade and consider the future of planning in England. Specifically, they present reviews of different aspects of planning and whether critiques of planning and any observable issues in performance derive from failings in the planning system and profession, failings of the state and its approach to planning, or a combination of these and other factors., After 13 years of Conservative-led governments and the political turbulence of the latter part of 2022, when this book was being completed, this is a particularly appropriate point of time for such a reflection.

The remainder of the chapters in this book address the following themes. Chapter 2 – 'The (housing) numbers game', by Richard J. Dunning and Tom Moore – addresses perhaps the key area of planning and development that has sat at the heart of debates about the fitness for purpose of planning in England over recent decades. Since the latter decades of the 20th century, there has been an annual shortfall in the number of new homes constructed relative to housing demand. As detailed earlier in this chapter, the planning system has often been accused of being the primary cause of this by governments of different political complexions. Chapter 2 examines the evidence that exists to back or refute this claim, and offers reflection on the future trajectories of this debate in light of proposed reforms.

Chapter 3 – 'Localism: the peccadillos of a panacea', by John Sturzaker and Olivier Sykes – examines the experience of localism posited since 2010 as a privileged scale and alternative to the regional planning structures established in England under the New Labour governments of the 1990s and 2000s. Localism's most tangible effect on planning has been the rights conferred on local communities and businesses to prepare neighbourhood plans. The chapter reflects on the legacies and lessons of a decade of experience of neighbourhood planning and its future prospects, and considers the experience and impacts of localism in planning and its prospects in light of the evolving government reform agenda for planning.

Chapter 4 – 'Planning at the "larger than local" scale: where next?', by Alex Nurse – charts the evolution of different initiatives that have sought to address the 'larger than local' scale since the abolition of the regional scale of planning in England in 2010. The policy of the 2010–15 Coalition government, with its economically focused and partnership-based model of sub-regional spatial governance, with weak ties to statutory planning, is reviewed. The gradual 'hardening' of sub-regional governance arrangements in some places during the 2010s with the creation of combined authorities (CAs), mostly focused on city-regional areas, is also observed. The accompanying emergence of strategic planning processes under different powers and models, seen by some as heralding a return to strategic planning reflection and capacity, is also noted. The chapter reflects on the experience of the past decade and the current prospects for planning at the 'larger than local' scale in light of the proposed reforms of planning in England.

Chapter 5 – 'PD games: death comes to planning', by Richard J. Dunning, Alex Lord and Mark Smith – explores the extension of permitted development (PD) rights to make the conversion of buildings to residential use easier, presenting a typical example of the faith in deregulation as a pathway towards aligning development with demand. The chapter critically reviews the impacts of this experimentation from a health perspective, asking whether it has resulted in good-quality housing and what the impacts of any extension of such rights might be on residential quality.

Chapter 6 – 'Building beauty? Place and housing quality in the planning agenda', by Manuela Madeddu – focuses on the 'achievement of place and housing quality' through the planning system since 2010. It starts by looking at initial attitudes towards achieving 'quality' through planning, regulation or self-certification (in the development sector). It reflects on the work of the Commission for Architecture and the Built Environment (CABE) and the government's attitude towards the work of this body, asking what its dismantling (and integration into the Design Council) said about the government's approach to place quality and its commitment to quality, as opposed to quantity (of housing). It traces the development of a more neoliberal approach to development and place quality (letting the market find its quality benchmark), followed more recently by moves to codify place and development quality. The chapter contrasts approaches to place quality based on partnerships between planning teams and developers, sometimes grounded in frameworks of described standards, development briefs and design manuals, with a codified and prescribed approach.

Chapter 7 – 'Zoning in or zoning out?', by Sebastian Dembski and Phil O'Brien – contextualises the debate of recent years about the introduction of a (more) regulatory or 'zonal' planning system in England. Arguments that this will create a faster and better planning system than the existing discretionary approach are reviewed. With reference to the experience of other states that operate a zoning-based planning system, the question of whether such proposals are based on an oversimplified understanding of the differences between discretionary and regulatory models is explored. One theme that is emphasised is the negotiation between stakeholders and the flexibility that also exists in regulatory planning systems.

Chapter 8 – 'Planning and the environment in England, 2010– 22: cutting "green crap", Brexit and environmental crises', by Richard Cowell, Thomas B. Fischer and Urmila Jha Thakur – responds to the fact that reforms of planning and narratives of planning failure have often been laced with a critique of the impacts of environmental regulation on the speed of decision making on development. The trope of 'counting newts' being a constraint on development has been a popular refrain in this narrative, used again by last-but-one Prime Minister Boris Johnson. Such criticism of environmental protection has been partly allied with the move to leave the EU, deploying similar narratives of 'constraint' warranting deregulation. The chapter reviews the planning and environment relationship in light of such changes as the retreat of the UK state from the EU, key legislation in the environmental domain and proposals for planning reform.

Chapter 9 – 'Stuck on infrastructure? Planning for the transformative effects of transport infrastructure', by Chia-Lin Chen – examines the role that transport, as an exemplar of public investment, can play in addressing regional inequalities. It tracks the effects of previous large-scale transport infrastructure on economic growth, both in general and sectorally, and looks at the tortured history of the High Speed Two (HS2) project. The intersections between planning, transport and other forms of public investment are explored, and the viability of 'levelling up' without complementarity between these sectors of activity is questioned.

Chapter 10 reviews the findings of the separate chapters and synthesises them across four themes, aiming in particular to understand the collective impact of planning reforms on the poorest in society. It then provides some closing reflections on the central question of the book: whether any observable issues and challenges faced by planning in England reflect failings of the planning system, profession and 'discipline', failings of the state within which planning has to operate (which then uses planning as a scapegoat for its own failure to deliver), or a combination of both state and planning failure.

Notes

[1] See: https://dictionary.cambridge.org/dictionary/english/state
[2] It is interesting to set this text alongside the Foreword to the 2020 Planning White Paper from then Prime Minister Boris Johnson reproduced later in this chapter.
[3] See: www.communities.gov.uk/documents/localgovernment/pdf/1872724.pdf

References

Allegretti, A. (2021) 'Conservative MPs put pressure on government to scrap planning reforms', *The Guardian*, 21 June. Available at: https://www.theguardian.com/uk-news/2021/jun/21/conservative-mps-put-pressure-on-government-to-scrap-planning-reforms

Allen, R. (ed.) (2001) *The Penguin English Dictionary*, London: Penguin Books.

Allmendinger, P. and Haughton, G. (2013) 'The evolution and trajectories of English spatial governance: "neoliberal" episodes in planning', *Planning Practice and Research*, 28(1): 6–26.

Barker, K. (2004) *Review of Housing Supply – Delivering Sustainability: Securing Our Future Housing Needs*, London: HMSO.

Barker, K. (2006) *Review of Land-Use Planning: Final Report – Recommendations*, London: HMSO.

Byers, S. (2001) 'Foreword', in Department of Transport, Local Government and the Regions (ed) *Planning: Delivering a Fundamental Change*, London: Department of Transport, Local Government and the Regions.

Conservative Party (2010) *Open Source Planning Green Paper*, Policy Green Paper No. 14, London: The Conservative Party.

DCLG (Department for Communities and Local Government) (2011) *National Planning Policy Framework: Myth Buster*, London: DCLG. Available at: http://www.communityplanning.net/pub-film/pdf/DraftNPPF_Myth_Buster.pdf

DCLG (2012) *National Planning Policy Framework*, London: DCLG. Available at: www.gov.uk/government/uploads/system/uploads/attachment_data/file/6077/2116950.pdf

DTLR (Department of Transport, Local Government and the Regions) (2001) *Planning: Delivering a Fundamental Change*, London: DTLR.

Gayle, D. (2021) 'UK at risk of becoming failed state says Gordon Brown', *The Guardian*, 25 January. Available at: https://www.theguardian.com/politics/2021/jan/25/uk-at-risk-of-becoming-failed-state-says-gordon-brown

Hall, P. (2014) 'Sir Peter Hall: reflections on a lifetime of town planning', *The Guardian*, 1 October. Available at: https://www.theguardian.com/cities/2014/oct/01/sir-peter-hall-reflections-on-a-lifetime-of-town-planning

Heseltine, M. (1979) *Secretary of State's Address, Report of Proceedings of Town and Country Planning Summer School: 8–19th September 1979*, London: Royal Town Planning Institute.

HM Treasury (Her Majesty's Treasury) (2015) *Fixing the Foundations: Creating a More Prosperous Nation*, London: HM Treasury.

HM Treasury and BIS (2013) *Plan for Growth Implementation Update*. Available at: https://assets.publishing.service.gov.uk/government/uploads/system/uploads/attachment_data/file/200019/growth_implementation_upd ate_mar2013.pdf

Hutton, W. (1995) *The State We're In*, London: Jonathan Cape.

Lord, A. and Tewdwr-Jones, M. (2014) 'Is planning "under attack"? Chronicling the deregulation of urban and environmental planning in England', *European Planning Studies*, 22(2): 345–61.

Marshall, T. (2020) 'The White Paper's ideological core', *Town and Country Planning*, September–October: 304–6.

MHCLG (Ministry of Housing, Communities & Local Government) (2020) *Planning for the Future White Paper*, August, London: MHCLG.

Monbiot, G. (2016) 'Neoliberalism: the ideology at the root of all our problems', *The Guardian*, 16 April. Available at: https://www.theguardian.com/books/2016/apr/15/neoliberalism-ideology-problem-george-monbiot

ODPM (Office of the Deputy Prime Minister) (2005) *Planning Policy Statement 1: Delivering Sustainable Development*, London, ODPM.

Pritchard, A. (2022) 'A planning bill in all but name', *Town and Country Planning*, July–August: 244–5.

Rotberg, I. (ed) (2003) *State Failure and State Weakness in a Time of Terror*, Cambridge, MA: World Peace Foundation and Washington, DC: Brookings Institution Press.

Schön, D.A. (1983) *The Reflective Practitioner*, London: Temple Smith.

Smith, L. (2016) *Briefing Paper, Number 06418*, 22 February 2016, Planning Reform Proposals, London: House of Commons Library.

Snow, J. (2023) *The State of Us: The Good News and the Bad News about Our Society*, London: Penguin.

Stead, D. and Nadin, V. (2014) 'Spatial planning in the United Kingdom, 1990–2013', in M. Reimer, G. Panagiotis and H. Blotevogel (eds) *Spatial Planning Systems and Practices in Europe: A Comparative Perspective on Continuity and Changes*, London: Routledge, pp 189–214.

Sturzaker, J. and Nurse, A. (2020) *Rescaling Urban Governance: Planning, Localism and Institutional Change*, Bristol: Policy Press.

Taylor, N. (1998) *Urban Planning Theory Since 1945*, London: Sage.

Tewdwr-Jones, M. (2011) *Urban Reflections: Narratives of Place, Planning and Change*, Bristol: Policy Press.

UNHSP (United Nations Human Settlements Programme) (2018) *Leading Change: Delivering the New Urban Agenda through Urban and Territorial Planning*, Kuala Lumpur: UNHSP.

Waterhout, B., Othengrafen, F. and Sykes, O. (2013) 'Neo-liberalization processes and spatial planning in Northwest Europe', *Planning Practice and Research*, 28(1): 141–59.

Winter, G., Smith, L., Cave, S. and Rehfisch, A. (2016) *Comparison of the Planning Systems in the Four UK Countries*, Commons Library Briefing Paper 0745920, January, London: House of Commons Library.

2

The (housing) numbers game

Richard J. Dunning and Tom Moore

Introduction

In April 2010, the average house price in England was £177,000; by April 2021, it was £268,000 (HM Land Registry, 2021) – an increase of more than double the average annual inflation of 2 per cent (Bank of England, 2022). Private rents have increased in line with incomes by an average of 1.9 per cent per annum since the start of the Conservative–Liberal Democrat Coalition government (ONS, 2021a). In 2010, the average weekly local authority rent was £68; in 2020, it was £86. Over the same period, registered-provider rents increased from an average of £78 to £94 (MHCLG, 2021a), both inflating above earnings. Between 2012[1] and 2020, homelessness increased by 40,000 households, and projections are for this to continue rising under the current welfare and housing system (Fitzpatrick et al, 2021). In 2010, 65.2 per cent of dwellings were owner-occupied; in 2020, that had fallen to 63.8 per cent (MHCLG, 2021b). Affordable housing has been officially redefined so that new housing statistics include dwellings at 80 per cent of market rent and price, which remain unaffordable for low-income earners in many parts of the country. First-time buyers have been given support since 2013 through two new help-to-buy schemes, with the government effectively underwriting mortgages, though with little impact on housing affordability. Taxes on private landlords and second homeowners have increased, while local authority borrowing restrictions have been partially relaxed to enable further local authority housing delivery. The threshold for stamp duty land tax was lowered by the Coalition government in 2010, then the system was changed from a slab to a slice approach in 2015. In 2020, following the growth in COVID-19, a stamp duty land tax 'holiday' was introduced to encourage house sales to continue through the pandemic.

This list reveals that there are numerous challenges associated with housing numbers across accessibility, availability and supply. In this chapter, we explore the current state of planning for housing in England, focusing on one of the key reductionisms: housing numbers. Housing numbers have become the dominant discourse in local and national housing and planning policies, and are a colloquial euphemism for variously the amount of housing supply required, permitted and delivered. At the time of writing, one of the Conservative government's flagship bills (the Levelling-Up and Regeneration Bill) has suffered a broadside attack from one side of the Conservative Party, with the issue being housing numbers.

The planning system is widely castigated as 'problematic' for housing. It is blamed for allowing housing that is substandard, of poor quality and in the wrong places. It is also blamed for restricting housing supply and increasing house prices, being a drag on the free market delivering housing. Yet, it is not always clear that planning is the root cause of these problems, and planning is rarely celebrated for its achievements in enabling the nation's housing to meet the population's needs. We frame the changes in policy that have occurred since 2010 in light of longer-term housing trends in England to ask whether state planning for housing has indeed failed. We recommend that the reader considers this chapter in light of Chapter 1, which highlights key trends in the political planning discourse that we refer to here.

This chapter considers housing policy and numbers in England as distinct within the UK. While there are overarching housing trends within the UK, there are substantive enough differences between the economics, demographics and housing policies of England, Wales, Scotland and Northern Ireland to warrant individual treatment (McKee et al, 2017). Indeed, while we draw evidence, argument and conclusions at the national scale, both housing and planning are always local, and for households in inadequate housing or with limited access to a home, the complexities of state planning for housing are intensely experienced at the micro-spatial scale, whether or not the state seeks to reconstitute spatial governance structures.

The next section considers the last ten years of housing supply within the historic context of household growth, housing stock, house prices and housing supply. We then consider the meaning of 'home' to create a framework with which to analyse the planning system, before providing concluding thoughts.

Housing numbers

In this section, we explore housing in relation to its quantitative aspect from a national perspective. Questions about the number of new homes required and the price of these homes recur regularly in the news and public discourses. Such is the public interest that political parties compete with house-building targets. The Conservative Party is currently struggling with these numbers, but in their 2019 manifesto, they committed to an increase in annual house building, simultaneously highlighting planning as a major barrier:

> we will continue our progress towards our target of 300,000 homes a year by the mid-2020s. This will see us build at least a million more

homes, of all tenures, over the next Parliament – in the areas that really need them. And we will make the planning system simpler for the public and small builders, and support modern methods of construction. (Conservative and Unionist Party, 2019: 31)

The time frame over which housing numbers are analysed is evidently crucial to the outcome of that analysis. Too short a time frame and we miss the wall for the bricks; too long a time frame and our analysis can be out of touch with contemporary housing preferences and needs. In this chapter, we present the data from 1971 to 2020 as an attempt to balance these competing jeopardies. It covers periods of political control by the Conservatives (1971–74, 1979–1997 and 2015–present), Labour (1974–79 and 1997–2010) and the Conservative–Liberal Democrat Coalition (2010–15). Thus, the current state of planning for housing is contextualised within a 50-year history, with six periods of alternative state leadership.

By 1975, English politicians largely agreed that housing need was met by the existing housing stock, which had expanded remarkably following the Second World War. Significant programmes of house building in the post-war period, coupled with the development and growth of new towns, tackled issues of housing disrepair and supply. Attention then shifted to changing the tenure mix through housing policies that reflected broader trends of privatisation and neoliberalisation, including the introduction of the Right to Buy policy in 1980 and the reduced regulation of private rental tenancies in the Housing Act 1988. While initially introduced by a Conservative government, the commitment to a property-owning democracy has run consistently through Conservative, New Labour and Coalition governments ever since (Lund, 2017). This ideological continuity has also been reflected in commitments to increase housing supply. As house prices rose relative to incomes, concern for housing supply numbers grew. Quickly, and with limited evidence, the planning system was identified as a constraint to housing development (Barker, 2004). The Barker Review (Barker, 2004) sparked a resurgence of alternative economic and demographic models for calculating housing requirements, which have been vying for political dominance through to today. While there have been substantive differences in the method for calculating housing supply targets and some policy variation introduced by successive governments throughout this period, ideological continuity is clear in identifying supply as a key focus of housing policy.

The standard method for calculating housing numbers

As described earlier, recent governments have been very specific in setting housing targets per annum; yet, there is limited agreement about how housing need should be quantified and limited clarity as to how this national target is arrived at. Over the last decade, England has had centralised responsibility for determining housing need (McGuinness et al, 2018). At one level, this makes sense, as the nation scale is reportedly a defined geography within which policy can be enacted to meet need; thus, it makes sense to know how much housing a nation needs. However, this is not the sense in which housing need is calculated in England; instead, the national government defines a national housing target (often with limited clarity regarding the evidence and method to calculate it) and then determines a calculation to distribute that requirement to local planning authorities to enact.

Before this Conservative government, local authorities were tasked with calculating housing need, but this process was considered lengthy, costly and, at times, too subjective (Ferrari et al, 2011). Introducing a method that was easier to calculate was supposed to save time, money and give an objective number. Thus, the standard method was implemented in a revision of the National Planning Policy Framework (NPPF) in 2018 (then clarified in February 2019). However, the initial formula was widely ridiculed, and by late 2020, the government was consulting on a revised methodology.

The standard method is predicated on estimates of household growth, with an additional uplift based on a ratio of the unaffordability of local authority house prices to income. The method has three steps:

1. Setting the baseline: the estimated ten-year increase in households sets the baseline (for example, projected number of households in the local authority in 2030 minus the projected number of households in the local authority in 2020).
2. An adjustment to take account of affordability: the baseline is then adjusted to reflect a nationally consistent uplift based on the local ratio of house prices to placed incomes. This adjustment factor is not well justified but has largely been accepted as an arbitrary uplift in the hope of increasing supply (and supposedly therefore making housing more affordable).
3. Capping the level of any increase: in order to prevent a massive increase in housing need from the local authority's previous local plan, the method caps the increase at 40 per cent above the existing requirement figure – an arbitrary cap.

The focus on national housing numbers has, however, highlighted the limited basis of this method in evidence. When the 2016 household projections were released, they showed household growth as lower than previously thought and therefore resulted in a significantly decreased annual housing figure for many local authorities (and nationally when each local authority's target is aggregated). Therefore, the government updated the 2019 planning policy guidance to mandate the use of the previous iteration of household projections (the 2014-based projections), despite them being less likely to be accurate. This highlights a tension between the pursuit of a national housing target that has been set by politicians and the more likely requirements of local housing need.

England has used household projections to estimate housing need for nearly three decades (Holmans, 2014), and it has gained more appeal through the standard method as a nationally prescribed mechanism to determine 'objective' local authority housing requirements and force local authorities to provide more planning permissions (Meen and Whitehead, 2020), with the explicit aim of increasing supply to meet the nation's housing need (DCLG, 2017). The standard method is not alone, with many policies considered by the Conservative government to increase housing delivery, such as financial incentives for neighbours (Inch et al, 2020), financial incentives for local authorities (Dunning et al, 2014) and derestricting development (Clifford et al, 2020).

The dominance of a quantitative measure of housing need within the standard method hides other equally important issues, including the type, tenure, size, quality and specific location of the dwellings. As we argue further on in this chapter, these aspects of housing and homes are important yet neglected aspects of the debate around housing numbers.

What is the relationship between households and housing?

A nation's housing supply should surely have some relationship to the number of households it has. Yet, determining what that relationship should be and how planning policy should manage that relationship is a political decision.

In 1971, there were 16.2 million dwellings in England, nearly 200,000 more dwellings than households (see Figure 2.1). Some 50 years later, there were 24.7 million dwellings, which is over 1.1 million more dwellings than households. This is because the dwelling stock has increased by about 0.9 per cent per annum since 1971, while households have only increased by 0.8 per cent per annum (though household growth is twice population growth, at 0.4 per cent per annum). The nature of housing is that it is designed to last for many years; hence, in most nations, new housing supply will only be a small proportion of stock. At the national scale, the number of households also tends to grow at only a low proportion of the overall population. These two immediate points are clear from the data: that the housing stock has grown at a low rate; but that it has grown at a faster rate than households.

Why is there concern regarding the number of homes in England if stock is above the number of households? Retaining a supply of vacant houses is necessary to enable household mobility and as a natural consequence of our finitude as humans. To enable household mobility, some vacancies are needed. While many housing sale chains enable households to move on the same day, other processes are at play that require some vacancy, such as the

Figure 2.1: Dwelling stock and households in England, 1971–2020

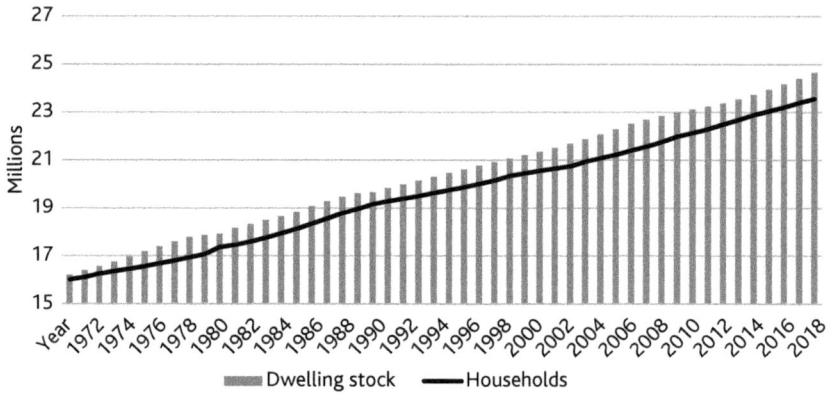

Source: MHCLG (2020b: Table 104) and Office for National Statistics household estimates and projections based on 2016 and 2018 data (ONS, 2018)

refurbishment of a dwelling prior to reoccupation or enabling a household to move from a low-demand location to a higher-demand location without finding a replacement household. Regarding our finitude as humans, it is a tragedy that any baby should be born to a household without a home (that is, at birth, we need a home ready for us), yet it is normal for a dwelling to be empty for a period after our death; thus, the dwelling stock needs to be higher than the number of households. Indeed, if there are few vacancies (and other difficulties in accessing housing), then the formation of new households will be suppressed (Bramley, 2013).

While some vacancy is to be expected, Dorling (2014) argues that there has been an increase in housing space per capita and an underutilisation of some of the housing stock through non-transitional uses (such as second home and overseas vacant ownership). Dorling goes on to argue that the affordability crisis and housing shortage is not a supply but rather a distributional crisis.

Who is responsible for increasing the housing stock and what type of housing are they delivering?

The neoliberalisation of housing delivery in England since the early Thatcher years has resulted in a diminution of direct housing delivery by the state and an increase in the proportion of supply provided by private actors (chiefly large house builders). Figure 2.2 shows how the number of dwellings supplied by private enterprise has varied from 83,000 to 176,000, but for housing associations and local authorities combined, it has varied from 13,000 to 140,000 (ONS, 2021b).

Figure 2.2: Permanent dwelling completions, by tenure, in England since 1971

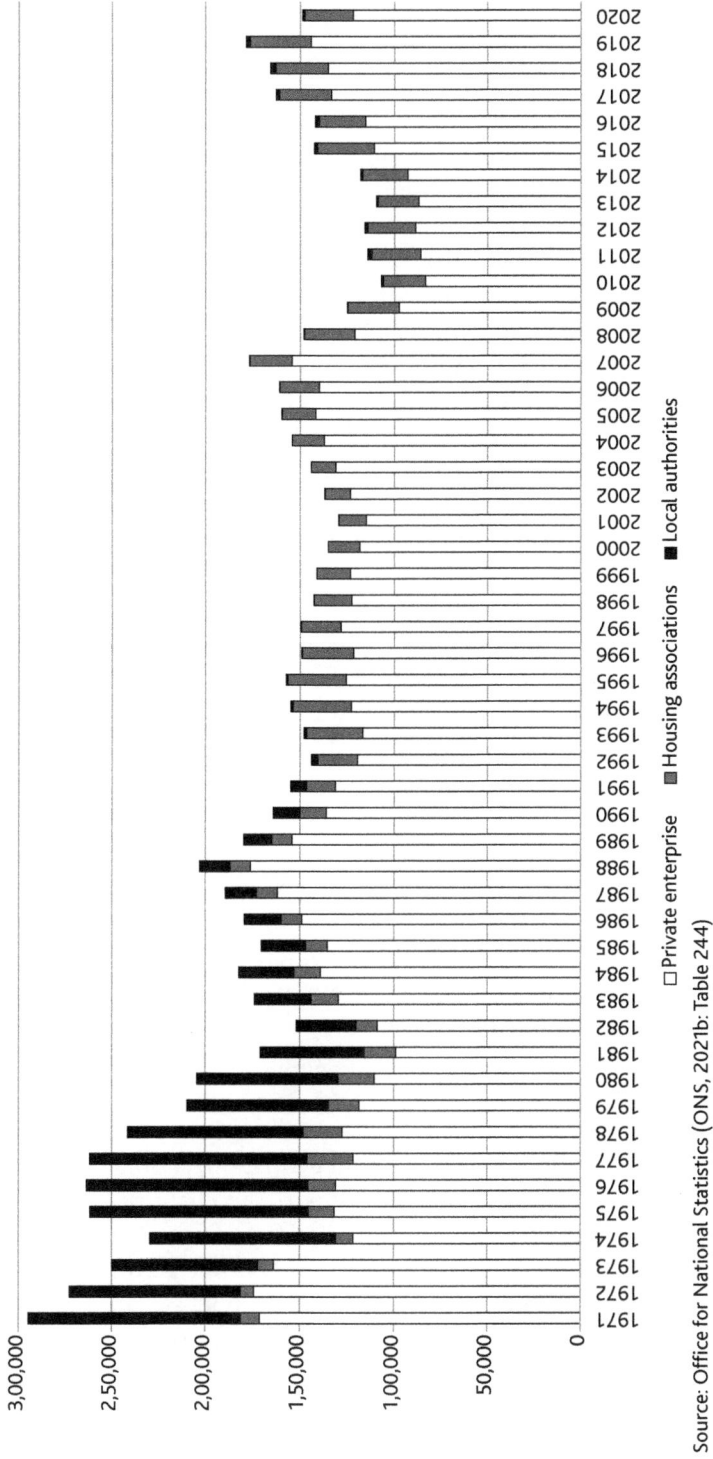

Source: Office for National Statistics (ONS, 2021b: Table 244)

Legend: ■ Local authorities ■ Housing associations □ Private enterprise

In 1977, housing associations and local authorities were responsible for 54 per cent of the dwelling completions, but as state funding decreased, this fell to just 9 per cent in 2003. Since 2010, this figure has remained at levels much below the significant volumes of local authority and housing association development in the 1970s, fluctuating between 18 and 25 per cent. Since the introduction of the Right to Buy, housing association and local authority housing has decreased as a proportion of the overall stock in England (between 2010 and 2020, the number of dwellings grew but as a proportion of total stock decreased from 17.7 to 16.8 per cent), having a decreasing impact on the total cost of housing in England.

These trends reflect ideological perspectives as to how housing should be planned, developed, distributed and consumed, which have concomitantly seen increasing affordability problems. There is a diminished role for the state in housing provision, with local authorities largely transitioning from the role of provider to that of enabler of housing and an increased emphasis on market provision and an expectation that individuals will navigate private housing markets to find housing rather than rely on state-funded or -managed homes.

What causes house price growth above household growth?

Discussion of housing supply is often framed in relation to both household formation and housing affordability. Indeed, these are the twin tenets of the current government's housing need calculations (albeit using a rather vague justification for the precise values in the calculations [see Lord et al, forthcoming]). The discussion belies an assumption that increasing housing supply above the household formation rate will reduce house prices. Duncan Bowie (2017: 54) wrote of the New Labour government's view 'that all they needed to do was set higher housing targets, make councils grant more planning permissions and the new homes would be built – the more homes were built, the more affordable they would be, and the more social rented and shared-ownership homes would be built'. This has largely been repeated since by all governments.

The economic argument put forward is that, all other things being equal, an increase in supply (above household formation) should reduce real house prices. There is some evidence to support the claim that restrictive land-use regulation can increase house prices (see, for example, Gyourko and Molloy, 2015; Hilber and Vermeulen, 2016), but arguments in favour of relaxing planning constraints and increasing supply are contingent upon the sensitivity of house prices. Studies have repeatedly suggested a sensitivity in the region of -1.1 to -2.2, meaning that a 1 per cent increase of stock above household growth would decrease prices by 1.1 to 2.2 per cent (Mulheirn, 2019). However, stock has been increasing at a faster rate than households over the last 50 years, yet house prices have continued to rise significantly faster than household incomes (see Figure 2.3). The overarching picture of house price changes is clear from Figure 2.3: even accounting for short-term cycles, most notably, the declines in the late 1980s and after the Global Financial Crisis of 2007–08, the increase in median incomes is much more modest over this period.

We are left with two alternatives: either stock has not been increasing sufficiently above household formation (that is, England needs significantly more than 1.1 dwellings per household to satisfy demand) or house price increases have not primarily reflected the change in household numbers. International evidence suggests that we should not rule out the first option (a counterfactual question is often raised here in defence of relaxing planning to increase supply: 'What would the impact have been on house prices without even this increase in stock?' [Been et al, 2019]); however, we can explore the second option and identify other factors that influence prices.

While the price of purchasing a dwelling may have increased substantially, the availability and cost of credit to purchase a home became significantly more advantageous for households through the 20th century. In the 19th and early 20th centuries, interest rates fluctuated between approximately 4 and 10 per cent. In 1979, the Conservative government sought to reduce inflation through a sizeable increase in interest rates (up to 17 per cent), and in the 1980s, they repeated the increase, partly to limit house price growth. The New Labour government devolved responsibility for interest rates to the Bank of England, which oversaw historically lower rates of between 3.75 and 6 per cent. Yet, these rates were slashed in response to the Global Financial Crisis of 2007–08, where rates fell to 0.25 per cent and remained below 1 per cent for over a decade. The correlation between the ease of access to finance and the cost of mortgages has regularly been identified as an explanatory variable for house price growth (Jones and Watkins, 2009). Most recently, Miles and Monro (2021: 6) found that 'the key factor in reconciling the divergent trends between house prices, incomes and consumer prices is that there has been a substantial decline in real interest rates, spanning decades, which was consistently not expected'. The diminution of below-market housing provision (that is, social housing), combined with the increasing availability of low-cost credit, has surely exacerbated affordability issues regardless of housing supply and planning policy. The year 2022 represents a period where concerns over increasing interest rates might limit house price inflation, or possibly reverse it. Crucially, while there is a substantial academic literature that identifies the role of planning in making the housing market (Adams and Watkins, 2014; Lord and O'Brien, 2017), there is very little discussion in government of planning's role in controlling interest rates or the supply of finance.

Figure 2.3: Indices of average house prices and median household incomes since 1977

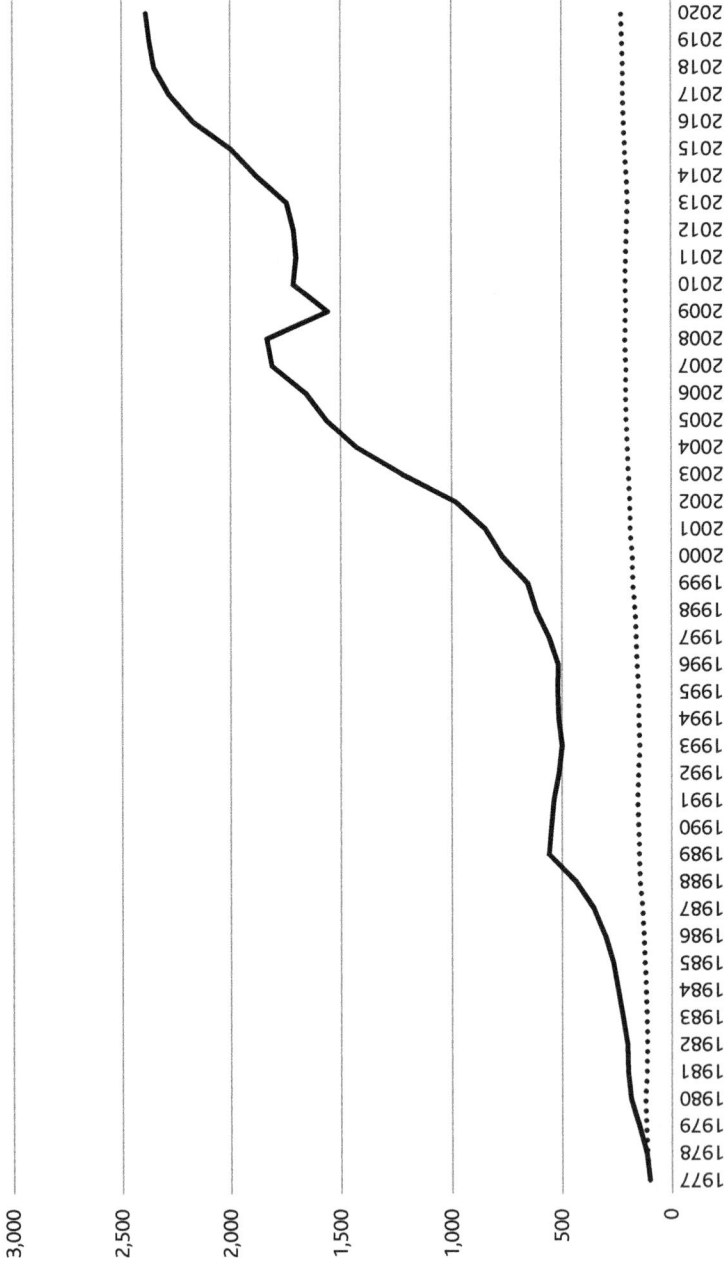

Source: Authors' calculation using data on simple average house prices (April) and the wages and salaries growth rate from the Office for National Statistics (ONS, 2020)

— Average house price index (1977 = 100) ••••• UK median household income (unadjusted) index (1977 = 100)

Planning permissions

Historic data on the number of dwellings permitted are sparse, as local authorities were required to provide information on the number of planning applications rather than the number of units in each application. However, between 2017 and 2021, the number of housing units granted permission has been modelled, indicating that, on average, 316,000 new dwellings were granted permission each year (MHCLG, 2021c). The number of planning applications received, decided and granted annually decreased significantly after the Global Financial Crisis but has remained relatively stable since 2010 (MHCLG, 2021c). As will be discussed further in Chapter 5, the number of applications for prior approvals for permitted development rights increased substantially after the government extended what could be permitted in subsequent phases from 2013 onwards.

Regional variation

As discussed earlier, the national picture of housing numbers masks a diversity of situations across the country (see Figure 2.4). In London, the median house price has increased from 8.8 times median income to 12.5 times between 2010 and 2020, and in the South East, it went from 7.7 times to 9.6 times. In fact, the ratio has worsened for every region except the North East.

Producing estimates of housing need and the impact on house prices at the national scale is a necessity for wise state action. However, there needs to be an awareness of the regional and local impacts of nationally determined parameters for planning. The current dispute regarding the top-down determination of local housing requirements is a clear example of this disconnect. The circularities that exist in a housing system between prices, supply, household formation and relative demand highlight that obsessing over the delivery of a national housing target is unlikely to meet the nation's housing needs by itself. To do that, we need a more nuanced grasp on what housing is for – something that planning has regularly grappled with.

What is housing? And what is housing for?

In the preceding sections, we began by identifying a range of housing challenges related to affordability, access and availability, each of which may be considered to be interrelated, before discussing the political preoccupation with increasing the numerical output of housing to solve these issues. While we do not question that more homes need to be built, it is also the case that the top-down determination of local housing requirements may fail to take account of local circumstances, distinctions and needs (McGuinness et al, 2018). Furthermore, in addition to the need for spatial nuance in planning

Figure 2.4: Regional ratios of median house prices to median residence-based earnings, 2002–20

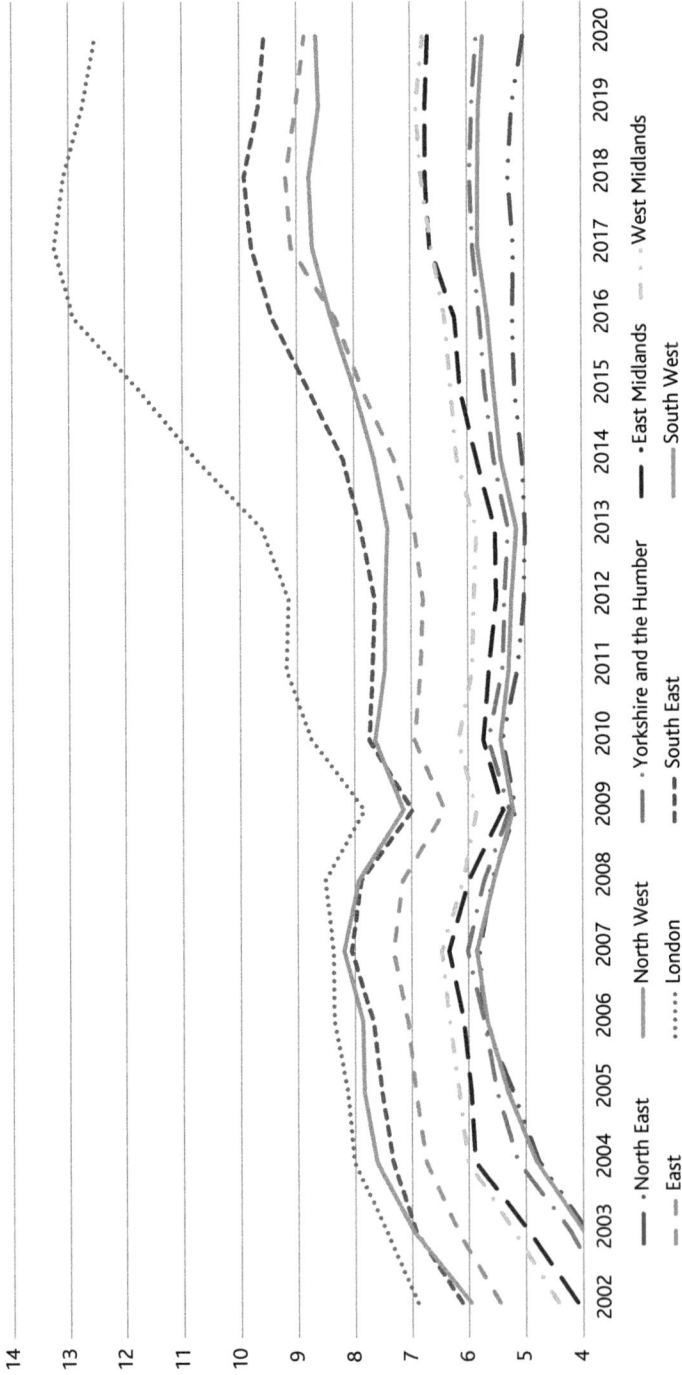

Source: Office for National Statistics (ONS, 2021a)

for housing, it is also important to consider *what* is constructed in terms of the type, tenure and quality of housing, and the extent to which it meets the various needs that housing serves. In this section, we identify different functions of housing and discuss the ways in which current approaches to planning for housing meet these needs or not.

A fundamental conception of housing is as shelter, or, as Fox O'Mahony (2012: 232) puts it, 'the existence of, and adequacy of, the roof over the occupier's head'. As Fox O'Mahony identifies, and as we discuss later, reducing housing to a concern with its physicality overlooks dimensions of home that are integral to the ways in which people experience and relate to their shelter and places of residence. However, ensuring that there are sufficient units of housing in which the population can shelter should be a basic starting point for approaches to planning for housing, and it could be argued that the preoccupation with increasing housing numbers reflects this concern, notwithstanding the persistence of housing precarity and homelessness, and the inadequacy of government responses to this. Approaches like the standard method for calculating housing need, the pressure on local authorities to identify a five-year land supply and the expansion of permitted development rights reflect an attempt to ensure that there is capacity in terms of land and housing stock for projected household growth. Yet, housing also serves needs that extend beyond the provision of shelter. As outlined in the following, housing can also be understood as 'home', from which a number of social, economic and cultural benefits can be derived by, or denied to, occupiers beyond the 'bricks and mortar'.

Scholars have identified different meanings and values of home, including but extending beyond its conception as a physical structure. Such meanings may include: an understanding of home: as a financial asset or constraint (such as the relative value of owning versus renting); as a site of ontological safety, security, control and autonomy; in its territorial role in providing a space for continuity, roots and permanence for occupiers; and as a site where social and cultural attachments can develop (Fox O'Mahony, 2012; Hoolachan, 2022). It is important to note that 'home' is a contested concept. The meanings and values ascribed to home can be socially, economically, politically and culturally contingent (Meers, 2023), and access to, or experience of, the apparent benefits of home may be shaped by gender, race, sexuality and household relationships (see, for example, Matthews et al, 2019).

Notwithstanding this contestation, the importance of home was brought into sharp focus during the outbreak of the COVID-19 pandemic. Homes simultaneously assumed many different functions: designated not only as sites of security and safety through public health control measures but also, simultaneously, as places of risk and danger, such as risks of infection within households, rising domestic violence and mental health and well-being issues. Poor housing conditions, including quality, affordability, space and security, impacted well-being (Jacoby and Alonso, 2022). Issues like overcrowding and high-density living became associated with increased risk of infection (Tinson and Clair, 2020), and the ontological security of households weakened as a result of poor-quality housing. While many of these issues were exacerbated during the COVID-19 pandemic, they were not necessarily new. Tenants in the lightly regulated and insecure private rented sector have been identified as having diminished feelings of home due to the insecurity of their tenancies (Soaita and McKee, 2019), and housing quality and cost have been linked to feelings of stress (Clair and Hughes, 2019).

While increasing housing numbers may be important in tackling housing shortages, it is clear that the type, quality and location of housing are also important. The planning system is sometimes critiqued for its failure to ensure that these broader functions of housing beyond its physicality are delivered, but it is important to remember that planning systems are shaped and enabled or constrained by national policy objectives. Many local planning authorities have experienced significant reductions in funding and resources during periods of austerity (Hincks et al, 2020), while methods of calculating housing need are set nationally and, as discussed earlier, have been critiqued for failing to take sufficient account of local nuance. In addition, a key pillar of the state's response to housing shortages has been the expansion of permitted development rights, encouraging the conversion of offices to residential use through significantly streamlined planning processes. While this may increase the supply of housing and contribute to broader objectives related to the reuse of empty buildings and regeneration, studies have highlighted that some housing delivered through permitted development rights is of poor quality. In relation to this, Ferm et al (2021: 2040) argue that 'a focus on housing numbers is eclipsing problems of housing quality, the type of housing being made available and whether it is in sustainable locations'. Furthermore, classification of office-to-residential conversions as permitted development is thought to have diminished the ability of local authorities with respect to place making (House of Commons, 2021: 64). While permitted development rights are not the only tool through which housing is delivered, their expansion highlights the prioritisation of increasing housing supply above other objectives that would ensure or contribute to feelings of home, including housing quality, condition and location.

This is not to suggest that planners and planning are entirely powerless in the planning and delivery of housing. At a local level, there are examples of interventions to ensure that housing development and management are considered in relation to place making, such as the use of local policies to control or shape occupancy (Gallent et al, 2019; Brookfield, 2022), though these policies can have discriminatory effects (Sturzaker, 2010). However, while the planning system is often identified as a blockage and barrier to the delivery of new housing, it is key to remember that planning systems are not inherently flawed in and of themselves but rather designed and resourced to reflect and deliver prevailing political ideologies and ambitions.

Conclusion

It is too simplistic to say that more rather than less planning is needed. However, the Conservative critique that more housing is needed in the right places does imply a more detailed level of analysis, thought and engagement than a national housing target can provide. If there is a disconnect between the national target and local implementation, then increasing the capacity of planning to grapple with this would be a good place to start.

Increasing the capacity of planning will not by itself produce more housing, nor more affordable housing. However, the state has the power to provide financial resources for local authority housing delivery and to enable the replacement of Right to Buy sales so that genuinely affordable housing accounts for a greater proportion of the housing stock. In this chapter, we have argued that existing methods of calculating and delivering housing targets fail to account for issues of housing tenure, size, quality and location, and that national housing targets do not effectively account for the need for spatial nuance and support the relationship between housing and place making. In part, this is reflective of prevailing political ideologies as to the role of housing in society, the economy and the level of state intervention that is thought appropriate. However, until attractive and affordable alternatives are offered across England, it is unlikely that the political problem of increasing house prices will diminish.

Note
[1]   The year 2012 is used here because it is the earliest estimate in the *Homelessness Monitor: England 2021* (Fitzpatrick et al, 2021) for projecting to 2020.

References
Adams, D. and Watkins, C. (2014) *The Value of Planning*, RTPI. Available at: https://www.rtpi.org.uk/media/1548/value-of-planning-full-report-2014.pdf
Bank of England (2022) 'Inflation calculator'. Available at: www.bankofengland.co.uk/monetary-policy/inflation/inflation-calculator
Barker, K. (2004) 'Barker review of housing supply', HM Treasury. Available at: https://webarchive.nationalarchives.gov.uk/ukgwa/+/http:/www.hm-treasury.gov.uk/barker_review_of_housing_supply_recommendations.htm
Been, V., Ellen, I.G. and O'Regan, K. (2019) 'Supply skepticism: housing supply and affordability', *Housing Policy Debate*, 29(1): 25–40.
Bowie, D. (2017) *Radical Solutions to the Housing Supply Crisis*, Bristol: Policy Press.

Bramley, G. (2013) 'Housing market models and planning', *The Town Planning Review*, 84(1): 9–35.

Brookfield, K. (2022) 'Planned out: the discriminatory effects of planning's regulation of small houses in multiple occupation in England', *Planning Theory & Practice*, 23(2): 194–211.

Clair, A. and Hughes, A. (2019) 'Housing and health: new evidence using biomarker data', *Journal of Epidemiology & Community Health*, 73(3): 256–62

Clifford, B., Canelas, P., Ferm, J., Livingstone, N., Lord, A. and Dunning, R. (2020) *Research into the Quality Standard of Homes Delivered through Change of Use Permitted Development Rights*, London: Ministry of Housing, Communities and Local Government.

Conservative and Unionist Party (2019) *Get Brexit Done: Unleash Britain's Potential*, London: The Conservative Party.

DCLG (Department for Communities and Local Government) (2017) 'Fixing our broken housing market'. Available at: https://www.gov.uk/government/publications/fixing-our-broken-housing-market

Dorling, D. (2014) *All That Is Solid: How the Great Housing Disaster Defines Our Time, and What We Can Do about It*, London: Penguin.

Dunning, R., Watkins, C.A., Inch, A., Payne, S., While, A., Young, G. et al (2014) *The Impact of the New Homes Bonus on Attitudes and Behaviour*, London: Department for Communities and Local Government.

Ferm, J., Clifford, B., Canelas, P. and Livingstone, N. (2021) 'Emerging problematics of deregulating the urban in England: the case of permitted development in England', *Urban Studies*, 58(1): 2040–58.

Ferrari, E., Laughlin-Levy, D. and Watkins, C. (2011) 'Planning and the housing market: reflections on strategic housing market assessment in England', *Town Planning Review*, 82(4): 393–423.

Fitzpatrick, S., Watts, B., Pawson, H., Bramley, G., Wood, J., Stephens, M. et al (2021) *The Homelessness Monitor: England 2021*, London: Crisis.

Fox O'Mahony, L. (2012) 'Meanings of home', in S. Smith (ed) *International Encyclopaedia of Housing and Home*, Oxford: Elsevier, pp 231–9.

Gallent, N., Hamiduddin, I., Stirling, P. and Kelsey, J. (2019) 'Prioritising local housing needs through land-use planning in rural areas: political theatre or amenity protection?', *Journal of Rural Studies*, 66: 11–20.

Gyourko, J. and Molloy, R. (2015) 'Regulation and housing supply', in G. Duranton, V. Henderson and W. Strange (eds) *Handbook of Regional and Urban Economics*, Vol 5, Oxford: Elsevier, pp 1289–337.

Hilber, C.A. and Vermeulen, W. (2016) 'The impact of supply constraints on house prices in England', *The Economic Journal*, 126(591): 358–405.

Hincks, S., Dunning, R., Moore, T., Young, G. and Watkins, C. (2020) 'A view from the North: understanding housing and planning capacity in an era of austerity', Northern Housing Consortium. Available at: www.north ern-consortium.org.uk/wp-content/uploads/2020/02/A-View-from-the-North-Summary-Report.pdf

HM Land Registry (Her Majesty's Land Registry) (2021) 'Simple average house prices in England', Office for National Statistics. Available at: www. gov.uk/government/statistical-data-sets/uk-house-price-index-data-downloads-april-2021

Holmans, A. (2014) *Housing Demand and Need in England 1996–2016*, London: Town and Country Planning Association and National Housing Federation.

Hoolachan, J. (2022) 'Making home? Permitted and prohibited place-making in youth homeless accommodation', *Housing Studies*, 37(2): 212–31.

House of Commons (2021) 'The future of the planning system in England: first report of Session 2021–22'. Available at: https://committees. parliament.uk/work/634/the-future-of-the-planning-system-in-england/

Inch, A., Dunning, R., While, A., Hickman, H. and Payne, S. (2020) '"The object is to change the heart and soul": financial incentives, planning and opposition to new housebuilding in England', *Environment and Planning C: Politics and Space*, 38(4): 713–32.

Jacoby, S. and Alonso, L. (2022) 'Home use and experience during COVID-19 in London: problems of housing quality and design', *Sustainability*, 14(9): 5355.

Jones, C. and Watkins, C. (2009) *Housing Markets and Planning Policy*, Malaysia: Wiley-Blackwell.

Lord, A. and O'Brien, P. (2017) 'What price planning? Reimagining planning as "market maker"', *Planning Theory & Practice*, 18(2): 217–32.

Lord, A., Cheang, C.-W. and Dunning, R. (forthcoming) 'Exception and rule: how the "standard method" fails to govern England's housing requirement', *Town Planning Review*.

Lund, B. (2017) *Housing Politics in the United Kingdom: Power, Planning and Protest*, Bristol: Policy Press.

Matthews, P., Poyner, C. and Kjellgren, R. (2019) 'Lesbian, gay, bisexual, transgender and queer experiences of homelessness and identity: insecurity and home(o)normativity', *International Journal of Housing Policy*, 19(2): 232–53.

McGuinness, D., Greenhalgh, P. and Grainger, P. (2018) 'Does one size fit all? Place-neutral national planning policy in England and its impact on housing land supplies and local development plans in North East England', *Local Economy*, 33(3): 329–46.

McKee, K., Muir, J. and Moore, T. (2017) 'Housing policy in the UK: the importance of spatial nuance', *Housing Studies*, 32(1): 60–72.

Meen, G. and Whitehead, C. (2020) *Understanding Affordability*, Bristol: Bristol University Press.

Meers, J. (2023) '"Home" as an essentially contested concept and why this matters', *Housing Studies*, 38(4): 597–614.

MHCLG (Ministry for Housing, Communities and Local Government) (2021a) 'Live tables on rents, lettings and tenancies'. Available at: www.gov.uk/government/statistical-data-sets/live-tables-on-rents-lettings-and-tenancies

MHCLG (2021b) 'Live tables on dwelling stock: Table 104: by tenure, England (historical series)'. Available at: www.gov.uk/government/statistical-data-sets/live-tables-on-dwelling-stock-including-vacants

MHCLG (2021c) 'Planning applications in England: January to March 2021, statistical release'. Available at: https://assets.publishing.service.gov.uk/government/uploads/system/uploads/attachment_data/file/996115/Planning_Application_Statistics_-_January_to_March_2021_-_Statistical_Release.pdf

Miles, D. and Monro, V. (2021) 'UK house prices and three decades of decline in the risk-free real interest rate', *Economic Policy*, 36(108): 627–84.

Mulheirn, I. (2019) *Tackling the UK Housing Crisis: Is Supply the Answer?*, UK Collaborative Centre for Housing Evidence. Available at: https://housingevidence.ac.uk/wp-content/uploads/2019/08/20190820b-CaCHE-Housing-Supply-FINAL.pdf

ONS (Office for National Statistics) (2018) National population projections: 2018 based. Available at: https://www.ons.gov.uk/peoplepopulationandcommunity/populationandmigration/populationprojections/bulletins/nationalpopulationprojections/2018based

ONS (2020) Avergae household income (UK), Available at: https://www.ons.gov.uk/peoplepopulationandcommunity/personalandhouseholdfinances/incomeandwealth/bulletins/householddisposableincomeandinequality/financialyearending2021

ONS (2021a) 'Index of private housing rental prices, UK: monthly estimates'. Available at: www.ons.gov.uk/economy/inflationandpriceindices/datasets/indexofprivatehousingrentalpricesreferencetables

ONS (2021b) 'House building, UK: permanent dwellings started and completed by country'. Available at: www.ons.gov.uk/peoplepopulationandcommunity/housing/datasets/ukhousebuildingpermanentdwellingsstartedandcompleted

Soaita, A.M. and McKee, K. (2019) 'Assembling a "kind of" home in the UK private renting sector', *Geoforum*, 103: 148–57.

Sturzaker, J. (2010) 'The exercise of power to limit the development of new housing in the English countryside', *Environment & Planning A*, 42(4): 1001–16.

Tinson, A. and Clair, A. (2020) 'Better housing is crucial for our health and the COVID-19 recovery', The Health Foundation. Available at: www.health.org.uk/sites/default/files/2021-01/2020%20-%20Better%20housing%20is%20crucial.pdf

3

Localism: the peccadillos of a panacea

John Sturzaker and Olivier Sykes

Introduction

The final revisions to this book were drafted at the end of 2022, a year in which the UK had three different prime ministers, all from the same political party, inhabiting 10 Downing Street within a period of 45 days. In that context, it is almost surreal to remember the atmosphere in the Rose Garden of that premises on 12 May 2010. In a scene later described as 'sick-inducing' (Merrick, 2014), new Prime Minister David Cameron and Deputy Prime Minister Nick Clegg launched their agreed programme for government following the general election. In a very unusual outcome for the UK, that election had led to a coalition government between the Conservative Party of Cameron and Clegg's Liberal Democrats. While fractures between them appeared quickly, their initial coalition agreement was full of inspirational rhetoric about the 'common ground' between the parties:

> We share a conviction that the days of big government are over; that centralisation and top-down control have proved a failure. We believe that the time has come to disperse power more widely in Britain today; to recognise that we will only make progress if we help people to come together to make life better. In short, it is our ambition to distribute power and opportunity to people rather than hoarding authority within government. That way, we can build the free, fair and responsible society we want to see. (HM Government, 2010: 7)

While the language about the 'failure' of 'big government' can, perhaps rightly, be seen as part of a continuum with neoliberal anti-state orthodoxy of the previous 30 years, the emphasis on dispersing power through what Cameron (2010) called the 'Big Society' is arguably different, ostensibly leaning more in the direction of social liberalism. What is certain is that the Coalition government embarked, through such legislation as the Localism Act 2011, on a programme of changes to governance, including planning, which had the potential to 'disperse power more widely' and certainly changed the planning system in fundamental ways.

It has been argued that localism and the Big Society were of only transient significance, indelibly associated with Cameron and of little interest to the subsequent Conservative governments (Lowndes and Gardner, 2016). This may be true, but neighbourhood planning, introduced by the Localism Act, remains in place, and some within the Conservative Party are lobbying for this and other powers to be extended – a report by a group of backbench Conservative members of parliament (MPs) and a 'localist campaign group' (Gardiner, 2021) has argued for neighbourhood planning to be universal rather than optional, as is the case at present (Baillie et al, 2021). The current secretary of state of the government ministry in charge of planning, Michael Gove MP, appeared at the launch of the report at the 2021 Conservative Party conference, hence being perceived to 'cast his weight behind' the ideas within it (Gardiner, 2021). The state of failure of the UK government being what it is, Gove was sacked by ex-Prime Minister Boris Johnson the day before the latter resigned, to be replaced by Greg Clark MP, who was subsequently replaced by Simon Clarke MP during Liz Truss's doomed period as prime minister, who was replaced in due course, again, by Michael Gove as Rishi Sunak took office. The rapidity of these changes is clearly unusual, but there is something of a revolving door at this department at the best of times – at the last count, there have been eight changes in secretary of state since 2015. It is therefore extremely difficult to predict what the latest result of the ongoing tussle between localism and centralism within the Conservative Party is going to be. Nevertheless, it is appropriate to reflect on the legacies and lessons of a decade of experience of neighbourhood planning and to consider its future prospects. In doing so, it is important to state that we are not blind to its many faults, nor do we see localism, per our title, as a panacea for planning. As we will quickly return to, some of problems with neighbourhood planning can be related to detailed design and implementation issues, which could be resolved. Other flaws are more fundamental, and one position could be to argue that these mean that neighbourhood planning can never succeed, so should be abandoned. Whether or not we might agree with this position, given that neighbourhood planning is part of the planning system and appears likely to be for some time yet, we need to know who is benefiting from it and how.

The Localism Act 2011 and house building

As discussed in Chapter 2, reforms to planning in England are often introduced as part of wider efforts to build more houses. The Localism Act 2011 was no exception. The secretary of state at the time, Eric Pickles, acted quickly after the Coalition government came to power to abolish the previous 'failed Soviet tractor style top-down planning targets ... [in] Regional Strategies [which] built nothing but resentment – we want to build houses' (DCLG, 2010). The Localism Act put this on a legislative footing, abandoning the short-lived experiment with statutory regional planning that had been introduced in 2004 (for more on planning at the 'above local' scale, see Chapter 4) and introducing neighbourhood planning alongside other powers and 'incentives for local people so they support the construction of new homes in the right places' (DCLG, 2010). These incentives included the New Homes Bonus – a grant paid by central government to local authorities based on how many new homes were built in their area – and reform to the Community Infrastructure Levy to require a proportion of income from that development tax to be made available to communities if they adopted a neighbourhood plan (DCLG, 2011).

In the context of mainstream land–use planning, neighbourhood plans are in some ways quite revolutionary. They are optional, that is, communities decide whether they want to produce them. If they are produced, before they can come into use, they must be approved through a referendum of all those who live and work in the area. If they pass that referendum, then the local authority must 'make' the plan and adopt it as part of the 'development plan', that is, the policies against which planning applications for new developments must, by law, be determined.

The hope of the UK government was that the introduction of neighbourhood planning would lead to the construction of 31,000 additional homes over the first 11 years of the policy's operation (DCLG, 2012). This has not transpired. As discussed in Chapter 2, the implications of removing housing targets from the planning system (that many local authorities would seek to reduce the quantum of houses they were planning for) were swiftly recognised by the government, leading to their reintroduction through the Standard Method. Other research has shown that fiscal incentives for communities are unlikely to achieve any significant increase in support for new house building (Inch et al, 2020). Therefore, localism has evidently not worked on the grounds it was intended to. What, if anything, has it achieved?

Quantitative evidence on the take-up of neighbourhood planning

The government was extremely optimistic that neighbourhood planning would be widely taken up. The 'impact assessment' undertaken when the Localism Act was introduced (DCLG, 2012) estimated that within 11 years of the introduction of the act, 55 per cent of communities would have adopted a neighbourhood plan – 4,190 of them. By the end of 2021, only 1,200 neighbourhood plans had been adopted (Locality, 2022). Before trying to unpick why this might be, in this section of the chapter, we explore data on which types of communities are using the neighbourhood planning powers.

Table 3.1: (Un)Changing patterns of neighbourhood planning activity over time

	IMD Q1 (wealthiest)	IMD Q2	IMD Q3	IMD Q4	IMD Q5 (poorest)	Totals
January 2016	414	424	410	255	122	1,625
	25.5%	26.1%	25.2%	15.7%	7.5%	
November 2011	674	749	645	396	235	2,699
	25.0%	27.8%	23.9%	14.7%	8.7%	

Source: Adapted from Locality (2022) and Parker and Salter (2016)

In this book's sister volume on the impacts of localism across urban governance (Sturzaker and Nurse, 2020: 158), we concluded that in relation to reforms at a range of scales, 'places that are richer are tending to do well, and places that are poorer are tending to do badly'. Neighbourhood planning exemplifies this trend. In their study of the first five years of neighbourhood planning, Parker and Salter (2016) found that more than 50 per cent of neighbourhood planning areas were in the lower two quintiles of the Index of Multiple Deprivation (IMD) (the least deprived areas) and only 23 per cent were from the upper two IMD quintiles (the most deprived areas). Our analysis of the data from the end of 2021 shows that the picture is largely unchanged: the proportion in the least deprived areas has increased slightly to nearly 53 per cent, while the proportion in the most deprived areas remains at 23 per cent (see Table 3.1).

This suggests that the argument made by some in the earlier days of neighbourhood planning – that wealthier communities had a 'head start' in neighbourhood planning but that other areas might catch up – has not come to pass. It remains the case that people in poorer areas are much less likely to embark upon the process of producing a neighbourhood plan. We explore the reasons for, and problematic implications of, this trend in the following. However, we can also now draw on more data to explore how successful those communities who have begun the process of producing a neighbourhood plan have been at navigating the 'complex statutory scheme' (Sturzaker and Gordon, 2017: 1329) and passing the referendum at the end of that process. At the time when Parker and Salter did their initial analysis, only 130 neighbourhood plans had been approved at referendum. By the end of 2021, this number had increased to 1,204, allowing us to analyse how deprivation has affected the likelihood of success in completing a neighbourhood plan. Table 3.2 shows the proportion of plans in each quartile that have passed the referendum, are in progress (being at an intermediate stage of completion) or are still at the 'designated' stage. The latter is the first step in preparing a neighbourhood plan and denotes that the local authority has designated a neighbourhood forum and approved the area

Table 3.2: Pattern of neighbourhood plans and progress

	Passed referendum	% passed referendum of quartile total	In progress	% in progress of quartile total	Designated	% designated of quartile total	Total
IMD Q1 (wealthiest)	325	48.7%	48	7.2%	294	44.1%	667
IMD Q2	334	44.8%	39	5.2%	373	50.0%	746
IMD Q3	329	51.4%	44	6.9%	267	41.7%	640
IMD Q4	143	36.2%	16	4.1%	236	59.7%	395
IMD Q5 (poorest)	73	31.3%	19	8.2%	141	60.5%	233
All IMDQs	1,204		166		1,311		2,681

Source: Adapted from Locality (2022)

of a neighbourhood plan. This is an essential first step, so some of those in this category have been designated only recently; however, a proportion of them represent communities who have started the neighbourhood planning process at some point since 2011 but not progressed beyond designation. We explore the reasons for this in the following, but Table 3.2 shows that a significantly larger proportion of neighbourhood plans in more deprived areas remain at the 'designated' stage and, conversely, that a significantly smaller proportion have passed the referendum.

These figures starkly illustrate the impact of deprivation upon the likelihood of successfully completing a neighbourhood plan. In IMD Quartiles 1–3, between 45 and 51 per cent of neighbourhood plans have passed their referendum, and 41–50 per cent remain at the 'designated' stage. In IMD Quartiles 4 and 5, these proportions are 31–36 per cent and 60 per cent, respectively. Putting it more simply, if you live in a less deprived area, around half of the neighbourhood plans that have been started since 2011 have passed referendum, while if you live in a more deprived area, this falls to around a third.

We can further supplement this with data from one region of England, the North West. Full analysis of those data can be found in Sturzaker and Nurse (2020), but here we present some key 'headlines'. First, we found that patterns found in relation to local authority data at the national level were largely replicated in the North West: a greater proportion of activity was found in more deprived parts of the region than at the national scale (28 per cent in the most deprived local authorities, compared to 23 per cent found by Parker and Salter [2016] and in our more recent analysis). In large part, this is due to the fact that the North West is a comparatively deprived region – only one North West local authority (Ribble Valley, with three neighbourhood planning areas at the time of this analysis) is in the top quintile, that is, the least deprived 20 per cent of local authorities nationally. The North West also contains four of the ten most deprived local authorities in the country by this measure.

Analysis at the local authority level blurs the picture of what is happening in neighbourhoods, so we also undertook analysis at that scale (for more details, see Sturzaker and Nurse, 2020). This again illustrated that most activity is in less deprived areas, as shown in Figure 3.1. It also shows that the level of activity has increased over time, with more activity as the system 'beds in', though no dramatic increase is visible in more deprived areas.

Why are poorer places less likely to undertake neighbourhood planning?

We suggest that there are various factors behind the persistent and enduring patterns in neighbourhood planning take-up just discussed. Some of these

Figure 3.1: Deprivation at neighbourhood level, activity type and activity over time

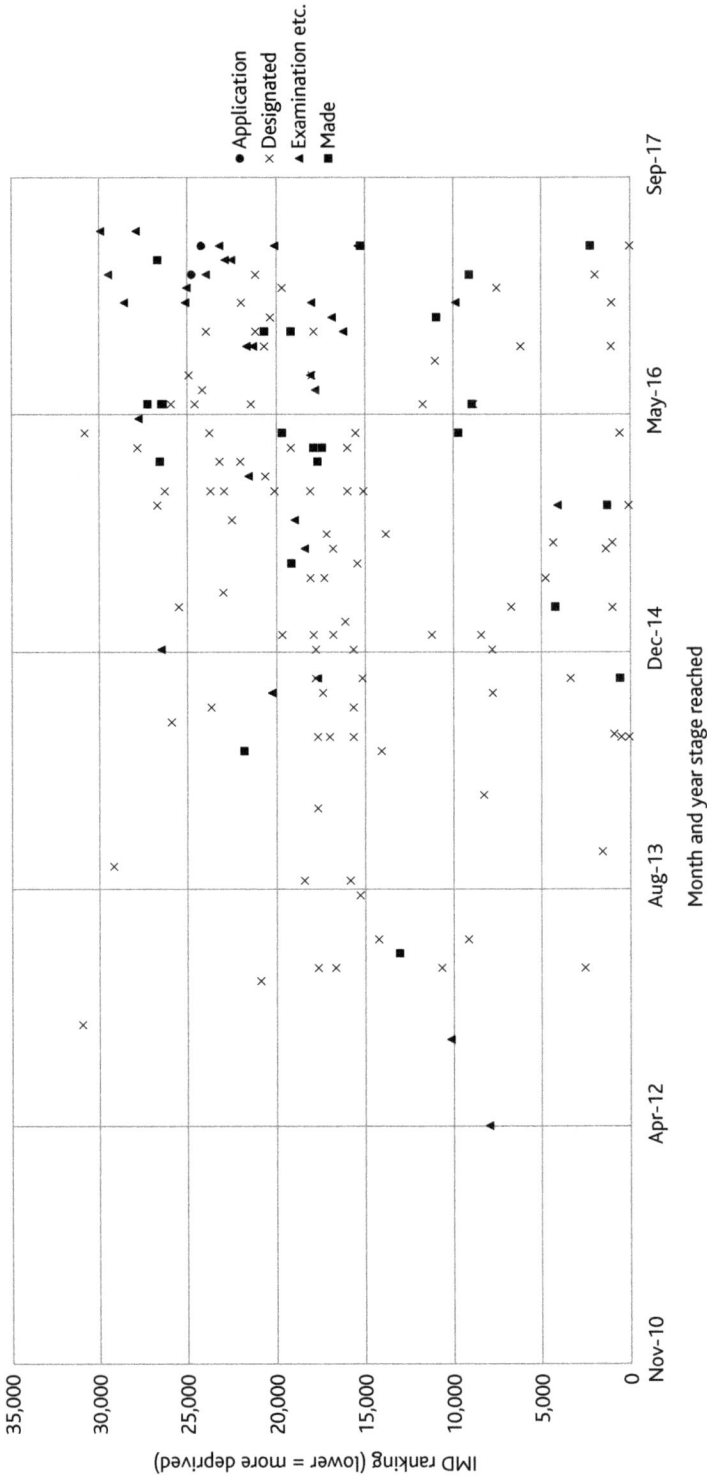

- Application
- × Designated
- ▲ Examination etc.
- ■ Made

Month and year stage reached

IMD ranking (lower = more deprived)

Source: Sturzaker and Nurse (2020: 138)

are inherent to the very nature of this form of community- (as opposed to expert-)led planning, and others are a result of interactions between the details of the statutory process and several groups of key actors in that process.

To take the inherent factors first, it has long been observed that wealthier individuals and communities are more likely to (successfully) engage with planning, whether in England or elsewhere. Proposed reasons for this differential engagement have included: variations in time and inclination to engage with planning, for example, that retired people are more likely to have the time needed to participate (Sutcliffe and Holt, 2011); a greater ability on the part of middle-class people to interact with the complexities of planning language and systems (Matthews and Hastings, 2012); and the 'collective action' problem (Pennington, 2000), that is, that the poor 'do not have sufficient unity to form a power-coalition that can insist on its interests being served by town planners' (Simmie, 1974: 139). Thus, the great and much-missed Professor Sir Peter Hall (2011: 60) suggested that neighbourhood planning was most likely to be taken up by middle-class people living in 'nice places'. This likelihood, however, was not predestination, and as the statistical evidence outlined earlier shows, some poorer communities have produced neighbourhood plans. There is a growing body of evidence that casts light on why more of them have not done so.

To organise this evidence, we present it in the sequence of steps necessary to produce a neighbourhood plan (for more detail, see Sturzaker and Gordon, 2017: 1328–29). The first step is the 'designation' of a body to prepare a neighbourhood plan. In areas where parish and town councils exist, these bodies, and their spatial boundaries, are by default the plan-making body. This has been identified as a considerable advantage in the neighbourhood planning process, as parish and town councils have a pre-existing governance architecture (committees, volunteer members and a budget drawn from the precept they can add to local council taxation) and often existing staff to help support the process (Taylor et al, 2019). The data reflect this advantage, with 91 per cent of the earliest neighbourhood plans designated in rural areas (Parker and Salter, 2016). In areas without parish and town councils, a wholly new body must be created, a neighbourhood forum, and a boundary for the neighbourhood agreed. The forum must be constituted of at least 21 people who live, work or are elected council members in the area. Pulling together such a group of volunteers takes time and effort, which, as noted earlier, might be easier in wealthier areas. That apart, however, the privileging of parish and town councils introduces explicit bias in favour of wealthier areas, as parish and town councils are almost exclusively in rural parts of England and, in general, rural areas are less deprived than are urban areas. A second potential barrier in relation to designation is that the membership of the forum and the boundaries of the neighbourhood plan area must be agreed by the local authority, and there is a body of evidence showing local authorities being reluctant to agree to the proposed forum membership or the area boundaries at all, or intervening to amend the proposed boundaries (Geoghegan, 2013; Parker et al, 2017; Sturzaker and Gordon, 2017). Our recent research suggests that this might be more likely in urban areas, where local authorities may not welcome complications to their 'painstakingly assembled entrepreneurial urban regimes and partnerships' (Sturzaker et al, 2022: 53).

The next step in the preparation of a neighbourhood plan is the process of actually writing it. As with all forms of plan making, this is a complex and lengthy exercise, despite a coalition minister in 2011 saying 'Planning "isn't brain surgery"' (Carpenter, 2011). Neighbourhood planning was introduced through legislation described by the government as 'light touch' (DCLG, 2017), but it has been observed that laying more expectations on 'ordinary citizens' to actively participate in planning places often substantial burdens upon them (Inch, 2015). Local authorities are required by law to support communities in preparing neighbourhood plans, but there are large variations in the extent of support local authorities (find themselves able to) offer (Parker et al, 2020), with some funding one or more officers specifically to work with neighbourhood plan groups, and others offering very little in terms of meaningful support. Some local authorities appear to be antagonistic towards neighbourhood planning, whether due to political opposition to the Conservative Party's policy, concerns over the democratic legitimacy of groups undertaking neighbourhood planning or more opaque, perhaps troubling, reasons (Sturzaker et al, 2022). The level of support able to be offered by local authorities is, in large part, connected to how well resourced individual local authorities are. Local authority budgets have been cut by at least half since 2010, with cuts falling disproportionately on more deprived areas (Lowndes and Gardner, 2016) – so the poor have got poorer. When some local authorities are being forced to make decisions about the delivery of critical social care support (Harris, 2020), it is unsurprising that planning budgets have seen significant reductions (Kenny, 2019), with support for neighbourhood planning hard to prioritise over caring for vulnerable people. This, of course, means that in some places with pre-existing disadvantages as regards the institutional capacity for neighbourhood planning, there is less support available than in wealthier areas (Sturzaker and Nurse, 2020).

With or without support from their local authority, there are grants available from central government to help communities prepare their neighbourhood plans. Much of this funding is tied to the delivery of additional housing, in line with the continuing focus of UK governments on this subject. Our previous work (Sturzaker and Nurse, 2020: ch 6) has drawn on interview testimony with those supporting neighbourhood plan groups (usually funded through grants from the government), some of whom argued that the focus on housing was unhelpful. Returning to the transcripts of those interviews, we can find more detail behind that argument. One neighbourhood planning support worker referred to the work they were doing in a major northern city, wherein "Housing isn't a challenge.... The vast majority of housing needed already has planning permission.... The issue of people getting housing is bigger economic opportunity.... It's pointless building more housing ... if they [local people] haven't got employment." Therefore, in areas where there may also be an ample stock of housing – indeed, according to some, an oversupply of certain types of homes – if neighbourhood planning funding is directed largely towards increasing house building, communities working on neighbourhood plans in those areas are less likely to receive funding.

As referred to several times earlier, neighbourhood planning is only the latest form of planning, both in England and beyond, to suffer from asymmetric participation due to the institutional capacity of communities. A particular issue in relation to neighbourhood planning, however, is that as it involves, in theory, citizens planning for themselves, knowledge and understanding of planning is clearly advantageous, and various authors have noted the prominence of professional planners in many neighbourhood planning groups (Sturzaker and Nurse, 2020; Sturzaker and Shaw, 2015; Vigar et al, 2017). While, of course, members of a profession and discipline as committed to social justice as planning may live in a huge range of neighbourhoods, it is unsurprising to find that they, or others with experience of the built environment, such as architects or surveyors, more commonly reside in less deprived areas and are thus able to add their voluntary capacity to the neighbourhood planning process in those areas.

Through all these issues and more, the inherent imbalance in neighbourhood planning capacity has been exacerbated by choices made in the design and implementation of the neighbourhood planning process. In the following section, we reflect upon why this matters.

Planning for housing through neighbourhood plans and spatial exclusion

A significant problem highlighted by many in relation to neighbourhood plans is that they must be 'pro-growth'. Prompted perhaps by the reaction of the development industry to the draft legislation contained in the Localism Bill in 2010 (Tait and Inch, 2016), this requirement was introduced by the government into the final Localism Act. In practice, the requirement means that neighbourhood plans cannot be anti-development: they must not allocate less land for development than in the local plan that sits above them in the planning policy hierarchy. Understanding what neighbourhood plans are saying is an enormous task when compared to the analysis of where they are (discussed earlier). As yet, there has been relatively little work at scale on how neighbourhood plans are grappling with the pro-growth requirement. A study by the development consultancy Lichfields found that many of the 330 plans they looked at did not focus on housing, being more concerned with such issues as green space or infrastructure provision instead. They concluded that only 15 of those plans were planning for additional homes, an uplift of 3 per cent in the supply of homes in those communities (Lichfields, 2018).

Does this matter? Unlike the UK government, we are not concerned about increasing housing supply to the exclusion of all other issues. There is ample evidence that demand, rather than supply, is of equal importance (Gallent et al, 2017) in relation to questions of access to, and the affordability of, housing. However, when aligned with the evidence we discussed earlier around the types of communities who are dominating the production of neighbourhood plans and the reasons we have identified for that domination, we argue that the fact that neighbourhood planning is not leading to the hoped-for expansion of housing numbers *is* important.

When neighbourhood planning was being discussed and in the early stages of its introduction, we wrote in cautiously optimistic terms about it (Sturzaker, 2011). We drew on interview data in rural communities suggesting that there was some evidence that it *might* work, in that it could help address concerns about a 'democratic deficit' (Bell et al, 2005) and distrust of decision makers in planning. That article, in turn, drew on work exploring opposition to housing in rural areas (Sturzaker, 2010; Sturzaker and Shucksmith, 2011), through which we identified the use of power by elites to exclude poorer people from the countryside, summed up by an interviewee noting that he was in favour of using the planning system to 'keep riff-raff from [nearby city] out of the community' (Sturzaker, 2010: 1014). Therefore, our cautious optimism in 2011 was caveated, and we noted the need for those designing neighbourhood planning to think carefully about how the breadth of community interests could be involved and how conflict and self-interest could be overcome. Our views on this have not changed: we believe that carefully designed, implemented and funded neighbourhood planning could be a powerful tool. However, that is not what we have in the process as introduced in the Localism Act.

The problems we discussed earlier have led to a process for neighbourhood planning that has arguably exacerbated the issues we identified in 2010 and 2011, whereby the powerful are privileged in, through and by planning in England. As the data we have presented for the first time earlier illustrate, wealthier communities and, by extension, the people who live within them are far more likely to begin the process of neighbourhood planning and, once begun, more likely to complete it and have a plan passed at referendum and 'made' by the local authority. This matters because, first, to return to Arnstein's (1969: 216) famous words from 1969, 'Participation of the governed in their government is, in theory, the cornerstone of democracy.' Neighbourhood planning is unequivocally part of the 'government' in this sense: it is a part of the statutory planning system and used in the determination of planning applications for development proposals. If this is going to endure, then everyone should have an equal right and ability to take part in neighbourhood planning. However, it also matters because the pattern of engagement in neighbourhood planning that we have illustrated and discussed in this chapter is actively entrenching and exacerbating spatial inequality.

Those communities who are able to produce a neighbourhood plan are able to exert a stronger influence on the places in which they live than are those who are not. Despite the important framing noted earlier that neighbourhood plans must be 'pro-growth', many communities have been adept in using their neighbourhood plans to promote the form of growth *they* prefer. This might be done by: promoting particular locations over others for development; specifying what type or size of housing they will support (with other forms of development implicitly or explicitly discouraged); and expressing positive views about community-led or -owned forms of development. None of these are intrinsically regressive in nature; indeed, the opposite is often true. However, the point is that they *can* be regressive. As we wrote in 2010 in relation to the popularity of 'locals-only' policies in relation to new house building, such approaches, while often popular with communities and encouraged by national and local government, can be 'potentially discriminatory' (Sturzaker, 2010: 1012) and part of a general attitude of opposition to 'otherness'. Research on the content of neighbourhood plans has found evidence of support for non-standard forms of housing delivery (Bradley and Sparling, 2017), and while this has been seen as a positive thing, that is, a challenge to the hegemony of the market, it has the potential to be less positive. As noted by others: 'Distinctions will need to be carefully delineated between "community" (outward-looking, providing open access to resources) and "communal" (inward-looking, with limitations for wider access to resources)' (Field and Layard, 2017: 111).

This might matter less, or matter differently, if every community was able to express their views through a statutory neighbourhood plan. However, as we have seen, they are not. Therefore, the net effect of some communities having being able to produce neighbourhood plans and others not is that some communities are able to express disapproval of development and some are not. Unpopular developments may therefore be more likely to be located in places where there is no neighbourhood plan, maintaining a pattern observed in the US of 'locally unwanted land uses' (LULUs) being more likely to be located in more deprived places (Schively, 2007). The proposition noted in the introduction that neighbourhood plans be made mandatory would, in theory, level the playing field, but the stark patterns we have revealed in relation to deprivation suggest that without a significant injection of resources, it will be very difficult for poorer communities to fully embrace neighbourhood planning.

As we discussed in the introduction, the attitude of the UK government towards (neighbourhood) planning has changed somewhat during the period in which this book was written. In the concluding section of this chapter, we attempt to discern possible ways forward from the most recent policy announcements and ministerial pronouncements. As with the rest of the book, this is, of course, caveated by the fact that it is impossible to say with any certainty who will be prime minister in a year's time or, if there is a change of government, how the Labour Party might deal with neighbourhood planning.

Conclusion

In this chapter, we have assessed neighbourhood planning, the flagship element of the Localism Act 2011 and a new component of the planning system in England intended to increase community support for housing. As we have discussed, it has largely failed in that aspiration, but it has succeeded in giving some additional power to communities to plan for the future of their areas. The extent to which communities have been able to use that power has varied substantially, with poorer areas much less likely to begin, or finish, work on a neighbourhood plan. This mirrors experience elsewhere; in a recent review of trends, Nadin et al (2020) note that opportunities for citizen participation in planning have been expanded across Europe but that actual engagement with these opportunities remains weak in many places. They conclude that there is a 'need for further development of participatory planning practices' (Nadin et al, 2020: 799). Elsewhere (Sturzaker et al, 2022), we have explored the barriers to neighbourhood planning that have been established by politicians in some places and the need for other aspects of reform to the system (Taylor et al, 2019). Does the latest proposed legislation by the UK government address such concerns?

The Levelling-up and Regeneration Bill, published in May 2022, contains proposals to both change aspects of the neighbourhood planning approach and introduce a new element of community governance: 'street votes'. The changes do not 'fundamentally reinvent neighbourhood planning' (Eckford, 2022a); rather, they are intended to re-emphasise central government commitment to it and make it easier for communities to produce policy that is more positive and innovative. The scope for framing by local authorities would be slightly reduced and a new more streamlined alternative to full neighbourhood plans, 'neighbourhood priorities statements', may be more attractive to less well-resourced communities.

Street votes are a concept that has been promoted by the right-wing think tank the Policy Exchange (Hughes and Southwood, 2021) and 'has made rapid progress by Whitehall' (Blackman, 2022) to form part of the Levelling-up and Regeneration Bill. Street votes, as the name implies, would operate at a smaller scale than neighbourhood plans and would 'permit residents to propose development on their street, and then hold a vote on whether it should be given planning permission' (Blackman, 2022). As yet, the draft legislation is lacking in detail, but the scale of development would appear to also be small and is likely to take the form of residents extending or redeveloping their homes. As with neighbourhood planning, street votes seem highly unlikely to have a substantive effect on housing supply; indeed, some have argued that they will, in fact, make existing homes more expensive as they are extended and thus increase in value (Booth, 2022). The idea has been described as 'frankly nuts' by the head of policy of the Town & Country Planning Association (Eckford, 2022b).

It is hard, then, to argue that either neighbourhood planning, in its current or proposed amended form, or street votes are likely to increase the supply of housing in England in any meaningful way. Both aspects of policy do, to some extent, increase engagement and involvement with planning and so can be perceived as broadly positive. Street votes, however, can also be seen as another example of the deregulation of planning that has been pursued by Conservative governments since 2010, which is discussed in more detail in Chapter 5. These approaches can therefore be seen as emblematic of the tensions that characterise much of those governments' approach to planning: between centralisation and localism; between deregulation and protectionism; between high-quality design and housing supply; and between the speed of decision making and community engagement. The case study of neighbourhood planning illustrates that these tensions are extremely difficult to resolve and that glib pronouncements about dispersing power are all but meaningless without strong and meaningful commitment from those who currently hold power. As has been argued elsewhere (Lord et al, 2017), it would be difficult for a government of any political stripe to abolish neighbourhood planning – once the Pandora's box of 'empowerment' is open, it would take a brave politician to close it again. Therefore, if it is to remain part of the English planning system, it seems clear that fundamental changes are needed to make it work effectively.

References

Arnstein, S.R. (1969) 'A ladder of citizen participation', *Journal of the American Planning Association*, 35(4): 216–24.

Baillie, S., Cates, M., Fletcher, N., Gideon, J., Gullis, J., Howell, P. et al (2021) 'Trusting the people: the case for community-powered conservatism'. Available at: www.newsocialcovenant.co.uk/wp-content/uploads/2021/10/TrustingThePeople.pdf

Bell, D., Gray, T. and Haggett, C. (2005) 'The "social gap" in wind farm siting decisions: explanations and policy responses', *Environmental Politics*, 14(4): 460–77.

Blackman, D. (2022) 'What street votes would mean for councils and communities', Planning Resource, 23 June. Available at: www.planningr esource.co.uk/article/1791011/street-votes-mean-councils-communities

Booth, R. (2022) 'Street votes on England planning rules "will not increase affordable housing"', *The Guardian*, 11 May. Available at: www.theguard ian.com/society/2022/may/11/street-votes-on-planning-rules-will-not-increase-affordable-housing

Bradley, Q. and Sparling, W. (2017) 'The impact of neighbourhood planning and localism on house-building in England', *Housing, Theory and Society*, 34(1): 106–18.

Cameron, D. (2010) 'Big society speech'. Available at: www.gov.uk/gov ernment/speeches/big-society-speech

Carpenter, J. (2011) 'Planning "isn't brain surgery", says communities minister'. Available at: https://www.planningresource.co.uk/article/1093 322/planning-isnt-brain-surgery-says-communities-minister

DCLG (Department for Communities and Local Government) (2010) 'Eric Pickles puts stop to flawed regional strategies today'. Available at: https:// webarchive.nationalarchives.gov.uk/20120919160104/http://www.comm unities.gov.uk/news/planningandbuilding/1632278

DCLG (2011) *A Plain English Guide to the Localism Act*, London: DCLG.

DCLG (2012) *Localism Act: Neighbourhood Plans and Community Right to Build: Impact Assessment*, London: DCLG. Available at: https://assets.pub lishing.service.gov.uk/government/uploads/system/uploads/attachment_ data/file/8447/2100392.pdf

DCLG (2017) 'Post implementation review of the Neighbourhood Planning (General) Regulations 2012 SI 2012/637'. Available at: www.gov.uk/gov ernment/consultations/technical-consultation-on-planning

Eckford, S. (2022a) 'The implications of the Levelling Up Bill's proposed changes to neighbourhood planning', Planning Resource. Available at: www.planningresource.co.uk/article/1793171/implications-levelling-bills-proposed-changes-neighbourhood-planning

Eckford, S. (2022b) 'TCPA policy chief describes government's street vote proposals as "frankly nuts"', Planning Resource. Available at: www.plann ingresource.co.uk/article/1806371/tcpa-policy-chief-describes-governme nts-street-vote-proposals-frankly-nuts

Field, M. and Layard, A. (2017) 'Locating community-led housing within neighbourhood plans as a response to England's housing needs', *Public Money & Management*, 37(2): 105–12. Available at: https://doi.org/10.1080/ 09540962.2016.1266157

Gallent, N., Durrant, D. and May, N. (2017) 'Housing supply, investment demand and money creation: a comment on the drivers of London's housing crisis', *Urban Studies*, 54(10): 2204–16. Available at: https://doi.org/10.1177/0042098017705828

Gardiner, J. (2021) 'Gove backs MPs' report that calls for "universal" neighbourhood planning', Planning Resource. Available at: https://www.planningresource.co.uk/article/1729372/gove-backs-mps-report-calls-universal-neighbourhood-planning

Geoghegan, J. (2013) 'Hackney refuses neighbourhood plan bids over community tension fears', Planning Resource. Available at: www.planningresource.co.uk/article/1192867/hackney-refuses-neighbourhood-plan-bids-community-tension-fears

Hall, P. (2011) 'The Big Society and the evolution of ideas', *Town and Country Planning*, 80(2): 59–60.

Harris, J. (2020) 'Austerity is grinding on: it has cut too deep to "level up"', *The Guardian*, 10 February. Available at: www.theguardian.com/commentisfree/2020/feb/10/austerity-level-up-newcastle-budget-cuts

HM Government (Her Majesty's Government) (2010) *The Coalition: Our Programme for Government*, London: HM Government Cabinet Office.

Hughes, S. and Southwood, B. (2021) 'Strong suburbs enabling streets to control their own development', London: Policy Exchange. Available at: https://policyexchange.org.uk/wp-content/uploads/2022/10/Strong-Suburbs.pdf

Inch, A. (2015) 'Ordinary citizens and the political cultures of planning: in search of the subject of a new democratic ethos', *Planning Theory*, 14(4): 404–24.

Inch, A., Dunning, R., While, A., Hickman, H. and Payne, S. (2020) '"The object is to change the heart and soul": financial incentives, planning and opposition to new housebuilding in England', *Environment and Planning C: Politics and Space*, 38(4): 713–32.

Kenny, T. (2019) *Resourcing Public Planning: Five Stories about Local Authority Planning in England and Recommendations for the Next Chapter*, London: Royal Town Planning Institute.

Lichfields (2018) *Local Choices? Housing Delivery through Neighbourhood Plans*, London: Lichfields. Available at: https://lichfields.uk/media/4128/local-choices_housing-delivery-through-neighbourhood-plans.pdf

Locality (2022) 'Key neighbourhood planning data'. Available at: https://neighbourhoodplanning.org/toolkits-and-guidance/key-neighbourhood-planning-data/

Lord, A., Mair, M., Sturzaker, J. and Jones, P. (2017) '"The planners' dream goes wrong?" Questioning citizen-centred planning', *Local Government Studies*, 43(3): 343–63.

Lowndes, V. and Gardner, A. (2016) 'Local governance under the Conservatives: super-austerity, devolution and the "smarter state"', *Local Government Studies*, 42(3): 357–75. Available at: https://doi.org/10.1080/03003930.2016.1150837

Matthews, P. and Hastings, A. (2012) 'Middle-class political activism and middle-class advantage in relation to public services: a realist synthesis of the evidence base', *Social Policy and Administration*, 47(1): 72–92.

Merrick, J. (2014) 'Cameron/Clegg Rose Garden love-in was "sickening", says Lib Dem adviser Julia Goldsworthy', *The Independent*, 16 March. Available at: www.independent.co.uk/news/uk/politics/cameron-clegg-rose-garden-lovein-was-sickening-says-lib-dem-adviser-julia-goldswor thy-9194832.html

Nadin, V., Stead, D., Dąbrowski, M. and Fernandez-Maldonado, A.M. (2020) 'Integrated, adaptive and participatory spatial planning: trends across Europe', *Regional Studies*, 55(5): 791–803.

Parker, G. and Salter, K. (2016) 'Five years of neighbourhood planning: a review of take-up and distribution', *Town and Country Planning*, 85(5): 181–8.

Parker, G., Lynn, T. and Wargent, M. (2017) 'Contestation and conservatism in neighbourhood planning in England: reconciling agonism and collaboration?', *Planning Theory & Practice*, 18(3): 446–65.

Parker, G., Wargent, M., Salter, K., Dobson, M., Lynn, T., Yuille, A. et al (2020) *Impacts of Neighbourhood Planning in England: Final Report to the Ministry of Housing, Communities and Local Government*, Reading: University of Reading.

Pennington, M. (2000) *Planning and the Political Market: Public Choice and the Politics of Government Failure*, London: Athlone.

Schively, C. (2007) 'Understanding the NIMBY and LULU phenomena: reassessing our knowledge base and informing future research', *Journal of Planning Literature*, 21(3): 255–66.

Simmie, J.M. (1974) *Citizens in Conflict: The Sociology of Town Planning*, London: Hutchinson Educational.

Sturzaker, J. (2010) 'The exercise of power to limit the development of new housing in the English countryside', *Environment and Planning A*, 42(4): 1001–16.

Sturzaker, J. (2011) 'Can community empowerment reduce opposition to housing? Evidence from rural England', *Planning Practice and Research*, 26(5): 555–70.

Sturzaker, J. and Gordon, M. (2017) 'Democratic tensions in decentralised planning: rhetoric, legislation and reality in England', *Environment and Planning C: Politics and Space*, 35(7): 1324–39.

Sturzaker, J. and Nurse, A. (2020) *Rescaling Urban Governance: Planning, Localism and Institutional Change*, Bristol: Policy Press.

Sturzaker, J. and Shaw, D. (2015) 'Localism in practice: lessons from a pioneer neighbourhood plan in England', *Town Planning Review*, 86(5): 587–609.

Sturzaker, J. and Shucksmith, M. (2011) 'Planning for housing in rural England: discursive power and spatial exclusion', *Town Planning Review*, 82(2): 169–93.

Sturzaker, J., Sykes, O. and Dockerill, B. (2022) 'Disruptive localism: how far does clientelism shape the prospects of neighbourhood planning in deprived urban communities?', *Planning Theory & Practice*, 23(1): 43–59.

Sutcliffe, R. and Holt, R. (2011) *Who Is Ready for the Big Society?*, Birmingham: Consulting InPlace.

Tait, M. and Inch, A. (2016) 'Putting localism in place: conservative images of the good community and the contradictions of planning reform in England', *Planning Practice and Research*, 31(2): 174–94.

Taylor, E., Santamaria, F. and Sturzaker, J. (2019) 'Localism: a planning panacea?', *Town Planning Review*, 90(5): 481–96.

Vigar, G., Gunn, S. and Brooks, E. (2017) 'Governing our neighbours: participation and conflict in neighbourhood planning', *Town Planning Review*, 88(4): 423–42.

4

Planning at the 'larger than local' scale: where next?

Alexander Nurse

Introduction

The last century of English sub-national (that is, regional) planning has been defined by two core themes. The first theme is that there is a persistent North–South divide (Dorling, 2010) that has fairly consistently been characterised by an overperforming South East and an underperforming Northern England. This first began to emerge as a serious spatial issue in the 1930s, when Northern industrial areas did not emerge from the Great Depression at the same rate as others. The second is the persistent, if varied, efforts to close that divide, which have appeared on a semi-regular basis across the last century or so.

There are some common characteristics as to how this issue has been approached. For one, successive governments have been consistent in diagnosing the problem. From the Barlow Report of 1940 (Barlow, 1940) and the Redcliffe-Maud Report of 1966 (Wise, 1969), through John Major's government office regions and John Prescott's Northern Way in the 1990s (The Northern Way, 2004; Goodchild and Hickman, 2006; Taylor et al, 2010), to the Northern Powerhouse and levelling up discussed in this chapter, all have recognised sclerotic growth away from London and have in some form advocated for a 'regional' form of governance to sit between the 'local' and the 'state'. Yet, unlike other national contexts with perhaps more settled sub-national structures (Desjardins and Géneau de Lamarlière, 2016; Demazière and Sykes, 2019), British 'regionalism' is not stable. Rather, over the decades, regional and metropolitan thinking has fallen in and out of favour, and the recent (that is, post-2010) sub-national environment is as much characterised by the introduction of 'new' forms of governance as by their subsequent abolition and a retrenchment towards centralisation (Sturzaker and Nurse, 2020). Ultimately, therefore, the thing that unites most forays into British regionalism is: (1) that they are short-lived; and (2) that, thus far, no scheme can claim success in solving one of British planning's grandest and long-running challenges.

This chapter explores the latest forays into this field undertaken by the Conservative-led governments of the 2010s and early 2020s. It first charts the abolition of regional governance in 2010 and its gradual replacement with city-region-focused combined authorities and subsequently democratically elected 'metro mayors' to lead those constructs. Then, following a period of torpor in the aftermath of the 2016 European Union membership referendum, it discusses how this movement pivoted to one that focused on 'levelling up', which moved away from those sub-regional constructs and towards centrally administered funding streams.

The fall and (partial) rise of regional thinking

In sub-national (that is, regional) planning terms, the first few weeks of the Coalition government in June 2010 were abrupt. On 6 July, mere weeks after coming to office, the incoming Secretary of State for Communities and Local Government Eric Pickles had abolished regional development agencies and regional spatial strategies (RSSs). In doing so, and fairly or otherwise, Pickles admonished what he perceived as a 'Soviet tractor style' (DCLG, 2010a) approach to governance. His intent was clear: regional planning in England was dead.

Shortly after, Pickles, along with Business Secretary Vince Cable, would signify their new approach in the form of local enterprise partnerships (DCLG, 2010c). These new organisations would be self-identified, based at the scale of the functional economic area (DCLG, 2010b), and be business led. In practice, and reflecting the reality of most functional economic areas, many of the new LEPs would coalesce around city regions, though fundamental questions remained, not least regarding the democratic accountability of these organisations (Bentley et al, 2010; Pugalis, 2011). In planning terms, the new LEPs had no planning powers, and the strategic approach of the RSSs would be gone for now. Although few would realise it at the time, these actions in the first few weeks of the Coalition government would set the tone for sub-national governance for much of the next decade.

While sub-national planning stayed in abeyance for much of the Coalition's time in office, a programme of devolution (with a lower-case 'd') slowly began to emerge. Initially, this was enacted through a suite of bespoke 'city deals' (DCLG, 2012) made with the core cities that provided for some modest transport and economic planning powers in return for referenda on moving to a directly elected mayoral model of governance. In the case of the latter reforms, only two cities (Bristol and Liverpool) adopted this mayoral model, with voters in all others rejecting the proposals (Marsh, 2012).

The next major shift in Coalition thinking came in 2014, when, during a speech in Manchester, Chancellor George Osborne (2014) announced proposals to create a 'Northern Powerhouse', which would align the economic powers of the Northern English cities to counterbalance the growth of London. In doing so, after spending most of the duration of their first term intervening in cities, the Northern Powerhouse would represent the Coalition's first overt attempt at tackling British planning's Gordian knot that is the North–South divide (Nurse, 2015b).

The Northern Powerhouse, and its similarly named sibling, the 'Midlands Engine', were premised on combined authorities – largely city-region/ metropolitan constructs comprising multiple local authorities, many of which bore a striking resemblance to the metropolitan counties abolished by Margaret Thatcher's government in 1986 (Flynn et al, 1985; Leach and Game, 1991). To access any reforms/funding, combined authorities would be expected to agree a 'devolution deal' with central government, on the understanding that elections (not referenda) would subsequently be held for a directly elected 'metro mayor'. This new mayor would receive £300 million in funding over 30 years and a potential suite of powers that could include transport, economic planning, education and skills, policing, and, in some cases, healthcare (Nurse, 2015b). In the first indication of something resembling a replacement for regional planning since the abolition of RSSs, the metro mayors would also have powers to convene a statutory spatial strategy, gaining powers previously only enjoyed by the Mayor of London (Haughton, 2020). Importantly, however, with the broad rejections of city mayors under the city deal and the anaemic response to elections for police and crime commissioners in 2012, the insistence on directly elected mayors was viewed as an imposition of new democratic norms on local areas, rather than something that was desired by the public (Sturzaker and Nurse, 2020).

The first raft of combined authorities was largely self-identified and uncomplicated in nature. This included Greater Manchester, the Liverpool City Region, the West Midlands and the West of England. Teesside was also among the early intake and remains one of the few combined authorities that is not ostensibly a city region. Yet, as other putative combined authorities came forward, it became clear that devolution would be on the government's terms. For example, the North East had its devolution deal withdrawn (Halliday, 2016), while proposals with broad local support for a combined 'One Yorkshire' devolution deal were rejected (Singh, 2018) in favour of the government's favoured two combined authorities based around Sheffield and Leeds. The implication here was clear: devolution is available, but it must be conducted in a way that is palatable to the state. This leads to the obvious question: under such conditions, is this truly devolution?

Those debates notwithstanding, in May 2017, the first intake of metro mayors was elected and began getting to grips with their new powers. In most areas, this manifested in a slow start, as the mayors had to lead a process of institution building from an effective standing start, in which they had to establish internal capacity and working relations with their constituent districts, and an external profile, both of which relied heavily on their charisma (see Weber, 1968). This was perhaps exemplified in the development of the statutory spatial strategies, as by the end of the first term in 2021, only Greater Manchester had made serious progress (Haughton, 2020), even if these efforts became bogged down in the same arguments over housing provision that similarly stymied London's planning process (Morphet, 2011) and the perennial British planning issue that is building on the 'green belt' (Sturzaker and Mell, 2016). By comparison, other combined authorities took a more cautious approach, opting to 'watch and learn' from pioneer authorities instead in order to avoid making the same mistakes (Sturzaker and Nurse, 2020).

The metro mayors also sought to exercise their powers in other areas. For example, by the end of their first term, four of the seven metro mayors (Greater Manchester, the Liverpool City Region, the West Midlands and Sheffield) had appointed a walking and cycling commissioner to champion active travel as part of their broader transport powers. Greater Manchester also announced plans to franchise its own bus network – the first of its kind in the UK outside of Transport for London. Elsewhere, the mayor of Tees Valley fulfilled a campaign pledge to bring Tees Valley Airport into public ownership.

Despite this, at the end of their first term, questions remained with regards to the role and remit of the metro mayors, especially in terms of their hierarchical relationship with the structures above and below them. For example, while the metro mayors hold the right to convene statutory spatial strategies, they have no real right to intervene in the day-to-day planning process within the districts. The issue here is that the nature of the British planning system means that the local authority, not the combined authority, is the local planning authority that determines applications. This means that the metro mayors often have little/limited say in planning decisions that may affect their strategic ambitions. This is exemplified in a row between the then mayors of Liverpool City and of the Liverpool City Region over the future of the major Liverpool Waters development scheme (Nurse, 2015a), as well as Stockport Council's decision to withdraw from the Greater Manchester Spatial Framework (Richardson, 2021), which shows that while these scenarios may be rare, they are not unprecedented.

The combined authorities are also intensely reliant on their relationship with central government. Not only must they first negotiate the devolution of powers – and the initial devolution deals suggest that this is a bespoke process, where some areas can attract more powers than others – but like the rest of local government, they are also heavily reliant on central funding – indeed, perhaps more so, as combined authorities have little to no capacity for revenue generation. This means that major projects like transport investment must largely rely on central funding streams or settlements like those in the 2021 Autumn Statement (HM Treasury, 2021b). Similarly, and perhaps even more tellingly, the combined authorities have little say in strategic national transport decisions that affect them (for example, the decision to scrap the eastern leg of High Speed 2 [HS2] or to dilute west–east Northern Powerhouse Rail), leading some leaders to abandon the sub-national structures set up to provide strategic oversight (Anderson, 2018).

This reliance on central government was brought into sharp relief by the COVID-19 pandemic when, amid a succession of localised 'lockdowns' – effectively restrictions on meeting in private spaces and the operating of business – a number of metro mayors, led by Mayor of Greater Manchester Andy Burnham, pushed back against the scale of support offered to local areas by central government. Their argument was comparatively simple: *both* the funding provided to local businesses to support them through a prolonged and uncertain period of closure, *and* the funding provided to the combined authorities for other localised support through the pandemic, were not sufficient (Nurse, 2020). This disagreement took place in full view of the public and, at times, on live television. In doing so, the row over finances and a very-public challenge to the authority of central government bore a striking resemblance to the events in the mid-1980s that precipitated the abolition of the metropolitan counties (Frost and North, 2013) and led to questions regarding the longer-term repercussions for the combined authorities. At the time, it was argued that the varied political composition of the metro mayors (in 2020, four were Labour and three were Conservative) would serve as a barrier against short-term repercussions for this kind of 'pushback' (Sturzaker and Nurse, 2020); yet, as the government's sub-national agenda has continued to develop in the early part of the 2020s, and amid some electoral losses in 2021, it is not clear if that truly is the case.

From the Northern Powerhouse to levelling up

Like so many other facets of British politics, the 2016 referendum on Britain's membership of the European Union became a critical turning point in the development of sub-national governance structures under the post-2010 Conservative governments. Although the period in the immediate aftermath of the referendum was politically tumultuous for the country at large, the sub-national debate could largely be characterised by torpor.

The Northern Powerhouse and Midlands Engine, which had quickly developed in the period since 2014, effectively stalled. The first serious blow came when George Osborne, widely seen as the champion of the Northern Powerhouse, was removed from government by incoming Prime Minister Theresa May, who indicated a shift in focus away from Osborne's agenda (Mance and Bounds, 2016). The second serious blow was more prolonged and stemmed from May's increasingly beleaguered attempts to negotiate the processes of 'Brexit'. In doing so, May and her government were forced to devote increasingly large amounts of parliamentary time to passing Brexit-related legislation, in turn, meaning that there was less time for other matters. This included the primary legislation needed to transfer devolved powers to the metro mayors (Sturzaker and Nurse, 2020), meaning that while having to build institutions (see earlier), they had to do so without the full legislative capabilities they might have expected.

Beyond this, and despite broad overtures that the May administration was committed to the idea of rebalancing power away from London, during her three years in office, little else happened in sub-national terms. Indeed, barring the installation of several more combined authorities and the election of additional metro mayors in Sheffield City Region and North of Tyne, the situation at the end of May's term in office was much the same as it was at the beginning.

Instead, much time during this period was given to the 'post-mortem' of the referendum and understanding the dominant narratives surrounding the causes of the 'Brexit' vote. Specifically, the dominant argument held that the vote for Brexit was a populist pushback (Eatwell and Goodwin, 2018) of a 'left-behind Britain' (Burrell et al, 2018; Sykes, 2018; Tomaney and Pike, 2018), primarily located in towns and coastal areas, who felt disconnected from metropolitan areas and, perhaps, the overt focus placed on them over previous decades (Jennings et al, 2017). However, others disagreed (Dorling, 2016; Dorling and Tomlinson, 2019), while others argued that such binary narratives masked a significantly more complex picture (Nurse and Sykes, 2019). Nonetheless, it was the narrative of left-behind Britain that dominated and, as we will now discuss, went on to heavily inform the next phase of sub-national governance in England.

In practice, the next fundamental shift in the sub-national policy landscape would come in June 2019, when, following the resignation of Teresa May and a leadership contest within the Conservative Party, Boris Johnson was installed as prime minister. In a speech days after becoming prime minister (Johnson, 2019), perhaps ironically in the same place as George Osborne launched the Northern Powerhouse, Johnson gave rise to the phrase that would encapsulate the next phase of sub-national thinking: 'levelling up'. In initially launching his vision, Johnson directly engaged with the narrative of left-behind Britain, arguing for other places across England to enjoy the same types of devolution and reform brought forward post-2014 via the combined authorities. Later in the year, Johnson would also use this approach during the 2019 general election, where – in tandem with a campaign slogan of 'Get Brexit Done', in reference to ending the political logjam that ultimately brought down the May government – the Conservative Party explicitly targeted those 'left-behind' places felt to hold the sentiments discussed earlier (Ford et al, 2021a). The result was a landslide victory driven by a collapse of the Labour Party's 'red wall' of heartland votes in Northern

England (Ford et al, 2021b), which placed Johnson in a strong position to deliver his legislative vision.

However, while 'levelling up' became the clarion call of Johnson's administration, the range of schemes and projects brought forward under its name gave rise to confusion. Examination of the rhetoric of levelling up (Jennings et al, 2021) revealed inherent contradictions between an at-times place-based approach and an at-times broad-brush approach that relies on a rising tide to lift all boats. As an illustration of this, one scheme announced by the Department for Transport focused on reopening disused train lines for passenger services in both the North East and the Oxford–Cambridge arc (Gov.uk, 2020). Under the accepted rhetoric, only one would be accepted as 'left-behind' under any reasonable circumstances. Similarly, an examination of the some of the mechanisms designed to deliver the UK's long-term economic growth, such as the *Industrial Strategy* (HM Government, 2017, 2018), suggests that the high-tech industries being prioritised by the government are almost uniquely located in metropolitan areas, and areas characterised as 'left behind' have neither the industrial base nor the skills base to capitalise on potential growth in those sectors (Nurse and Sykes, 2020). In their assessment of the contradictions of levelling up, Jennings et al (2021: 303) invoked Stuart Hall's (1979) analysis of Thatcherism, saying: 'Just as Stuart Hall clarified about Thatcherism, so we argue about levelling up: "this is no rhetorical device or trick, for this populism is operating on genuine contradictions, and it has a rational and material core".'

If the Cameron-era devolution programme would be characterised by deal making, the Johnson-era levelling-up programme would largely be articulated through a swathe of funding schemes. The first to be announced was the 'Towns Scheme'. Launched on the same day Johnson announced levelling up in June 2019, the Towns Fund would comprise £3.6 billion of infrastructure funding – both physical and sociocultural – for 100 towns in England (Johnson, 2019). The criteria for this funding prioritised income and skills-based deprivation, economic productivity, and exposure to both 'Brexit' and broader economic shocks. In doing so, the rhetorical intention was clear: levelling up was about targeting the places in most need and building a resilience to the economic ruptures that drove decline in many of those places.

The other major scheme would be the 'Levelling Up Fund' (LUF) – announced in 2021 as a collaborative effort between the Treasury, Department for Transport and Ministry for Housing, Communities and Local Government (HM Treasury, 2021a). The LUF was initially announced as a £4 billion scheme for which only English local authorities would be eligible, before a further £400 million was added for the devolved nations. At first glance, the scheme was relatively simple: all local authorities in England would be divided into three 'tiers' based on subjective 'need'; after that point, local authorities would be invited to bid for monies, with local authorities able to prepare one bid for every member of parliament (MP) whose constituency lay wholly within the local authority boundary (HM Treasury, 2021a). In practice, however, this approach would represent a new way of approaching local government funding and would raise significant questions.

First, there was an issue regarding equity. Specifically, larger cities have more MPs by their very nature: London has 73, the West Midlands has 59 and Greater Manchester has 27. However, the places recognised as 'left behind' in the accepted narratives are, by and large, towns (Sykes, 2018; Nurse and Sykes, 2019). Many towns – particularly those that are unitary authorities – have one or two MPs. This immediately places them at a material disadvantage in terms of accessing LUF monies because they have less opportunities to do so.

Second, the novel nature of connecting local funding and parliamentary constituencies would expose the idiosyncratic way in which local authorities are administered in the UK. In practice, very few local authority districts would have MPs whose constituency boundaries would be totally analogous to any particular local authority. Indeed, many MPs might find their constituency spanning two separate local authority boundaries. In those instances, there are questions for both the local authorities (Who, if anyone, can 'claim' the MP for their LUF allocation?) and the MP in terms of which of their local authorities they might choose to side with. The idea that MPs can lobby for their preferred scheme also takes the competitive element of local government funding to a new extreme and deepens the entrepreneurial notion of 'winners' and 'losers' (Peck and Tickell, 1994). It also begs the question: what happens if 'left-behind' local authorities lack the institutional capacity to compile a 'winning' bid and thus miss out on a scheme that is intended to help them?

Many of these concerns were compounded when initial allocations for the Towns Fund and LUF began to be made across 2021. In the case of the Towns Fund, preliminary research of the first 45 allocations made by the Ministry for Housing, Communities and Local Government (MHCLG, 2021) revealed that of those 45, 39 (87 per cent) had gone to towns residing in Conservative-held constituencies (Walker and Allegretti, 2021). At first glance, it could be suggested that this might simply reflect the political landscape, in which many towns considered to be left behind may have voted Conservative in the 2019 general election. However, within those allocations, there was also evidence that government ministers had made some allocations against the advice of civil servants. For example, Cheadle was classified as a 'low-priority area' by civil servants but nonetheless received nearly £15 million of funding from the Towns Fund. These allocations gave rise to accusations that the Towns Fund was subject to 'pork-barrel politics' (Hanretty, 2021), in which funding was allocated for political expedience rather than to the places that needed it the most.

Table 4.1: LUF tiers and deprivation, by selected local authorities

Tier 1 funded		Tier 2 or 3	
Authority	IMD rank	Authority	IMD rank
18 of the 20 most-deprived authorities are Tier 1		Hackney	7
		Salford	20
		Tower Hamlets	27
St Helens	40	Halton	39
...	...	...	...
Lewes	194		
High Peak	202		
Richmondshire	251		
Derbyshire Dales	265		

Source: HM Treasury (2021a) and IMD (2019)

These concerns were deepened when the allocations for the LUF were made. The first concern came when all local authority areas were initially ranked into tiers (Tiers 1–3), reflecting high, medium or low priority in 2021 (DfT, 2021). When the tiers are analysed against the most recent Index of Multiple Deprivation (IMD) (MHCLG, 2019), at first glance, this may suggest that the LUF is hitting its core targets (see Table 4.1). For example, 18 of the 20 most deprived local authority areas in England are ranked as Tier 1. However, Hackney and Salford are omitted. The omission of Hackney, in particular, might suggest a wider pattern in which London-based local authorities were overlooked for Tier 1 status. However, while Tower Hamlets (IMD ranking = 27) was similarly excluded from Tier 1, Barking and Dagenham (IMD ranking = 5) is included, which immediately counters these notions. The exclusion of some London boroughs could, nonetheless, be understood in light of the LUF serving as an attempt to rebalance growth away from London, with London boroughs thus being excluded. However, authorities like Hackney and Tower Hamlets are objectively deprived and thus 'left-behind' places. This suggests that while levelling up has a place-based ethos, it is not in fact a place-based approach.

Further down the list, and away from London, there are other notable discrepancies in the allocation. For example, St Helens (IMD ranking = 40) and Halton (IMD ranking = 39) are ranked as Tier 1 and 2, respectively. This is despite the two authorities bordering each other and being part of the same combined authority area. There are also other areas that are less deprived but are nonetheless granted Tier 1 status. Like the Towns Fund, most of those less deprived areas were politically Conservative held. Here, Richmondshire

(IMD ranking = 251) was particularly notable as the parliamentary seat of the then Chancellor of the Exchequer Rishi Sunak. Again, this gave rise to accusations of pork-barrel politics, rather than a funding mechanism that targeted the places most in need.

Concerns were also raised regarding the LUF following the initial round of funding allocations in Autumn 2021 (DLUHC, 2021). Here, of the ten most deprived local authorities in England, five did not receive any funding. Most notably, this included Blackpool, the most deprived local authority in England. Reflecting the argument that the LUF overlooks London, neither Barking and Dagenham nor Hackney received any funding. Like with the initial allocation of the tiers, there were also anomalies at the other end of the scale. For example, Gloucester (IMD ranking = 138), the Forest of Dean (IMD ranking = 143) and Derbyshire (IMD rankings = 177, 218 and 265) all received LUF monies that exceeded that given to all but one of the ten most deprived areas (Birmingham). Going further, Central Bedfordshire (IMD ranking = 264) had two applications funded. This allocation raises real questions as to the nature of levelling up, particularly: how can it be that an area ranked in the top third best-performing local authorities can receive two bids, while the most deprived local authority can receive none? This discrepancy seems particularly stark when considering the specific case of Blackpool as a Brexit-voting coastal town that fits the 'pen picture' of left-behind places so neatly.

The reality of the allocations of the Towns Fund and LUF makes it difficult to avoid accusations of pork-barrel politics (Hanretty, 2021) when, simply put, funding is not going to places that need it most while, simultaneously, going to places that seemingly need it least but that appear politically convenient. There can be little doubt that this deepens, rather than resolves, the inconsistencies and irregularities of levelling up raised by Jennings et al (2021). Yet, it gives perhaps the clearest indication that levelling up is not a place-based initiative that focuses on the towns with the deepest need, nor is it the rising tide that will lift all boats. Rather, it is a rising tide that will lift *some* boats, while others remain beached or, worse, doomed to sink due to neglect. Crucially, the decisions of who remains in or out seem arbitrary and, perhaps ironically, a far cry from the mechanisms that govern funding allocations at the European scale.

Away from the funding announcements, long after Johnson first became prime minister (and even after his departure), levelling up existed in a dual state, being simultaneously talismanic of the government while remaining markedly undetailed. Such is the commitment to the idea that following a cabinet reshuffle in late 2021, the Ministry for Housing, Communities and Local Government was renamed the 'Department for Levelling Up, Housing and Communities'. Thus, the idea would have a secretary of state dedicated to its advancement – though there is also much that could be written about the rhetorical de-prioritisation of 'local government' in the department's name.

In early 2022, the government published its much-vaunted 'Levelling Up White Paper', which set out the government's vision in stark policy after several delays (DLUHC, 2022). In practice, the proposals in the White Paper were, by and large, comprised of funding that had been announced (that is, in the 2021 Spending Review) or teased. Among them was included the notion that the model of devolution and metro mayors would now be extended to all local authorities who wanted it – with county authorities having the option to elect a 'governor' rather than a mayor. Ultimately, the government would also commit to 12 levelling-up 'missions' – broadly analogous to those in the 2017 *Industrial Strategy* (HM Government, 2017) – which would be realised by 2030. There can be no doubt that this is an ambitious strategy, not least given that with the 'Northern Powerhouse' combined authorities existing for a similar timespan (2014–22 – or eight years), they have clearly not succeeded in rebalancing the country's economy. However, we must also note that the White Paper is effectively a consultation and some of these proposals remain off the statute books at this point in time.

At the time this chapter was originally written, the UK was amid yet another period of significant political flux. Following a period of extensive scrutiny regarding his conduct in office, the prime minister resigned and a leadership election to replace him was under way. At the original time of writing, one of either Rishi Sunak or Liz Truss would be the UK's next prime minister, with neither of their respective campaigns have paid much attention to 'levelling up' or setting out substantive policy positions to that end. Although Liz Truss won the leadership election, her tenure did not last long enough to set forth any serious policy position on the matter. However, it is likely that Truss will leave a legacy to local government by way of the fiscal disaster that preceded her political demise and that seems set to reintroduce a period of prolonged austerity and spending cuts.

The hesitancy to engage with levelling up by both Truss and Sunak might have been expected given the highly personalised nature of the levelling-up 'branding'. In time, it may be that the policy is revisited, or discarded altogether. Ultimately, it is therefore possible that it may come to pass that Boris Johnson's core domestic policy may come, and go, without ever evolving beyond a slogan. This would, perhaps, be fitting with the broader mannerisms of both Johnson and his government, which have, at times, relied heavily on short pithy slogans, such as 'Get Brexit Done', in support of their political and policy narratives. This would also align with the view of Johnson largely held by his critics that he is a politician who is high on rhetoric and devoid of detail. Here, one thing seems certain: levelling up is likely to be added to the pile of previous attempts to recast the UK's geographically skewed growth. However, the way in which this is recast and by whom currently remains to be seen.

Conclusion

It is perhaps cliche, but the story of sub-national governance under the Conservative government of the 2010s and early 2020s is one of two halves. The first half of the 2010s is characterised by deal making and devolution. Although the Northern Powerhouse will be considered as the flagship policy of this period, the reality goes much further than this. Indeed, the Coalition ushered out regional governance in order to effectively usher in the revitalisation of metropolitan governance. By the end of the decade, all but one (Nottingham) of the English core cities would be part of a combined authority and governed by a metro mayor. Within this, there is perhaps an irony that it would be a Conservative government that would undo one of the most infamous interventions in local government during the Thatcher years. Nonetheless, the city-regional reforms have, by and large, found their feet, and after a slow start, many of the metro mayors have grasped their mandate and are proving popular with their electorates. In doing so, however, this has created a fresh challenge for governance in a centralised state. In particular, the challenge of the next decade will be how this centre–local relationship is managed with metro mayors who have mastered their brief and may come to demand more powers.

However, there have been defective elements stemming from this period of sub-national reform. The Coalition's term, in particular, can be described as one of pursuing local democratic reform at all costs – even often ignoring the democratic wishes of local populaces who rejected successive proposals of reform. At the broader scale, the Coalition also drastically increased the clutter of local governance by failing to 'tidy up' overlapping governance structures as they introduced new ones (Sturzaker and Nurse, 2020). This led to situations where, for example, the city of Liverpool was subject to two separate mayors, each with distinct but overlapping remits, and who clashed regularly in trying to deliver those remits. Similarly, as the devolution agenda advanced, institutions became overshadowed to the point they became redundant, for example, the LEPs that established the city-regional thinking early in the Coalition's term became overshadowed by the more politically coherent combined authorities.

To extend the cliche of 'two halves', 'Brexit' was effectively half-time. It marked the end of the Cameron–Osborne approach, ushered in the May government (which was characterised by a torpor) and ended with the installation of the Johnson administration in 2019.

The Johnsonian approach to sub-national governance will undoubtedly be encapsulated with its slogan of 'levelling up'. Yet, like Jennings et al (2021), we find an agenda riddled with inconsistencies. On face value, Johnson's levelling up seeks to engage with the political landscape of Brexit and, in doing so, goes further than Cameron and Osborne's devolution – moving beyond the metropolises to the 'left-behind' towns of England. However, analysis of the funding allocations suggests that some of the most archetypal places that meet this rhetoric are overlooked. Here, there is a danger for the government. There is a broad sense that many of these places voted for 'Brexit' out of a (perhaps misplaced) sense of frustration at being overlooked by the broader forces for a sustained period and voted Conservative in the 2019 general election as an extension of this (Ford et al, 2021a). Indeed, Johnson's government is built on the strength of MPs in those places. Yet, if people in those places understand that they have, again, been overlooked by those forces, they may find retribution once more at the ballot box. Simultaneously, Johnson's pursuit of votes in Northern England's 'red wall' is increasingly being seen as to the cost of votes in traditionally 'safe' Conservative seats, as evidenced by heavy losses in recent by-elections for both Johnson and Sunak. In doing so, there are mirrors of how Tony Blair's government pursued votes in 'middle England' at the expense of heartland votes – something broadly viewed as precipitating the precise decline that led to Brexit.

It is said that history does not repeat itself, but it often rhymes. Elsewhere, it is said that it appears first as tragedy, then as farce. There are arguments that both sentiments can be found true of this decade of governance.

References

Anderson, J. (2018) 'Why I resigned from the Northern Powerhouse Partnership', CityMetric. Available: www.citymetric.com/transport/joe-anderson-why-i-resigned-northern-powerhouse-partnership-4387

Barlow, M. (1940) *Report of the Royal Commission on the Distribution of the Industrial Population*, London: HMSO.

Bentley, G., Bailey, D. and Shutt, J. (2010) 'From RDAs to LEPs: a new localism? Case examples of West Midland and Yorkshire', *Local Economy*, 25(7): 535–57.

Burrell, K., Hopkins, P., Isakjee, A., Lorne, C., Nagel, C., Finlay, R. et al (2018) 'Brexit, race and migration', *Environment and Planning C: Politics and Space*, 37(1): 3–40.

DCLG (Department for Communities and Local Government) (2010a) *Eric Pickles Puts Stop to Flawed Regional Strategies*, London: DCLG.

DCLG (2010b) *Functional Economic Market Areas*, London: HMSO.

DCLG (2010c) 'Letter to local authority leaders and business leaders', London: HMSO.

DCLG (2012) *Unlocking Growth in Cities: City Deals – Wave 1*, London: DCLG.

Demazière, C. and Sykes, O. (2019) 'The rise of the metropolitan city region? Exploring the establishment', in S. Armondi and S. De Gregorio Hurtado (eds) *Foregrounding Urban Agendas: The New Urban Issue in European Experiences of Policy-Making*, Cham: Springer, pp 185–209.

Desjardins, X. and Géneau de Lamarlière, I. (2016) *L'aménagement du territoire en France*, Paris: La documentation française.

DfT (Department for Transport) (2021) 'Levelling Up Fund: list of local authorities by priority category', London: HMSO.

DLUHC (Department for Levelling Up, Housing and Communities) (2021) 'Levelling Up Fund: first round successful bidders', London: HMSO.

DLUHC (2022) 'Levelling Up White Paper', London: HMSO.

Dorling, D. (2010) 'Persistent North–South divides', in N.M. Coe and A. Jones (eds) *The Economic Geography of the UK*, London: Sage, pp 12–28.

Dorling, D. (2016) 'Brexit: the decision of a divided country', *BMJ*, 354: i3679.

Dorling, D. and Tomlinson, S. (2019) *Rule Britannia: BREXIT and the End of Empire*, London: Biteback Publishing.

Eatwell, R. and Goodwin, M. (2018) *National Populism: The Revolt against Liberal Democracy*, London: Penguin.

Flynn, N., Leach, S. and Vielba, C.A. (1985) *Abolition or Reform? The GLC and the Metropolitan County Councils*, London: G. Allen & Unwin.

Ford, R. Bale, T., Jennings, W. and Surridge, P. (2021a) *The British General Election of 2019*, Cham: Palgrave Macmillan.

Ford, R., Bale, T., Jennings, W. and Surridge, P. (2021b) 'The Red Wall Falls', in R. Ford (ed) *The British General Election of 2019*, Cham: Palgrave Macmillan, pp 243–75.

Frost, D. and North, P. (2013) *Militant Liverpool: A City on the Edge*, Liverpool: Liverpool University Press.

Goodchild, B. and Hickman, P. (2006) 'Towards a regional strategy for the North of England? An assessment of "The Northern Way"', *Regional Studies*, 40(1): 121–33.

Gov.uk (2020) *Progress for Oxford–Cambridge Arc as Government Announces Preferred East West Rail Central Section*, London: Department for Transport.

Hall, S. (1979) 'The great moving right show', *Marxism Today*, 23(1): 14–20.

Halliday, J. (2016) 'Sajid Javid: devolution deal "off the table" for North-East of England', *The Guardian*, 8 September. Available at: https://www.theguardian.com/politics/2016/sep/08/north-east-england-devolution-deal-off-the-table-sajid-javid

Hanretty, C. (2021) 'The pork barrel politics of the Towns Fund', *The Political Quarterly*, 92(1): 7–13.

Haughton, G. (2020) 'Constrained governance rescaling and the development of a new spatial framework for Greater Manchester', in V. Lingua and V. Balz (eds) *Shaping Regional Futures: Designing and Visioning in Governance Rescaling*, Cham: Springer, pp 73–85.

HM Government (Her Majesty's Government) (2017) *Industrial Strategy: Building a Britain Fit for the Future*, London: The Stationery Office.

HM Government (2018) *Local Industrial Strategies: Policy Prospectus*, London: HMSO.

HM Treasury (Her Majesty's Treasury) (2021a) *Levelling Up Fund: Prospectus*, London: HMSO.

HM Treasury (2021b) *Autumn Budget and Spending Review*, London: HMSO.

Jennings, W., Brett, W., Bua, A. and Laurence, R. (2017) *Cities and Towns: The 2017 General Election and the Social Divisions of Place*, London: New Economics Foundation.

Jennings, W., McKay, L. and Stoker, G. (2021) 'The politics of levelling up', *The Political Quarterly*, 92(2): 302–11.

Johnson, B. (2019) 'PM speech at Manchester Science and Industry Museum', London: Gov.UK.

Leach, S. and Game, C. (1991) 'English metropolitan government since abolition: an evaluation of the abolition of the English metropolitan county councils', *Public Administration*, 69(2): 141–70.

Mance, H. and Bounds, A. (2016) 'Theresa May shifts focus from "Northern Powerhouse"', *Financial Times*, 2 August.

Marsh, A. (2012) 'Is it time to put the dream of elected mayors to bed?', *Policy and Politics*, 40(4): 607.

MHCLG (Ministry for Housing, Communities and Local Government) (2019) 'Index of Multiple Deprivation 2019', London: MHCLG.

MHCLG (2021) 'Towns Fund recipients March 2021', London: HMSO.

Morphet, J. (2011) 'Delivering infrastructure through spatial planning: the multi-scalar approach in the UK', *Local Economy*, 26(4): 285–93.

Nurse, A. (2015a) 'Bridging the gap? The role of regional governance in delivering effective public services: evidence from England', *Planning Practice & Research*, 30(1): 69–82.

Nurse, A. (2015b) 'Creating the North from the sum of its parts? Research questions to assess the Northern Powerhouse', *Local Economy*, 30(6): 689–701.

Nurse, A. (2020) 'Andy Burnham's standoff with London was always about more than just lockdown money', *The Conversation*, 23 October. Available at: https://theconversation.com/andy-burnhams-standoff-with-london-was-always-about-more-than-just-lockdown-money-148594

Nurse, A. and Sykes, O. (2019) 'It's more complicated than that! Unpacking "Left Behind Britain" and some other spatial tropes following the UK's 2016 EU referendum', *Local Economy*, 34(6): 589–606.

Nurse, A. and Sykes, O. (2020) 'Place-based vs. place blind? Where do England's new local industrial strategies fit in the "levelling up" agenda?', *Local Economy*, 35(4): 277–96.

Osborne, G. (2014) 'What we can do to make the cities of the North a powerhouse for our economy again', speech. Available at: https://www.gov. uk/government/speeches/chancellor-we-need-a-northern-powerhouse

Peck, J. and Tickell, A. (1994) 'Jungle law breaks out: neo-liberalism and global–local disorder', *Area*, 26(4): 317–26.

Pugalis, L. (2011) 'Look before you LEP', *Journal of Urban Regeneration and Renewal*, 5(1): 7–22.

Richardson, A. (2021) ' "Plan of nine" set to replace Greater Manchester Spatial Framework takes another step forward', *Manchester Evening News*, 23 March.

Singh, A. (2018) 'Leaders meet to discuss One Yorkshire devolution with unity tested by Ministers', *Yorkshire Post*, 16 July.

Sturzaker, J. and Mell, I. (2016) *Green Belts: Past; Present; Future?*, Abingdon: Routledge.

Sturzaker, J. and Nurse, A. (2020) *Rescaling Urban Governance: Planning, Localism and Institutional Change*, Bristol: Policy Press.

Sykes, O. (2018) 'Post-geography worlds, new dominions, left behind regions, and "other" places: unpacking some spatial imaginaries of the UK's "Brexit" debate', *Space and Polity*, 22(2): 137–61.

Taylor, P.J., Hoyler, M., Evans, D.M. and Harrison, J. (2010) 'Balancing London? A preliminary investigation of the "Core Cities" and "Northern Way" spatial policy initiatives using multi-city corporate and commercial law firms', *European Planning Studies*, 18(8): 1285–99.

The Northern Way (2004) *First Growth Strategy Report*, The Northern Way Steering Group.

Tomaney, J. and Pike, A. (2018) 'Brexit, devolution and economic development in "left-behind" regions', *Welsh Economic Review*, 26(1): 29–37.

Walker, P. and Allegretti, A. (2021) 'Sunak's £1bn of "town deals" will nearly all go to Tory constituencies', *The Guardian*, 3 March. Available at: https://www.theguardian.com/uk-news/2021/mar/03/ sunaks-1bn-of-town-deals-will-nearly-all-go-to-tory-constituencies

Weber, M. (1968) *On Charisma and Institution Building*, Chicago: University of Chicago Press.

Wise, M.J. (1969) 'The future of local government in England: "The Redcliffe Maud Report"', *The Geographical Journal*, 135(4): 583–7.

PD games: death comes to planning

Richard J. Dunning, Alex Lord and Mark Smith

Introduction

It is a truth universally acknowledged that a human must be in want of a healthy home. Planning has been tasked with enabling this want for over 70 years, yet in English planning's current emaciated state, it is struggling to ensure that housing is healthy. The fortunes of England's population are growing further apart (ONS, 2021). While all its citizens share the same human rights according to the International Convention on Economic, Social and Cultural Rights as part of the International Bill of Human Rights, the UK's unwritten constitution does not actually include the 'right to healthy housing'. Increasingly, it appears that the ability of citizens in England to actuate their international human right is devolved to their financial capacity. Variation in the quality of housing is not new, but the minimum quality for new housing development, which has been required since 1947, has been absent in much of a new form of housing development: permitted development.

Since 2010, there have been significant changes in the process of obtaining permission for much new housing development in England. Broadly, these deregulatory national changes have allowed the conversion and extension of housing that would not have been permitted through local planning permission.

This chapter explores the expansion of permitted development rights to allow the conversion of non-residential uses to homes. It does so with a particular focus on neighbourhood health, providing new evidence of the problematic assumption in permitted development that housing should be allowed regardless of local amenities and the built environment of existing buildings. Our neighbourhood-health-based approach should be considered complementary to the excellent extant analysis of the quality of the physical structures of dwellings by Clifford et al (2018), on which this analysis builds directly and for which it seeks to provide corroborating evidence (see, for example, Madeddu and Clifford, 2021).

A pastiche aside

Lizzy was looking forward to seeing her friend again. Travelling south from the fine county of Derbyshire, the train line cut through miles of green, purple and gold manicured moorland. Looking out the windows, which ran almost the full length of the train, Lizzy saw estates merge into pastureland, past isolated oaks and pylons strung together to provide electricity to disparate settlements. The train was quiet. In a moment, the density of sheep fell as the frequency of new homes, many even with the architectural delight of anthracite UPVC windows, increased. Somewhere on the journey, around Hertfordshire, Lizzy saw a large regency manor house flying the flags of a sprawling golf course, and a warm recollection of childhood security struck Lizzy.

After changing to an Uber at St Pancras and now heading back out of the city, Lizzy was on the final leg of her journey to see her good friends. It felt strange to have spent the same time travelling the first 100 miles as the last 10. After a mile or so of grey-white warehousing, the taxi turned round the edge of a call centre. Lizzy saw that the developer had not yet finished removing the middle word from the sign 'Rosings Industrial Park'.

Charlie and Colin appeared at the Uber door. After heartfelt but perfunctory pleasantries, Lizzy was given a tour of their new home. The glass entrance was neat enough, situated at the centre of a concrete building. It was hard to tell how big the building was inside without any windows to hint at the number of storeys. "They used to print some of the classics here", Charlie humbly explained as they climbed the metal stairs to the first-floor apartment. Inside, an odd light came from the ceiling, a mixture of the harsh strip fixture and dull light well. "We'll eat here this evening", Colin said; "Otherwise, we'd have to get a taxi back to town", he half-jokingly apologised. Lizzy had not noticed that the taxi had not passed even a corner shop for the last few minutes of the journey until now. "At least you're here while the garage over the Road isn't open. Sometimes, I can't even smell Colin's cooking", Charlie chimed in. Given that the entire apartment was smaller than her kitchen-diner, it was hard for Lizzy to imagine that. Stuck to the fridge, Lizzy could see, was the house-warming card she had sent, though someone had scrawled on it: 'An Englishwoman's home pays for her landlord's castle.'

What is permitted development?

Permitted development is a way of granting planning permission for development without the usual review and determination by the local planning authority. Since 1947, development has been controlled through nationalised rights that allow democratically elected councillors to judge the quality of a development proposal (albeit operating within national guidelines).

In this discretionary system, permission to undertake the development is granted if the local authority agrees that it is merited and, if necessary, any negative impacts of the development have been considered and mitigated. It can take time for a local authority to consider the proposal and any additional evidence necessary (viability assessments, health and environmental impact assessments, traffic routes and so on). Arguably, if a development lasts more than 100 years, then taking 1 per cent of that time to consider its merits is a sensible trade off. However, there is a widespread perception that this deliberative and discretionary process is cumbersome and slows down development, requiring an alternative approach to granting permission.

The argument for permitted development is that where a development clearly meets certain national guidelines, then permission may be granted through the General Permitted Development Order, which would therefore decrease the perceived burden on local authority planning officers and committees (DCLG, 2008). However, limitations to the ability of a local authority to influence a development outcome clearly does not equate to a reduced planning burden.

In England, permitted development has been a consistent part of planning law and practice since 1948 (following the Town & Country Planning Act 1947). In a discretionary planning system where each development is considered on its own merits through the planning permission process, it was necessary to avoid administrative sclerosis and have a mechanism to deal with evidently straightforward and very minor cases (for example, the erection of a small garden shed or a porch). However, these rights were significantly expanded in 2005, 2010, 2012, 2013, 2015 and 2016 to allow broader ranges of developments to take place without planning permission. The Town and Country Planning (General Permitted Development) (Amendment) (England) Order 2013[1] covered quite diverse development types, from the erection of telecoms masts to the wholesale conversion of offices to residential. It is this latter ability that we focus on in this chapter.

England is not alone in using a form of permitted development as a mechanism to regulate development. The expansion of permitted development rights has been attributed to a neoclassical narrative: 'that greater housing *supply* is the solution to the housing crisis and that planning regulation is the problem' (Ferm et al, 2021: 2043, emphasis in original). In this light, as a form of planning deregulation, permitted development is considered on the same trajectory as the broader critique of the neoliberal deconstruction of planning (see Chapter 1), even if planning is a site of contestation for this expansion of financial logics (Inch et al, 2021).

In 2011, at an early stage of the expansion of permitted development, Secretary of State for Communities and Local Government Eric Pickles gave the following, widely cited, justification: 'By unshackling developers from a legacy of bureaucratic planning we can help them turn thousands of vacant commercial properties into enough new homes to jump start housing supply and help get the economy back on track' (Russell, 2011). Pickles' priorities were clear: reduce regulation, permit more housing and support the economy. Concepts of quality, aesthetics, security, affordability and health were irrelevant in the drive to let former call centres boost housing-supply targets.

Allowing more permitted development in urban environments also had the perceived advantage of encouraging increased housing densities, including the introduction of residential uses in previously commercial and office areas. In the context of a political predilection for expanding housing supply (see Chapter 2), urban intensification has broad political appeal in supposedly easing pressure on greenfield sites and limiting other environmental impacts of development (Dembski et al, 2020). This logic was explicitly reported by Housing and Planning Minister Brandon Lewis in 2015, when the temporary changes to permitted development were made permanent: 'Today's measures will mean we can tap into the potential of underused buildings to offer new homes for first-time buyers and families long into the future, breathing new life into neighbourhoods and at the same time protecting our precious green belt' (MHCLG, 2015). However, where densification takes place in areas of denuded planning, it is liable to cause unintended consequences (Dunning et al, 2020). The purported 'new life into neighbourhoods' could now mean people living in retail centres or industrial warehouses, something that 'bureaucratic planning' had hitherto sought to regulate. To phrase it differently, permitted development removed the ability of a local authority to weigh up the advantages and disadvantages of a development, and to prevent it where the disadvantages were too high.

The unintended consequences of permitted development cover the whole gamut of social, economic and environmental life. Prior to the Conservative extension of permitted development in England, evidence from Scotland revealed that it could also have negative impacts because of its cumulative effect (Prior and Raemaekers, 2006).

Yet, there have been strong calls to consider health as a crucial factor in analysing the impact of permitted development (see, for example, Marsh et al, 2022). The impact of COVID-19 on the value and dangers of homes has exacerbated the need for understanding how health and permitted development rights collide (Madeddu and Clifford, 2021).

Planning and health

There is a long association between urban planning and public health. The first town and country planning acts were a public health intervention intended to end unsanitary living conditions, while John Snow became father to both epidemiology and geographic information systems (GIS) in tracing clinical statistics onto street maps to understand cholera outbreaks (Fischer and Muthoora, 2020). Although modern practitioners are thankfully less concerned with cholera and squalor, a growing range of chronic conditions and air pollutants continues to reaffirm the affinity between planning and health (Fawcett, 2019). Public health has been widely characterised as 'the science and art of preventing disease, prolonging life and promoting health through the organized efforts of society' (Acheson, 1988: 1). Urban planning represents one of these organised efforts through place-making/shaping functions that widely determine population health (Buck, 2020; LGA, 2020).

The National Planning Policy Framework directs planners to deliver safe and healthy communities that enable and support healthy lifestyles (MHCLG, 2021). The health success of a development thus rests on two assumptions: first, that the design and physical quality of the development are of a sufficient quality that they do not harm the occupants (and, more progressively, provide a platform for occupants to experience the dwelling as home); and, second, that the context of the development provides a positive bridge between the home and societal services, such as green spaces, employment sites, schools, transport hubs, shops and cultural activities. Both of these attributes contribute towards the wider determinants of our health and apply to all developments.

There are presently three general ways urban planners in the UK influence and improve these wider determinants of health. First, planners can use location policy in development plans to restrict development in unhealthy and unsanitary areas (Fawcett, 2019). Examples include keeping new housing away from traffic and industrial pollution, or from areas that might actively encourage unhealthy lifestyles due to having a high presence of pubs, off licences, tobacconists and so on.

Second, planners can impose national space standards on new development that stipulate minimum sizes for rooms (Fawcett, 2019). National space standards do now apply to permitted development conversions, though only since 2021. These national minimum standards can be supported with locally set codes on other aspects, including windows and open spaces. Examples here include the Housing Supplementary Planning Guidance (SPG) in Camden, which stipulates that residential development above ten units should have play areas for children and 5 m² of outdoor space per unit. The Residential Amenity Supplementary Planning Document (SPD) in Leicester meanwhile stipulates that new flats should offer 1.5 m² of private amenity space.

Planners' final option is to use developer contributions to harvest planning gain and pay for mitigation (Fawcett, 2019). This will usually be through either negotiated Section 106 agreements or via a hypothecated Community

Infrastructure Levy (CIL). For health, the measures funded might include (but are in no way limited to) the provision of/improvements to public spaces, healthcare services, active travel and/or flood defences. Examples here include the Green Spaces SPD in Leicester that requires developers to contribute to improving and enhancing open spaces, and provision in Croydon for developers to pay £100 per unit for air-quality improvements.

Could permitted development result in healthy outcomes?

There is a sizeable amount of evidence now emerging on the outcomes of permitted development rights, particularly residential developments. Much of this evidence has quite rightly focused on the quality of the housing itself in terms of both physical and aesthetic qualities, as well as the direct health and well-being aspects of occupying those dwellings (see, for example, Clifford et al, 2020). Some provisional analysis has considered our second earlier assumption of the context of development, for example, Clifford (2019) considers 30 examples of permitted development with regards to both the physical characteristics and the surrounding land use. However, there is little on the limitations of permitted development to enhance the health context for development – a common requirement under planning permission (Marsh et al, 2022).

The reason that these limitations are important is because permitted developments are not liable for developer contributions towards public needs in the same way as other planning permissions (Bibby et al, 2018). In a regular planning application, the local authority can add an agreement to the permission that requires the provision of health-supporting attributes (anything from bike lanes to general practitioner surgeries) or a financial contribution towards health services. In permitted development, this ability is removed; hence, the developer or landowner cannot be required to contribute to a healthy context for its residents. While CIL is, in theory, leveraged on permitted development conversions, in practice, developers can exploit various clauses in the regulations to reduce their obligations to zero.

In 2018, a report for the Royal Institute of Chartered Surveyors (RICS) argued that the majority of additional dwellings being delivered through permitted development rights were small-scale conversions from business uses and that large-scale office-to-residential conversions were less common (Bibby et al, 2018). However, the same report argued that the financial loss to local authorities from permitted developments was largely attributable to the loss of high-quality affordable housing on large-scale office-to-residential conversions. In other words, permitted development enabled large schemes to provide low-quality, insecure and potentially unhealthy housing at the cost of high-quality, secure-tenured and well-planned affordable homes.

Case study

We examine the health of neighbourhoods where residential conversions have occurred using permitted development rights. This is founded on a 2018 RICS report that considered the impact of permitted development conversions in selected local authorities (Clifford et al, 2018). We take some of these examples and identify the underlying health needs of the neighbourhoods affected using the Access to Health Assets and Hazards (AHAH) tool developed by Liverpool University (CDRC, 2022). This tool is a multidimensional index that uses various indicators to assess the state of community health at Lower Super Output Area (LSOA) level. The tool ranks each neighbourhood area's performance overall and on four specific measures, which are then placed on a decile scale between 1 and 10, where 1 is the top 10 per cent and 10 is the worst 10 per cent.

Camden

Camden is a borough authority in Central London. It has some of the highest residential land values in the UK, and there is considerable pressure from developers to convert offices into housing. Since the relaxation of office-to-residential permitted development rights in 2013, 832 residential units have been completed and another 605 are on the way (Clifford et al, 2018). The cost of this has been the loss of approximately 24,000 m² of office space and 2,570 jobs. The new residential units have increased pressure on public services, which is crudely estimated at £3.8 million. In excess of £9 million has been lost in Section 106 contributions (Clifford et al, 2018).

Examples of residential conversions using permitted development rights have all occurred in some of the unhealthiest neighbourhoods in the UK (see Table 5.1). It is apparent that all examples have some of the best access to healthcare services but experience some of the worst air pollution in the UK. The immediate retail environment is also recorded as poor due to the number of nearby pubs, takeaways and tobacconists, thus encouraging unhealthy lifestyles. Access to blue and green infrastructure for leisure and recreation is generally bad despite the proximity to Regents Park.

Croydon

Croydon is a borough authority just outside Central London. It has a large supply of vacant, dated office premises due to changes in the requirements and expectations of businesses. Being just outside Central London, the location has experienced significant demand for new housing stock and considerable pressure from developers to convert old offices into residential units. The authority has also encountered the highest number of applications

Table 5.1: Neighbourhood health scores for areas with permitted development conversions in Camden

Location	Scheme	AHAH overall index	Retail environment	Access to health services	Access to blue/green infrastructure	Air quality
116 Boundary Road	1 flat	10	10	1	6	10
2 and 4 Kings Terrace	Extension	10	10	1	10	10
68A Delancey Street	1 flat	10	10	1	10	10
48–56 Bayham Place	13 flats	10	10	1	10	10
5–8 Anglers Lane	27 flats	10	10	1	10	10
Merlin House	12 flats	10	10	1	9	10
Asher House	29 flats	10	10	1	10	10

Source: Data from Clifford et al (2018) and CDRC (2022)

for residential conversions using permitted development rights in England (Clifford et al, 2018). Up to 2017, 2,708 residential units had been completed or were under construction, while another 3,000+ had approval. The cost on public services from these new residential units is conservatively estimated as £12.5 million, rising to in excess of £27.6 million if all are completed (Clifford et al, 2018). The forgone Section 106 contributions are likely to be many millions.

The examples of residential permitted development conversions were all in very unhealthy neighbourhoods (see Table 5.2). While there is good access to healthcare services, the neighbourhoods suffer from poor air quality and a retail environment lending itself to unhealthy lifestyles due to the close proximity of pubs and fast-food outlets. Access to blue and green infrastructure for recreation and leisure was also very poor.

Leeds

Leeds is a relatively prosperous city authority in Northern England. It has one of the largest office markets outside of London and a growing demand for new residential development. A proportion of the office stock is antiquated, and developers are keen to convert it to residential use (Clifford et al, 2018). This has seen extensive use of permitted development rights: 2,170 units were completed under these rights in 2017, with another 715 under construction. These extra residential units were estimated to have cost public services £9.98 million (Clifford et al, 2018).

Most examples here of residential conversions from permitted development rights were in the unhealthiest of neighbourhoods (see Table 5.3). While they typically have good access to healthcare services, they suffer

Table 5.2: Neighbourhood health scores for areas with permitted development conversions in Croydon

Location	Scheme	AHAH overall index	Retail environment	Access to health services	Access to blue/green infrastructure	Air quality
Concord House	126 flats	10	9	1	10	9
Green Dragon House	111 flats	10	10	1	10	9
5 Sydenham Road	54 flats	10	9	1	10	9
3 Church Road	32 flats	10	10	1	10	9
St Annes House	197 flats	10	9	2	10	9
Delta Point	404 flats	10	10	1	10	10
Beech House	24 flats	6	7	2	8	6
Emerald House	121 flats	10	9	2	10	9
410 Brighton Road	6 flats	8	8	3	9	7
35A Brighton Road	10 flats	10	10	3	10	8

Source: Data from Clifford et al (2018) and CDRC (2022)

Table 5.3: Neighbourhood health scores for areas with permitted development conversions in Leeds

Location	Scheme	AHAH overall index	Retail environment	Access to health services	Access to blue/green infrastructure	Air quality
60 Upper Basinghall Street	5 flats	10	10	1	10	10
Meridian House	29 flats	9	9	2	8	9
117 The Headrow	27 flats	10	10	1	10	10
25 Queen Street	71 flats	10	10	1	9	9
Sunshine House	39 flats	9	9	2	9	8
Green Flag House, Pudsey	139 flats	8	3	7	9	8

Source: Data from Clifford et al (2018) and CDRC (2022)

from poor air quality and a built environment that encourages unhealthy lifestyles. Access to leisure and recreation in blue/green infrastructure was generally very poor. One notable example was Green Flag House, a conversion on an out-of-town business park. This seemed a much healthier retail environment, as there were some nearby shops and leisure outlets, but the area suffered from air-quality issues (due to a nearby major road),

Table 5.4: Neighbourhood health scores for areas with permitted development conversions in Leicester

Location	Scheme	AHAH overall index	Retail environment	Access to health services	Access to blue/green infrastructure	Air quality
MPK House	20 flats	7	8	3	4	9
Lionel House	15 flats	10	10	1	10	9
53a London Road	4 flats	10	10	1	9	9
75 London Road	2 flats	10	10	1	9	9
Allied Place	31 flats	10	10	1	9	10
Kimberley House	33 flats	8	8	4	7	9

Source: Data from Clifford et al (2018) and CDRC (2022)

had limited blue/green infrastructure accessibility and less than ideal access to health services.

Leicester

Leicester is a provincial city in the East Midlands. It has a high rate of empty offices, while the residential market is not particularly competitive. Despite this, the city has experienced one of the highest rates of residential conversions using permitted development rights among comparable cities (Clifford et al, 2018). Up to 2017, 637 residential units had been completed or were under construction using these powers. The cost to public services from these conversions is estimated in excess of £2.9 million, while the forgone Section 106 contributions are around £1.1 million (Clifford et al, 2018).

Examples here of residential conversions using permitted development rights take place in unhealthy neighbourhoods (see Table 5.4). Most have issues relating to poor air quality and a built environment that lends itself to unhealthy lifestyles, while there is less than ideal access to blue/green infrastructure, though there is generally very good access to healthcare services.

Reflection

While almost all examples of residential conversion using permitted development rights that we looked at had good access to healthcare services and also sometimes reasonable access to blue and green infrastructure, it is questionable whether these services and infrastructure can cope with extra demands from more residential development. It may well be necessary to expand healthcare services to cope with a larger residential population or to add more facilities to public spaces; otherwise, these public assets will become over-pressured and gradually deteriorate. However, permitted development conversions make no contributions to managing these demands.

Furthermore, residential conversions through permitted development do nothing to mitigate neighbourhood health conditions, such as investing in air-quality improvements or enhancing blue/green infrastructure provision. The practice also causes further health and well-being concerns, for example:

- Loss of employment sites and affordable housing provisions can increase stress and uncertainty for many, thus potentially contributing to mental health problems.
- The quality of conversions is often a concern, with developers sometimes doing the minimum work required to convert former offices into residential accommodation, leading to poor choice of materials and a lack of windows and soundproofing.
- Ventilation issues can cause damp and mould accumulation, which exacerbates respiratory concerns. This is a particular concern following the recent tragic death of a two-year-old boy from chronic exposure to mould (Brown and Booth, 2022). Although this incident occurred in a purpose-built flat, that permitted development conversions are likely to be more susceptible to these problems is especially worrisome.

Not all permitted development conversions are, however, a race to the bottom; some are prestigious and award-winning developments, particularly certain examples from Camden and Leeds (Clifford et al, 2018). It is unfortunate, however, that these exclusive developments make no contribution to addressing the wider underlying community health needs and problems.

Overall, the long-standing and fundamental dynamic between planning and health is challenged by the relaxation of planning powers on residential conversions, to the extent it becomes impossible to manage the wider determinants of health through appropriate planning strategies. Since our research, the central government has continued to expand permitted development rights. In 2021, it became possible to convert from Use Class E (a new class created in 2020, which is colloquially slandered as 'Class Everything', and covers commercial business and service use) to residential, with the intended purpose of reinvigorating the high street by increasing residential density. Local planning authorities retain some tools to prevent Class E permitted development conversions (Such as Article 4 Directions, which require approval from the secretary of state!), but their ability to plan for healthy neighbourhoods continues to be eroded by the egregious use of permitted development powers.

Death comes to planning

The question is not whether planning lives or dies, as if planning is an end to itself; rather, 'What happens if death comes to planning?' is the relevant question. Planning is about the lived outcome, but the process of planning matters when it is limiting healthy lives. This chapter has explored the question: if planning is deliberately inhibited, what is the outcome? The analysis adds to the already-extensive evidence that the death of planning through permitted development is producing dire outcomes; housing that is not healthy is not a home at all.

The introduction of permitted development rights into the English planning system turns on the logic that planning is a barrier to development. On this understanding, the problems of undersupply are erroneously displaced from the house-building industry, for which undersupply maintains prices and profits, to regulatory planning. Proponents of the case for less regulation point to the fact that, with only one exception (2005/06), the annual target number of new homes required has been missed. The result, it is argued, is that the level of new supply required in 2022 (around 300,000 new dwellings per annum) is far greater than the only time since 2000 that the government's target was met (200,000 in 2005/06). The introduction of permitted development rights within this context is correspondingly understood as removing a regulatory impediment to the supply of new homes.

However, as the preceding analysis shows, there is a cost to this approach: diminishing regulatory planning control has resulted in conversions that are often of poor quality in areas where large-scale residential development was not originally planned and that are underserved by new infrastructure and public goods, as they are not eligible for developer contributions. In accounting for the worst of what permitted development has delivered, it is essential not to lose sight of the underpinning argument that bypassing formal planning control would result in an increase in the supply of new homes. An alternative to this supply-side logic would be to instead think of planning as a 'market maker' (Lord and O'Brien, 2017). This demand-oriented perspective situates planning as an essential broker of the development process. Far from being an impediment to development, the regulatory activity of planning is more accurately conceptualised as one of persuasion, nudging market participants to development outcomes that maintain the profit motive for developers while securing public goods and attendant investments for wider society. Persuasive planning requires planners to act both as mediators between the competing interests in land and property development, and as guarantors of the public interest – not least through the recovery of development value for investment in public goods through developer contributions. The oversimplified understanding of planning as a barrier to development fails to understand that this economically significant role played by planning can, over time, have a positive impact on the creation and re-creation of development value (Lord et al, 2019). The failures of permitted development, which will cast a decades-long shadow in some English towns and cities, have their origins in the misapprehension of the planning system as a brake on, rather than an enabler of, development.

Madeddu and Clifford (2021: 46) argue that enhanced regulations regarding building design could drive up the health standards of development but are sceptical about whether permitted development will deliver this, as the permitted development right 'has always faced fierce criticism from lobby and interest groups who argue that quality and liveability in housing cannot be sacrificed in pursuit of a delivery target and that "home" has to deliver against health, well-being and social equity goals'. We echo their comments here and have provided additional evidence that when health outcomes are not well regulated, they are not provided through permitted development.

Permitted development rights are not the only aspects that are failing planning, as is explored elsewhere in this book, but they are radically altering health outcomes. Buildings with a quality that is so low that they harm their residents and homes built in the wrong places are not acceptable, yet both are currently allowed under guidelines set by the national government.

Note

[1] See: www.legislation.gov.uk/uksi/2013/1101/contents/made

References

Acheson, D. (1988) *Public Health in England: The Report of the Committee of Inquiry into the Future Development of the Public Health Function*, London: HMSO.

Bibby, P., Brindley, P., Dunning, R.J., Henneberry, J., McLean, A. and Tubridy, D. (2018) 'The exercise of permitted development rights in England since 2010', Royal Institute of Chartered Surveyors. Available at: www.rics.org/globalassets/rics-website/media/knowledge/research/research-reports/the-exercise-of-permitted-development-rights-in-engl and-rics.pdf

Brown, M. and Booth, R. (2022) 'Death of two-year-old from mould in flat a "defining moment", says coroner', *The Guardian*, 15 November. Available at: www.theguardian.com/uk-news/2022/nov/15/death-of-two-year-old-awaab-ishak-chronic-mould-in-flat-a-defining-moment-says-coroner

Buck, D. (2020) *The English Local Government Public Health Reforms: An Independent Assessment*, London: Kings Fund. Available at: www.kingsfund.org.uk/publications/local-government-public-health-reforms

Clifford, B. (2019) 'Healthy homes? Thirty examples of permitted development conversions'. Available at: https://discovery.ucl.ac.uk/id/eprint/10088243/

Clifford, B., Ferm, J., Livingstone, N. and Cenelas, P. (2018) *Assessing the Impacts of Extending Permitted Development Rights to Office-to-Residential Change of Use in England*, London: Royal Institute of Chartered Surveyors. Available at: www.rics.org/uk/news-insight/research/research-reports/assessing-the-impacts-of-extending-permitted-development-rights-to-office-to-residential-change-of-use-in-england/

Clifford, B., Caneleas, P., Ferm, J., Livingstone, N., Lord, A. and Dunning, R. (2020) 'Research into the quality standard of homes delivered through change of use permitted development rights', MHCLG. Available at: https://assets.publishing.service.gov.uk/government/uploads/system/uploads/attachment_data/file/902220/Research_report_quality_PDR_homes.pdf

CDRC (Consumer Data Research Centre) (2022) 'Access to Health Assets and Hazards dataset', University of Liverpool. Available at: www.liverpool.ac.uk/geographic-data-science/research/geographiesofresilienceexclusionandopportunity/healthy-assets-hazards/

DCLG (Department for Communities and Local Government) (2008) 'The Killian Pretty Review: planning applications: a faster and more responsive system', London: DCLG.

Dembski, S., Hartmann, T., Hengstermann, A. and Dunning, R. (2020) 'Introduction enhancing understanding of strategies of land policy for urban densification', *The Town Planning Review*, 91(3): 209–16.

Dunning, R., Hickman, H. and While, A. (2020) 'Planning control and the politics of soft densification', *Town Planning Review*, 91(3): 305–24.

Fawcett, P. (2019) 'Leveraging health: the urban planner's dilemma', PhD thesis, University of Liverpool. Available at: https://livrepository.liverpool.ac.uk/3076471/

Ferm, J., Clifford, B., Canelas, P. and Livingstone, N. (2021) 'Emerging problematics of deregulating the urban: the case of permitted development in England', *Urban Studies*, 58(10): 2040–58.

Fischer, T.B. and Muthoora, T. (2020) *Links between Health Issues and the Development of Strategic Plans*, London: Local Government Association and the Planning Advisory Service. Available at: www.local.gov.uk/sites/default/files/documents/PAS%20Strategic%20planning%20and%20Health%20final%20report.pdf

Inch, A., Dunning, R., While, A., Hickman, H. and Payne, S. (2021) '"The object is to change the heart and soul": financial incentives, planning and opposition to new housebuilding in England', *Environment and Planning C: Politics and Space*, 38(4): 713–32.

LGA (Local Government Association) (2020) *Public Health Transformation Seven Years on: Prevention in Neighbourhood, Place and System*, London: LGA. Available at: www.local.gov.uk/publications/public-health-transformat ion-seven-years-prevention-neighbourhood-place-and-system

Lord, A. and O'Brien, P. (2017) 'What price planning? Reimagining planning as "market maker"', *Planning Theory & Practice*, 18(2): 217–32.

Lord, A., Burgess, G., Gu, Y. and Dunning, R. (2019) 'Virtuous or vicious circles? Exploring the behavioural connections between developer contributions and path dependence: Evidence from England', *Geoforum*, 106: 244–52.

Madeddu, M. and Clifford, B. (2021) 'Housing quality, permitted development and the role of regulation after COVID-19', *Town Planning Review*, 92(1): 41–8.

Marsh, R., Chang, M. and Wood, J. (2022) 'The relationship between housing created through Permitted Development Rights and health: a systematic review', *Cities & Health*, 6(4): 833–52.

MHCLG (Ministry for Housing, Communities and Local Government) (2015) 'Thousands more homes to be developed in planning shake up'. Available at: www.gov.uk/government/news/thousands-more-homes-to-be-developed-in-planning-shake-up

MHCLG (2021) 'National Planning Policy Framework'. Available at www. gov.uk/government/publications/national-planning-policy-framework--2

ONS (Office for National Statistics) (2021) 'Household income inequality, UK: financial year ending 2020'. Available at: www.ons.gov.uk/peoplepop ulationandcommunity/personalandhouseholdfinances/incomeandwealth/ bulletins/householdincomeinequalityfinancial/financialyearending2020

Prior, A. and Raemaekers, J. (2006) 'Does planning deregulation threaten the environment? The effect of "permitted development" on the natural heritage of Scotland', *Journal of Environmental Planning and Management*, 49(2): 241–63.

Russell, V. (2011) 'Pickles plans to make it easier to turn offices into homes', *Public Finance*, 8 April. Available at: https://www.publicfinance.co.uk/ news/2011/04/pickles-plans-make-it-easier-turn-offices-homes

Building beauty? Place and housing quality in the planning agenda

Manuela Madeddu

Introduction

The starting point, and also the end point, for this chapter is that government in England has established the Office for Place and signalled its confidence in the use of design codes as a foundation for building more 'beautiful' places. There is nothing new in having a dedicated body to oversee development and place quality, and this is not the first time that design strictures have been codified. Reform is often about returning to the past and applying old ideas to today's challenges. Institutional and political memory is short, while the processes that underpin development outcomes have greater longevity. Governments, of different stripes and ideologies, are inclined to return to the same problems time and again, and the odds are that their prescriptions, drawn from a limited repertoire, will be strangely similar. They are also compelled to offer fresh solutions to the challenges of the day – a prerequisite of electoral success in a parliamentary democracy.

In this chapter, I contend that the challenge confronting planning is often the pace and regularity of change – rooted in the oscillations of political rhythm – rather than the apparently 'substantive' dilemmas inherent in development. The chapter is organised into two principal parts. In the first, I will sketch what I see as the antecedents of contemporary debate over the long and short run; this is presented as the road to, and recurring interest in, 'beauty'. In the second, I reflect on the last ten years of engagements with place quality – the shorter run of political rhythm. My argument is that the failure of planning is a political failure to think strategically and long term, rather than being buffeted by fashion and, in recent years, by the revolving door of 'political advice' and its perennial rebadging of old ideas. I argue for the need to acknowledge the value of foundational ideas that have been tested and retested over the years, and from which important principles can be distilled.

The road to beauty

The current place quality agenda in England is a mishmash of inconsistency. On the one hand, coding will deliver a uniformity of quality to be prescribed in local plans. However, on the other, decisions will be divorced from planning control through the distribution of permitted development rights (PDR). This is part of the recent narrative of 'building beauty', to which I will return shortly. But what of the longer run?

The codification of design, now outlined in the National Model Design Code (NMDC) for England, pre-dates any notion of modern or comprehensive planning, having been a feature of urban planning for centuries in a wide variety of settings. In all periods of planning history, local rules and pattern books – different forms of 'large-scale urban coding' (Talen, 2009: 147) – have been foundational to the designing and building of towns and cities. These have been culturally contingent, seeking to give physical form to otherwise abstract ideas and belief. In ancient China, for example, Feng Shui principles influenced the siting and layout of imperial capitals. The *Zhou Li* ('Rite of Zhou'), an ancient ritual text that shares much with Feng Shui cosmology and was applied as a building code, stipulated the precise orientation of cities according to a north–south axis, the arrangements of their streets along a regular grid, the number of gates on their surrounding walls, and the location of central palaces and markets. This codification of design expressed the power of the emperor, and it was inconceivable that Feng Shui principles were not respected (Madeddu and Zhang, 2021).

The use of codes is also evident in the development of ancient Roman colonial cities, which represent an embodiment of the typical Roman 'model city', built according to the criteria of order and functionality (Maganzani, 2015). Often growing from military camps, these planned cities were connected to Rome via 'consular roads' that formed part of the new city's regular grid plan, organised around two main axes and centred on the *forum* ('main square') and *capitolium* ('temple'). The 'beauty' of these cities was a celebration of the achievement of the empire, of which the inhabitants were sharing (Zanker, 2013). Strict codes governed the cities' built fabric, with Emperor Augustus (27 BCE–14 CE) decreeing that the height of buildings should not exceed 20 m (that is, six storeys) to ensure sufficient light to streets. The widths of principal thoroughfares – the east–west *decumanus* and north–south *cardus* – were set at 12.2 m and 6 m, with all other roads 4.5 m wide (Southworth and Ben-Joseph, 2003). These codes make Roman cities immediately identifiable, providing the essential framework for their development and urban form.

Similar codes were used throughout the Renaissance; the fort city of Palmanova in Italy, for instance, with its concentric layout, is a striking example. In France, codes were introduced in the 1780s that linked building heights to street widths, the intention being to promote a particular 'urban aesthetic' and create 'scenic views' (Talen, 2009: 156). Early French codes anticipated Haussmann's comprehensive Parisian regulations of the 1850s, which sought to realise Napoleon III's ambition to transform medieval Paris into a modern and monumental city. Widened streets became open boulevards that offered new perspectives on grand squares and important public buildings. This was achieved through prescribed floor and building heights, through the coordination of facades, and through a level of detail that guided the depths of balconies and the presence of ornamental ironwork (Jordan, 2004).

Across the Channel in England, design coding guided the rebuilding of London after the Great Fire of 1666, resulting in straightened and paved streets, flanked by buildings of coordinated heights and materials (Hebbert, 1998). Later on, pattern-book designs and coded layouts were agreed with landowners when Thomas Cubitt advanced schemes for Bloomsbury, Belgravia and Pimlico; these comprised 'grand terraces of white stucco houses of uniform mass, height (mainly four- and five-storey) and architectural treatment (Italianate)' (Knox, 2012: 31). At the turn of the 20th century, the construction of garden cities and suburbs relied on similar pattern books. These were used by the architects Raymond Unwin and Barry Parker to give physical form to Ebenezer Howard's marriage of town and country at Hampstead Garden Suburb, achieved through the narrowing of roads to give more space to green and open areas, and allowing for a variety of housing types, often according to the 'arts and crafts' style (Hall, 2014). Arguably less successful was the deployment of pattern books to guide the expansion of 'metro-land' into Hertfordshire and Buckinghamshire at around the same time, resulting in endless streets of semi-detached houses in mock-Tudor style, built with 'steep roofs, bay windows and half-timbered gables' (Forrest, 2015: para 5), and with near-identical floor plans (Barratt, 2012). Later in the 20th century, European modernism gained a foothold in England: notions of 'existenzminimum' (minimum dwelling) and the advantages of industrial production found their way into public housing schemes, including those of London County Council, whose architects drew inspiration from Le Corbusier's *Unité d'Habitation* (housing unit) (Murphy and Orazi, 2015).

In more recent times, the centrality of design codes has been maintained in the 'urban villages' promoted in England during the 1990s as part of the broader 'Urban Renaissance' agenda. These found a parallel in America's 'New Urbanism' (Neal, 2003). In England, the goal of revitalising and repopulating inner urban areas was pursued by the Urban Task Force, chaired by the architect Richard Rogers, which advocated design excellence and gave 'a massive boost to the urban design dimension of planning and development' (Punter, 2010: 3). Design coding was presented as a key implementation tool and a means of strengthening 'quality control, particularly on larger-scale, multi-phased developments' (Punter, 2010: 21). Indeed, the approach won many plaudits, including from then Deputy Prime Minister John Prescott: 'Coding can produce the regularity of a London square or the variety of Seaside in Florida. Instead of spending money on lawyers and planning enquiries, developers can spend it on planning and design – and everyone benefits' (quoted in Dewar, 2003: 4). The Labour government promoted the idea that 'good design is indivisible from good planning' (ODPM, 2005: 14), charging the Commission for Architecture and the Built Environment (CABE) to become its design champion from its creation in 1999. CABE advised government on architecture and urban design matters, undertook assessments of the quality of the built environment, and contributed to the 'development and delivery of best practices in urban design' (Punter, 2010: 13). As part of its remit, CABE, together with the government and with English Partnerships, undertook an evaluation of design codes and prepared a manual for their use between 2004 and 2005 (DCLG and CABE, 2006). The manual, written for local authorities, developers and practitioners, explained how coding could be woven into the development planning process and play a leading role in the delivery of place quality. Used in 'appropriate circumstances', they were deemed to be 'valuable tools' (DCLG and CABE, 2006: 14). Researchers examining the use of codes at the time agreed that while they do not offer a 'panacea' to the challenge of upping design quality, they have considerable efficacy if used in the right way and alongside other design tools (Carmona et al, 2006: 221). It was in the context of this debate and the emergence of CABE that codes became the means of ensuring design coherency at the Greenwich Millennium Village and in the redevelopment of Hulme in Manchester, where the codification of design principles provided the core of a planning framework to guide the replacement of a 1960s' public housing estate with a mixed development – mixed in terms of tenure and use – which played an important part in 'demonstrating the potential of coding' (Carmona et al, 2006: 259).

This brief overview has shown that at all times and in many different circumstances, it has been accepted good practice to formalise and codify design. Throughout the history of urban planning, design codes, with their explicit rules on the urban fabric and their attention for the aesthetic of development, have produced what are widely considered desirable places to live and work. The application of rules has happened at a variety of scales – from individual buildings and plots, to settlements and cities – generating design codes that are very different in nature from each another but that share a common purpose in ensuring a high degree of coherency in place making (see Carmona et al, 2006). This codification can be more or less prescriptive. The more prescriptive codes tend to seek monumental spaces as expressions of civic power (for example, Haussmann). The less prescriptive give flexibility and seed intimacy, recognising that places develop over long periods and in order to meet the needs of different groups. This is often the case in domestic spaces, where planning on a more human/community scale is needed. In recent times, the use of more prescriptive design codes has generally accompanied large phased projects and those where more actors are in charge of the development, with codes emphasising their role as a coordinating tool – between public and private sectors, and between landowners, land developers and planners – and driving the realisation of a coherent design vision (Carmona et al, 2006).

CABE and design codes emerged from the Urban Renaissance agenda of the late 1990s, though CABE took on a broader role in design governance, seeking to encourage greater concern for place quality across the planning and development sectors rather than officiating over outcomes. By the end of the first decade of the 21st century, the agenda nurtured by CABE looked to have gained some foothold in local development debates, with some evidence that its Building for Life standards were providing a blueprint for many new developments (Building for Life, 2009). Success on a number of high-profile projects had also demonstrated the effectiveness of design codes, deploying these in fast-tracked schemes in which the codification of agreed principles across multiple development phases (in the case of Hulme) substituted for standard management practices. Rather than requiring any fundamental shift in development control, coding could easily be accommodated within existing planning processes; indeed, it is able to transcend local processes, as it has done throughout history.

Yet, CABE was not without its critiques, being accused in some quarters of acting as a sort of 'design police force' (Sharro, 2010), applying inflexible and subjective notions of quality to the exclusion of alternative architectural ideas, and 'colonising' rather than engaging with built environment professionals (Carmona et al, 2017). In the space of ten years, CABE has been dismantled, design codes have gone out and back into vogue, and the Office for Place has been set up and offers what is an arguably more subjective guide for future place quality: the notion of beauty (see Araabi et al, 2022). These ten years are critical in the unfolding narrative of design quality in England and a period of significant oscillation: from external judgements over development quality, through a localisation of planning and through the dismantling of planning control, back to new external oversight and a return to exogenous notions of quality.

The last ten years

The last ten years of planning and design governance in England have a clear beginning, middle and end. In this section, I recount the shift away from, and return to, stronger design governance, with the manner of that return shaped by the intervening localist and deregulatory focus of planning reform.

The foundations of the *beginning* were laid with the relatively high-level master-planning and design-code recommendations originating in the report of the Urban Task Force and experimented with on the Greenwich Peninsula and elsewhere (see earlier). The creation of CABE as an independent guardian of place quality was also part of this foundation. While its predecessor, the Royal Fine Art Commission (RFAC), aimed to 'beautify England' through a focus on art and architecture, the new juxtaposition of 'built environment' with 'architecture' signalled a shift 'away from purely aesthetic preoccupations to a more integrated approach to urban development' (Ryser, 2017: 545). For more than ten years, from its creation in 1999 to its dismantling in 2011, CABE 'sought to understand, campaign for and prescribe solutions to the delivery of better architectural, urban and public space design to the nation at large' (Carmona et al, 2017: vii). The role of planning, and the design process therein, was seen as key to the achievement of quality in the built environment. That quality was to be sought through: the gathering of 'evidence' and the accumulation of 'knowledge' on the back of that evidence; the 'promotion' of exemplars revealed through the 'evaluation' of schemes; and 'assistance', which included, among other things, the use of design codes (Carmona et al, 2017). Despite criticisms from some quarters (focused largely on the inevitable subjectivities of quality), a comprehensive review of recent design governance has argued that the 'CABE experiment has shown widespread, tangible and positive results, leading to a long-term legacy of better projects, places and process than would otherwise have been the case, and with positive impacts across England on local population, the environment, and society at large' (Carmona et al, 2017: 247).

The focus on higher-level design oversight and governance, however, receded under the Conservative-led Coalition government after 2010, being seen as overly prescriptive and remote from communities. The last ten years started with an assault on this kind of expert oversight: CABE was accused of operating as an 'authoritarian taste police' (Sharro, 2010). The knowledge produced and exemplars promoted came to be seen as 'elitist and exclusive' (Ryser, 2017: 545). The new government presented CABE as a legacy of the steering centrism of the previous administration, which it pledged to eliminate through its return of power to town halls. With experts, or at least experts with ties to the Labour government, out of favour with the Conservatives, CABE was derided as another Labour quango, to be cast onto David Cameron's 'bonfire of the quangos'. While some of its functions were incorporated into the work of the Design Council (itself downgraded and reinvented as a charity), Design Council CABE – now a private subsidiary – lost government sponsorship and funding, and was no longer driving the design and design leadership agenda for the built environment (Carmona et al, 2017). CABE had been visibly out of step with the incoming government's localist agenda – it was another planner to 'get off our backs'. However, its denigration and demise at a national level did not end its influence. Its presentation of good design as being central to planning inspired many local groups and projects, which continued to use CABE tools, including codes, to deliver better design outcomes.

The protracted *middle* of this ten-year narrative has been localism and its many inconsistencies. The Conservatives claimed to have three priorities for government: localism, localism, localism (Pickles, 2011). More specifically, the rhetorical claim was that Labour's years of 'big' and intrusive government would be substituted with the 'Big Society', in which a great many challenges would be addressed through locally designed solutions. Neighbourhood development planning would provide the framework for collaborative design, with then Housing Minister Grant Shapps calling on architects and house builders to 'think outside the identikit Legoland box' and work with local communities to develop innovative ideas and designs more attuned to local character and neighbourhood identity (DCLG, 2011a). The government repeated this commitment to good design in the 2012 National Planning Policy Framework (NPPF), which was badged as 'a key aspect of sustainable development', 'indivisible from good planning' and fundamental to 'making places better for people' (DCLG, 2012: 14). This rhetoric, however, was not matched with resources. Professional groups quickly flagged a lack of investment in requisite skills, alongside inconsistencies in official messaging (see Brown, 2012; Lowe, 2012), with design presented as integral to effective planning but *planning* then lambasted as unnecessary bureaucracy, as government sought to denigrate and undermine the system ahead of its extension of PDR. Slow progress on the roll-out of neighbourhood development plans also meant that 'the knock-on potential to reinvigorate a new interest in design at the local level did not quickly materialise' (Carmona et al, 2017: 126). Government was also busy dismantling the apparatus of design oversight at a regional level, prioritising *any* development over good development. The regional development agencies (RDAs) had actively promoted and invested in design (Carmona et al, 2017). It was claimed that the closure of RDAs, and the other elements of regional planning would remove the unnecessary 'regional bureaucracy that imposed decisions on communities' (DCLG, 2011b) and substitute it with the opportunity for communities 'to exercise meaningful choice over the look and feel of the places where they live' (DCLG, 2011a). However, without the redirection of resources to neighbourhood groups, the real winners were developers, set to 'benefit from a smoother process for obtaining planning permission' (DCLG, 2011a). The rhetoric said that this would happen by creating 'the conditions where people begin to welcome rather than resist growth' (DCLG, 2011b) because of a combination of local empowerment and fiscal incentive. The latter was financed through creative accounting: a sleight of hand that cut local authority budgets but then occasionally returned a portion of the withheld funding through a 'Homes Bonus', though only if localities accepted additional development. Since 2013, the reality has been to smooth the pathway for development by eliminating the requirement to seek planning permission, thereby bypassing local people altogether, undermining both the democratic and quality goals of local planning.

PDR, alongside the removal of quality checks, mainly from CABE but also the regional agencies, have been the core element of planning reform over the last ten years. Conservative governments have been keen to tout the virtues of neighbourhood planning. However, this has been a sideshow rather than the major direction of change. This form of deregulation has been diametrically opposed to any quality agenda, contributing little or nothing to place making. The theory has been that planning is a cost on developers, limiting the extraction of value from development. Sometimes, there is little value to be extracted (from an old warehouse or 1970s' office building sitting on an arterial road), but by eliminating everything that planning would normally require – linked to: acceptable *building reuse*, in terms of created space, light and functionality; *location*, in terms of proximity to services; or *impact*, in terms of infrastructure contribution – it is possible to leave a developer with just enough extractable value to make a conversion profitable. There is certainly no room for quality; in fact, the ad hoc, unregulated and incremental PDR approach stands in sharp contrast to the emergent 'beauty agenda' and its reverence of the iconic master-planned and codified developments of the past, some of which were referenced earlier.

However, the use of PDR to advance residential development conversions has greatly accelerated since 2015 (Clifford et al, 2019). That acceleration is presented as a response to England's 'housing crisis' (Gallent, 2019), with the removal of 'red tape' (or 'getting the planners off our backs') seen as a way of increasing the supply of available housing (Ferm et al, 2020). The suspension of the site-by-site scrutiny of development proposals, which thereafter require only technical consent, means that there is no consideration of broader design quality; PDR allows developers to build 'quickly and cheaply', often delivering substandard homes in the worst-possible locations (Madeddu and Clifford, 2021), well away from any accessible services and close to major sources of pollution. The process and its outcomes have been the subject of withering critique, with the government accused of greenlighting modern slums and lacking any empathy for the people whose lives are then blighted by poor housing (Ing, 2020). PDR is adding to, rather than resolving, the housing crisis. However, that critique has not stopped the Ministry of Housing, Communities and Local Government (MHCLG) (now the Department for Levelling Up, Housing and Communities [DLUHC]) from pressing on with its reforms, which by 2022, have lengthened the list of commercial buildings – including high-street shops and offices – that can be converted to residential use without a standard planning permission. The government contends that faster use changes will help revitalise high streets hit by the COVID-19 pandemic. However, the theory of conversion to 'best use' (that is, highest rent) tells us that this will only happen in failing high streets, where the subtraction of usual high-street uses will weaken agglomeration benefits and accelerate economic obsolescence (Hughes and Jackson, 2015). It will happen in already-deprived areas, where there is little extractable value, creating more low-quality housing, risking the health and well-being of residents, and further compromising the quality of the public realm (Clifford and Madeddu, 2022).

The middle narrative, following CABE's downgrading, is one of a diminishing role for planning in design governance. This has been rooted in austerity (and hence a lack of resourcing), in the wider dismantling of the planning apparatus and in the deregulation of development planning. The promise of greater attention to design through reinvigorated localism has been patchy, at best. The 2010s therefore saw continuing conflict around the quality of new development and the production of some of the worst commercial-to-residential conversions ever seen in the UK.

At the *end* of this narrative, the government has been keen to lay the blame for low development quality, of the type highlighted by Carmona et al (2020), at the door of local planning authorities rather than accept the role its own choices have played in this race to the bottom. CABE was populated by the 'wrong experts', who would undoubtedly have been critical of the planning system's reduced oversight over the form and quality of development through a combination of diminished resourcing and PDR. Its removal created a window in which the government could supercharge unfettered development without challenge from its own watchdog. However, the chorus of complaint from professional bodies has ultimately returned us to the case for clear design leadership. In 2018, the philosopher and social conservative Sir Roger Scruton was asked by the government to chair a forthcoming inquiry into housing design. After some controversy, Scruton became the co-chair, with Nicholas Boys Smith, of the Building Better, Building Beautiful Commission (BBBBC). That commission took as its starting point Scruton's own work on aesthetics and beauty – rooted in his conservative views on monarchy, religion and tradition – as the foundations of a better architecture. His writings on these subjects had demonstrated their popular appeal – or at least the popularity of 'beauty', if left as an idea without fixed definition. The commission reported its findings in 2020: *Living with Beauty* began by setting out how 'beauty' 'includes everything that promotes a healthy and happy life, everything that makes a collection of buildings into a place, everything that turns anywhere into somewhere, and nowhere into home [and] should be an essential condition for the grant of planning permission' (BBBBC, 2020: iv). While the commission was critical of PDR and its promotion of 'future slums' (BBBBC, 2020: 69), which was inevitable given the professional interests and affiliations of its commissioners and advisers, its major finding was that beauty can be codified and, through that codification, embedded in development projects. This view again seemed to reflect both the make-up of the commission and Scruton's architectural aesthetics, with its preference for traditional and monumental beauty – of the type found in the longer history of urban planning and urban codes sketched earlier in this chapter. Codes were presented as a crucial part of the planning process, though they should be 'tolerant of, and encouraging of, local forms' and 'reflect local preferences' (BBBBC, 2020: 37, 62). The proposals needed to fit with the government's reform agenda while balancing the case for new leadership with respect for localism.

In response to the work of the commission, amendments were made to the NPPF in 2021. New references to codes and coding were inserted, and the NMDC, in two parts, was published. At the same time, then Secretary of State for Housing, Communities and Local Government Robert Jenrick announced the creation of the Office for Place, with an advisory group comprising some members of the commission and some new industry and political appointees. Scruton had died in 2020, and so a new co-chair was appointed alongside Boys Smith.

Many of those who have drawn attention to the loss of design leadership offered a cautious welcome to the Office for Place: 'we have reached a moment of *potential* national change in the relationship between design, planning and development in England' (Carmona, 2021: 130, emphasis added). Seen in the context of declining quality (Bishop, 2021: 160) and the failure, at all levels, to follow existing NPPF guidance on design (Place Alliance and CPRE, 2020), the resumption of some element of leadership was perhaps bound to be seen as a good thing. The emphasis on codifying design and avoiding not only poor but also mediocre development has been welcomed (Carmona, 2021), but there is also a concern that a balance between prescription and respect for local character will be difficult to achieve, as the draft NMDC 'mentions community engagement a lot but fails to properly understand it, mentions local character but only minimally and misses out on its proper use, and fails to mention local distinctiveness at all' (Bishop, 2021: 160).

There are three very significant worries. The first, just conveyed by Bishop, is that the government is not really very serious about localism; rather, it has become a political necessity that sits uneasily with the overriding goal of supporting the development sector. While codes do not require reform of the existing (discretionary) approach to development management, there was a fear in 2020/21 that they might become part of a zoning system that would end local scrutiny at the application stage (MHCLG, 2020; Gallent et al, 2021). That fear has now receded: a new secretary of state (Michael Gove, who was appointed in September 2021, sacked in July 2022 and then returned to the role in October 2022) rejected the zoning plans of his predecessor and issued his own planning bill (the Levelling-up and Regeneration Bill [LURB] [HM Government, 2022]) in May 2022. There was a worry when the 2020 White Paper (which appeared to entirely forget about the existence of neighbourhood planning) was in circulation that coding would ride roughshod over local preference. There is still a concern that a technical focus on local codes – to be produced by every planning authority, either as part of the local plan or as a supplement to it – will sideline communities as authorities rush to get plans completed within a 30-month window. The second worry is that the 'current emphasis on "beauty" will not deliver housing fit for future generations' (RIBA, 2021: paras 9–10). This is because of the 'unnecessary centrality' of aesthetics and the sidelining of 'sustainability, accessibility, and adaptability' (RIBA, 2021: paras 9–10; see also Araabi et al, 2022). CABE engaged fully with these issues, but the Office for Place is linked – through the work of the BBBBC – with Scruton's architectural aesthetics. How the office will work and whether or not it will be faithful to Conservative ideology and its narrow preferences are significant unknowns. There is also evidence that place-based coding is possible only if 'local authorities are given resources to implement it' (UDG, 2021). The third major worry is therefore resourcing: improved quality, let alone a 'design revolution', will only be possible with substantial investment in the planning system and in local authorities (Carmona, 2021; RIBA, 2021; RTPI, 2021). There are particular concerns around local authorities' in-house design skills and whether these are sufficient to allow the effective local implementation of the NMDC (Carmona et al, 2022). A lack of investment has driven down development quality in England, and there is little indication that this is about to change.

At first sight, it appears that the design governance debate has gone full circle since 2010 and that the vacuum in design leadership is about to be filled. The government is looking at the independence of the Office for Place, but as it stands, this new design champion has a far narrower focus than CABE. Its emphasis on beauty and coding is in marked contrast to CABE's mixed approach to promoting, evaluating and supporting good design (Carmona et al, 2017: 244). Its capacity to shape the design agenda will also be greatly hampered by the government's insistence on extending PDR (Carmona, 2021: 131). While design coding has an important part to play in achieving greater consistency in place quality if it works with local character and preference, PDR is rooted in incoherent incrementalism, giving the market free rein to repurpose buildings irrespective of their locational or typological attributes. PDR is an example of actually existing neoliberalism and is emblematic of the government's underlying view of planning. Ten years ago, CABE sought a broader role for the planning system in design governance, with quality judged across multiple dimensions. That view was out of step with the incoming administration's market logic. Today, the Office for Place has been tasked to defend 'beauty', not through stronger, broader and better-resourced planning, but through the conscription of the development sector and the hope that it will embrace a codified aesthetic – in much the same way as Thomas Cubitt did when master-planning Bloomsbury and Belgravia nearly 200 years ago. The 2020 Planning White Paper proposed that the incentive to do so would come from a trimmed-back planning system, with development zoning supplanting the uncertainties of extant development management. Since government was unable to sell 'by right' permissioning to a sceptical electorate, suffering defeat in a local by-election when it tried, it has continued to extend PDR and claw back power over plan making, proposing the implementation of national development management policies (HM Government, 2022). It continues to target the delivery of faster and more standardised plans, providing the development sector with as much certainty as possible without outraging Conservative voters.

Conclusion

Despite the swing back to design leadership in England, the end point, where we are now, is not exactly the same as the point of origin. CABE and the Office for Place are different organisations, operating under very different conditions. The planning system is far more degraded and demoralised today than it was ten years ago. CABE emerged from the Urban Renaissance agenda, with its focus on the power of planning and design to change neighbourhoods and win support for development, mainly in the form of new housing (Carmona et al, 2017). It had a suite of tools at its disposal and took a broad view of place quality. In contrast, the Office for Place appears anachronistic, the white knight returning to save the day after a decade of famine. However, its appearance does not mark any sudden ideological shift. It is the product of a conservative mindset that regularly argues that the places we most value today, that is, those that are the most 'beautiful', are not the products of the '1947 system'. The staunchest planning critics will contend that nothing of quality has been built since the Second World War but that traditional urbanism, achieved through coding, holds lessons for today. This pared-down view of planning, which ignores its contribution to a massive increase in housing quality until the 1980s, sees all land policy as a leftist project that undermines propertied interests. These ideological oscillations are nothing new, but they are hugely disruptive to the operation of local planning, undermining the contribution that well-resourced departments could make to housing and place quality. At the beginning of this chapter, I argued: 'Governments, of different stripes and ideologies, are inclined to return to the same problems time and again, and the odds are that their prescriptions, drawn from a limited repertoire, will be strangely similar. They are also compelled to offer fresh solutions to the challenges of the day – a prerequisite of electoral success in a parliamentary democracy.' Chopping and changing, and occasional chaos, is the price paid for open democracy. However, in the case of design governance, it has an exclusively negative impact. The imprint of failure is borne heavily on the built environment, affecting lives and livelihoods for generations.

Yet, the return to design oversight by the Office for Place is to be cautiously welcomed. The organisation embodies a mix of views and is not entirely tied to the aesthetics of beauty. It is an organisation that will undoubtedly evolve, eventually concerning itself with a broader raft of design and place considerations. The political context will also evolve. There is a hope that PDR will burn itself out, that the chorus of condemnation it has faced will not be silenced and that the denigration of planning will come to an end. The 'art and science' of planning is about place design across multiple levels, and the cycle of political debate will recognise this reality at some future point.

References

Araabi, H.F., Hickman, H. and McClymont, K. (eds) (2022) 'On beauty', *Planning Theory & Practice*, 23(4): 601–33.

Barrat, N. (2012) *Greater London: The Story of the Suburbs*, New York: Random House.

BBBBC (Building Better, Building Beautiful Commission) (2020) *Living with Beauty*, London: Ministry of Housing Communities and Local Government.

Bishop, J. (2021) 'Cracking the code?', *Town & Country Planning*, 90(5–6): 160–5.

Brown, C. (2012) 'The community is the client', *Urban Design*, 123(Summer): 25–6.

Building for Life (2009) 'Some of the best housing this century', 3 December. Available at: https://webarchive.nationalarchives.gov.uk/ukgwa/2011010 7170020/http:/www.buildingforlife.org/news/some-of-the-best-hous ing-this-century

Carmona, M. (2021) 'Design quality: have we reached a moment of national change?', *Town and Country Planning*, 90(3–4): 130–3.

Carmona, M., Marshall, S. and Stevens, Q. (2006) 'Design codes: their use and potential', *Progress in Planning*, 65(4): 209–89.

Carmona, M., De Magalhaes, C. and Natarajan, L. (2017) *Design Governance: The CABE Experiment*, London: Routledge.

Carmona, M., Alwarea, A., Giordano, V., Gusseinova, A. and Olaleye, F. (2020) 'A housing design audit for England'. Available at: https://indd. adobe.com/view/23366ae1-8f97-455d-896a-1a9934689cd8

Carmona, M., Clarke, W., Quinn, B. and Giordano, V. (2022) 'National Model Design Code (NMDC) pilot programme phase one, monitoring & evaluation'. Available at: www.gov.uk/government/publications/natio nal-model-design-code-pilot-programme-phase-1-lessons-learned

Clifford, B. and Madeddu, M. (2022) 'Turning shops into housing? Planning deregulation, design quality and the future of the high street in England', *Built Environment*, 48(1): 123–40.

Clifford, B., Ferm, J., Livingstone, N. and Canelas, P. (2019) *Understanding the Impacts of Deregulation in Planning: Turning Offices into Homes?*, London: Palgrave Pivot.

DCLG (Department for Community and Local Government) (2011a) 'Think outside of "identikit Legoland homes"'. Available at: www.gov.uk/gov ernment/news/think-outside-of-identikit-legoland-homes

DCLG (2011b) 'Localism to spark growth revival'. Available at: www.gov. uk/government/news/localism-to-spark-growth-revival

DCLG (2012) *National Planning Policy Framework*, London: DCLG.

DCLG and CABE (Commission for Architecture and the Built Environment) (2006) *Preparing Design Codes. A Practice Manual*, London: RIBA Publishing.

Dewar, D. (2003) 'Prescott adopts coding to boost developments', *Planning*, 28: 4.

Ferm, J., Clifford, B., Canelas, P. and Livingstone, N. (2020) 'Emerging problematics of deregulating the urban: the case of permitted development in England', *Urban Studies*, 58(10): 2040–58.

Forrest, A. (2015) 'Metroland, 100 years on: what's become of England's original vision of suburbia?', *The Guardian*, 10 September. Available at: www.theguardian.com/cities/2015/sep/10/metroland-100-years-engl and-original-vision-suburbia

Gallent, N. (2019) *Whose Housing Crisis? Assets and Homes in a Changing Economy*, Bristol: Policy Press.

Gallent, N., De Magalhaes, C. and Freire Trigo, S. (2021) 'Is zoning the solution to the UK housing crisis?', *Planning Practice & Research*, 36(1): 1–19.

Hall, P. (2014) *Cities of Tomorrow: An Intellectual History of Urban Planning and Design since 1880*, 4th edn, Chichester: Wiley Blackwell.

Hebbert, M. (1998) *London: More by Fortune Than Design*, Chichester: John Wiley.

HM Government (Her Majesty's Government) (2022) *Levelling Up and Regeneration Bill*, London: HM Government. Available at: https://publi cations.parliament.uk/pa/bills/cbill/58-03/0006/220006.pdf

Hughes, C. and Jackson, C. (2015) 'Death of the high street: identification, prevention, reinvention', *Regional Studies, Regional Science*, 2(1): 237–56.

Ing, W. (2020) '"Immoral slums": Raynsford slams government over permitted development policy', *Architects' Journal*, 17 January. Available at: www.architectsjournal.co.uk/news/immoral-slums-raynsford-slams-gov ernment-over-permitted-development-policy

Jordan, D.P. (2004) 'Haussmann and Haussmannisation: the legacy for Paris', *French Historical Studies*, 27(1): 87–113.

Knox, P. (2012) *Palimpsests: Biographies of 50 City Districts: International Case Studies of Urban Change*, Berlin and Boston, MA: Birkhäuser.

Lowe, S. (2012) 'Localism vs NPPF', *Urban Design*, 123(Summer): 2.

Madeddu, M. and Clifford, B. (2021) 'Housing quality, permitted development and the role of regulation after COVID-19', *Town Planning Review*, 92(1): 41–8.

Madeddu, M. and Zhang, X. (2021) *Feng Shui and the City: The Public and Private Spaces of Chinese Geomancy*, London: Palgrave Macmillan.

Maganzani, L. (2015) 'Roma antica e l'ideale di città' ['Ancient Rome and the ideal city'], *Teoria e Storia del Diritto Privato*, VIII(Dicembre): 1–46.

MHCLG (Ministry of Housing, Communities and Local Government) (2020) 'White Paper: planning for the future'. Available at: www.gov.uk/government/consultations/planning-for-the-future

Murphy, D. and Orazi, S. (2015) 'Modernism in Britain: did it stand the test of time', *The Guardian*, 13 September. Available at: www.theguardian.com/artanddesign/2015/sep/13/60s-housing-dream-living-in-it

Neal, P. (ed) (2003) *Urban Villages and the Making of Communities*, London: Spon Press.

ODPM (Office of the Deputy Prime Minister) (2005) 'Planning Policy Statement 1: Delivering Sustainable Development'. Available at: https://webarchive.nationalarchives.gov.uk/ukgwa/20120920042341/http://www.communities.gov.uk/archived/publications/planningandbuilding/planningpolicystatement1

Pickles, E. (2011) 'Eric Pickles MP: The Localism Bill reverses a century of centralisation', *Conservative Home*, 18 November. Available at: https://conservativehome.com/2011/11/18/in-pursuit-of-localism-restoring-a-100-year-democratic-deficit/

Place Alliance and CPRE (The Countryside Charity) (2020) 'A housing design audit for England'. Available at: https://indd.adobe.com/view/23366ae1-8f97-455d-896a-1a9934689cd8

Punter, J. (2010) 'An introduction to the British urban renaissance', in J. Punter (ed) *Urban Design and the British Urban Renaissance*, London: Routledge, pp 1–34.

RIBA (Royal Institute of British Architects) (2021) 'Shaping the NPPF and National Design Code', 1 April. Available at: www.architecture.com/knowledge-and-resources/knowledge-landing-page/shaping-the-nppf-and-national-design-code

RTPI (Royal Town Planning Institute) (2021) 'RTPI response to MHCLG NPPF and Model Design Code consultation', 26 March. Available at: www.rtpi.org.uk/consultations/2021/march/rtpi-response-to-mhclg-nppf-and-national-model-design-code-consultation/

Ryser, J. (2017) 'Book review. Design governance: the CABE experiment', *Journal of Urban Design*, 22(4): 544–6.

Sharro, K. (2010) 'Why not abolish CABE altogether?', *Design Curial*, 14 September. Available at: www.designcurial.com/news/why-not-abol ish-cabe-altogether-

Southworth, M. and Ben-Joseph, E. (2003) *Streets and the Shaping of Towns and Cities*, Washington, DC: Island Press.

Talen, E. (2009) 'Design by the rules: the historical underpinnings of form-based codes', *Journal of the American Planning Association*, 75(2): 144–60.

UDG (Urban Design Group) (2021) 'The National Model Design Code'. Available at: www.udg.org.uk/directory/awards-finalists/national-model-design-code

Zanker, P. (2013) *La città romana* [*The Roman City*], Roma and Bari: Editori Laterza.

Zoning in or zoning out?
Lessons from Europe

Sebastian Dembski and Phil O'Brien

Introduction

> Thanks to our planning system, we have nowhere near
> enough homes in the right places. People cannot afford to
> move to where their talents can be matched with opportunity.
> Businesses cannot afford to grow and create jobs. The whole
> thing is beginning to crumble and the time has come to do
> what too many have for too long lacked the courage to do – tear
> it down and start again. (Boris Johnson, quoted in MHCLG,
> 2020a: 345)

Planning has long been 'under attack' (Lord and Tewdwr-Jones, 2014) – not
just since the publication of the highly controversial White Paper *Planning for
the Future* (MHCLG, 2020a). The prime minister's opening remarks in the
planning White Paper cited earlier are just some of many clearly laying
the blame with the planning system for all that is wrong. England is not
the only country struggling with a persistent housing crisis (Wetzstein,
2017) and using the planning system to address it, yet the debate seems
a little more adversarial there than elsewhere. In addition to housing
numbers, there is also a persistent issue in terms of design quality, with
many approved developments even contradicting national planning policy
(Carmona et al, 2020).

One of the key proposals of the White Paper (MHCLG, 2020a) was
the introduction of a zoning mechanism in all but name. Local plans
were supposed to zone land into three distinct categories: growth areas,
renewal areas and protected areas. Growth areas indicate sites of substantial
development, including both greenfield and brownfield land, which
automatically grant outline approval. Renewal areas would cover the existing
built-up area, where there would be a presumption in favour of sustainable
development, with fast-track planning permission. Only in protected areas,
which according to the White Paper, in essence, refers to open countryside
that is not designated as growth or renewal areas, would the planning system

continue to operate more or less as is, with each planning application being dealt with individually on its merits. Despite the attempt at a rule-based approach, the White Paper envisaged that planning applications that are different to the plan could nevertheless still be submitted (MHCLG, 2020a: 34).

The publication of the planning White Paper has shaken up the planning community in England. Although the debate on planning reform has since moved on following considerable backlash from the government's backbenches and a change in political leadership of the department that was reflected in the change of name, several reforms had already pointed in a similar direction: the introduction of rule-based instruments into what is essentially a discretionary system (Gallent et al, 2021). This included the extension of permitted development rights in 2013 and 2020, as well as permission in principle in 2016, and, more recently, the introduction of a National Model Design Code promoting local design codes (MHCLG, 2021). The 2022 Levelling-up and Regeneration Bill has dropped the zoning proposals, though it does require local planning authorities to establish area-wide design codes.

There is an explicit assumption that rule-based planning systems will deliver better outcomes, both in terms of certainty for developers and faster decision making, on the one hand, and place making or beauty, on the other. This false dichotomy of regulatory and discretionary planning systems and instruments has been with us at least since the introduction of simplified planning zones (SPZs) in the 1980s and is unlikely to go away. This chapter argues that most European zoning systems, at least for major planning applications, are no less flexible and provide no more certainty than the English system, but that the higher autonomy of local planning authorities in these countries to decide on planning matters leads to a far more cooperative process, potentially delivering better outcomes.

Regulatory versus discretionary systems, and British exceptionalism

Traditionally, a distinction has been made between regulatory (or zoning) and discretionary planning systems, which essentially focuses on whether building rights are granted at the moment the land use or zoning plan is approved (regulatory system) or the application is approved (discretionary system) (Booth, 1995). The terminology is somewhat clumsy, as discretionary planning systems also operate within a legal framework and either system ultimately regulates development activity (Booth, 2007). However, it is the non-binding nature of the development plan against which planning applications are tested, thus providing much greater discretion in decision making, that forms the key difference between the two systems. In the

English discretionary system, as well as those related to it, the land-use plan is largely a compendium of written policies applied when decisions are made that determine planning applications, together with maps that set out the local planning authority's preferred sites for development into different uses. While in regulatory systems, indicative plans showing preferred sites are often produced as a means to set out the local planning authority's preferences, zonal plans are also produced that automatically confer land-use and development rights for landowners.

Viewed globally, the discretionary planning systems in the UK are an exception, though this has not always been the case. The British exceptionalism emerged gradually over the course of the 20th century. British statutory planning started out with land-use plans in 1909, which were legally binding (Booth, 2003; Ward, 2020). By that time, planners were part of an international community and the British approach had been inspired by the extension plans in Germany and elsewhere in Europe, which specified functional land-use zones and included clear procedures for building permits (Ward, 2010, 2020). Unlike in Germany, municipal ownership of development land was not part of the 1909 act (Sutcliffe, 1988) and the fact that the landowners could claim compensation for loss of development value, a feature not present in the existing by-law system, limited the adoption of town-planning schemes to where landowners cooperated (Ward, 2020). Ultimately, this was viewed as a cumbersome process that delayed development (Crow, 1996).

Britain's departure from zoning started as early as the 1920s, when interim development control was introduced and expanded in subsequent years into the discretionary system, which was fully established in the Town and Country Planning Act 1947 and has essentially stayed the same since (Crow, 1996). Interim development control allowed local governments to approve development ahead of the formal approval of town-planning schemes to speed up development. Subsequently, the scope of town-planning schemes, and with them, interim development control, was extended to any area in the city and became concerned with land-use change too (Booth, 2003). Interim development control still meant that proposals needed to be in conformity with the final scheme or else the scheme itself must be modified, resulting in arguments to make plans more flexible. The 1947 act nationalised development rights and established a system whereby any development as specified by the act required planning permission to be granted by the local planning authority with regard to the statutory but indicative development plan and any other material considerations (Davies, 1998). The key principles of the planning system have remained unchanged until this day, despite numerous reforms.

For a long time, the flexibility of British planning has been valued nationally and internationally (Booth, 2003: 4), but it has since come under pressure. Critiques of planning in Britain have tended to come from two sources: economic research conducted in the neoclassical tradition (Cheshire et al, 2014; Hilber and Vermeulen, 2016); and the residential development industry's land acquisition and development perspective. The criticisms levelled from these sources have, to a degree, coalesced in policy reports published by liberal think tanks, in which the neoclassical focus on planning as a supply constraint that raises house prices combines with the industry notion of 'planning risk', or the risk of not obtaining permission to develop (Breach, 2019; Airey and Doughty, 2020). These criticisms are related but not analogous given that a planning system might be designed to grant outright certainty to developers for only a limited number of sites. Recent UK government efforts to increase the rate of private sector house building in England have addressed both concerns by way of a consultation exercise on proposed revisions to calculating housing need in local authorities, since abandoned, which would have substantially raised house-building targets in more heated markets (MHCLG, 2020b), alongside the White Paper's (MHCLG, 2020a) concern for reducing planning risk for developers through the introduction of a zonal planning system.

The proposed introduction of a zonal planning system in England, alongside the aforementioned notion of planning risk, is aligned with the balance between flexibility and certainty that has long been the main analytical line drawn to characterise the contrast between discretionary and regulatory planning systems (Muñoz Gielen and Taşan-Kok, 2010). Where the case-by-case decision making of England's discretionary system enables it to adapt to changing site and market conditions, regulatory systems effectively fix what is permissible at the point of plan publication and are therefore, barring exemptions from the plan, inflexible to change. However, the flexibility of the discretionary system comes at a price, in the form of a lack of certainty granted to developers, for whom the plan does not confer the right to develop. The weak relationship between development and the plan in England thereby raises risk for house builders. But is this analytical distinction an accurate one in practice?

According to the White Paper, in England, 'nearly all decisions to grant consent are taken on a case-by-case basis, rather than determined by clear rules for what can and cannot be done. This makes the English planning system and those derived from it an exception internationally' (MHCLG, 2020a: 10–12). This is certainly the received wisdom as regards the distinction between discretionary and zonal planning, but it addresses a theory of zonal planning that fails to match its practice in much of the world. Indeed, in practice, the prototypical zonal system, in which the whole plan area is divided into different possible land uses with clearly specified rules guaranteeing the development rights of landowners, is heavily reliant upon the granting of exemptions to the plan (Janin Rivolin, 2008; Moroni et al, 2020). These exemptions are regarded as necessary to give sufficient flexibility to developers, who would otherwise be constrained by a plan that, however up to date, is by its nature fixed and therefore unable to respond to changing conditions.

The level of control conferred on local authorities over individual planning decisions by use of exemptions to the plan is also used by planners to shape the pattern of urban growth. Booth (1995) sets out various mechanisms to demonstrate how this is achieved in France, such as by the use of a zoning designation that permits development only when necessary infrastructure has been agreed to be implemented and where a special case plan (the *Zone d'Aménagement Concerté* [ZAC]) can be used to supersede the land-use plan and put special conditions in place. Similarly, Buitelaar et al (2011), discussing how virtually all new development in the Netherlands diverges from the plan and therefore requires a new or amended plan, describe the land-use plan for an individual development as the formalisation of negotiated agreements between developers and planners, noting that it bears closer similarity to a contract than a plan.

A more illuminating dichotomy than that between regulatory (or zonal) and discretionary planning divides planning systems into those that are 'conformative' and those that are 'performative' (Janin Rivolin, 2008). Planning systems that use a legally binding zonal plan to establish current and possible future land uses are said to be conformative, in the sense that development must conform to the plan. Those that are responsive to development proposals and assess these on a case-by-case basis to ensure that what is developed will perform the local planning authority's strategy are said to be performative. However, as noted, few, if any, planning systems demand total adherence to the land-use plan and are therefore entirely conformative. The conformative–performative distinction is a continuum rather than a dichotomy, then. This is most aptly represented in the notion of 'neo-performative' planning systems, where binding zonal plans are produced but development rights are ultimately only conferred following final approval by the local planning authority, usually following negotiations with developers (Berisha et al, 2021).

This is suggestive of two important points. First, in many zonal planning systems local planning authorities arguably have much greater discretion than their UK counterparts and make wide use of it. Second, there is always a compromise to be reached between flexibility and certainty in planning systems. This compromise can be reached within a regulatory, or zonal, planning system by means of allowing developers to approach the local planning authority with an idea to develop a site in a particular way that is not permitted by the existing plan. The question that has been grappled with in England is one of how to build in greater certainty to a discretionary planning system in which land-use plans do not set out legally binding prescriptions. The White Paper proposed the replacement of the current discretionary system with a zonal system, while successive governments have attempted to achieve the same aims by the introduction of zoning tools, such as, most recently, the Local Development Order, into the current system.

Arguably, the point is not so much whether a discretionary or a regulatory planning system is in place but, rather, whether the planning system is configured towards the aims of providing homes of acceptable quality at sufficient quantities in the most appropriate locations. Granting control to local planning authorities over the location and design of new development is one part of the solution to this, while the incentivisation of the same bodies to allow house builders to deliver enough new homes is another. In the following section, we set out how the German, Dutch and Swiss planning systems are able to come closer to achieving this balance than has been the case in England in the recent past, highlighting the frameworks and tools that facilitate this.

Zoning in Germany, the Netherlands and Switzerland

Most European countries have regulatory planning systems, with binding land-use plans that directly grant building rights. They face similar challenges in balancing housing delivery with place making while being viable. Therefore, the question is how other European countries address the problems identified in the critique of the English planning system.

Germany's housing market has been remarkably stable compared with other European countries over a long period of time, which is why many have looked to find answers there, though over the last decade, metropolitan areas have seen significant increases in house prices. The Federal Building Code establishes a two-tier local planning system, consisting of a preparatory land-use plan that outlines the preferred development for the whole territory of the municipality and binding land-use plans that grant direct building rights for clearly demarcated areas within the municipality (see Figures 7.1 and 7.2). Initially, it was intended that, eventually, the whole built-up area would be covered by binding land-use plans, but this idea was soon abandoned and a perhaps surprisingly large part of the built-up area of German municipalities remains 'unplanned' (see Figure 7.3). Development in the unplanned built-up area is permissible as long as it blends in with the environment (for example, use class, massing, floor-space ratio, height and architecture).

Over the past decades, the German planning system has become increasingly development led, which has paradoxically strengthened the position of municipalities. Historically, Germany experienced a situation that has been described as the building land paradox of too much and not enough building land (Davy, 1996), as little attention was given to the implementation of land-use plans. With increasing pressure on public

Figure 7.1: Preparatory land-use plan Neuburg an der Donau, 2006 (detail) after 45th amendment

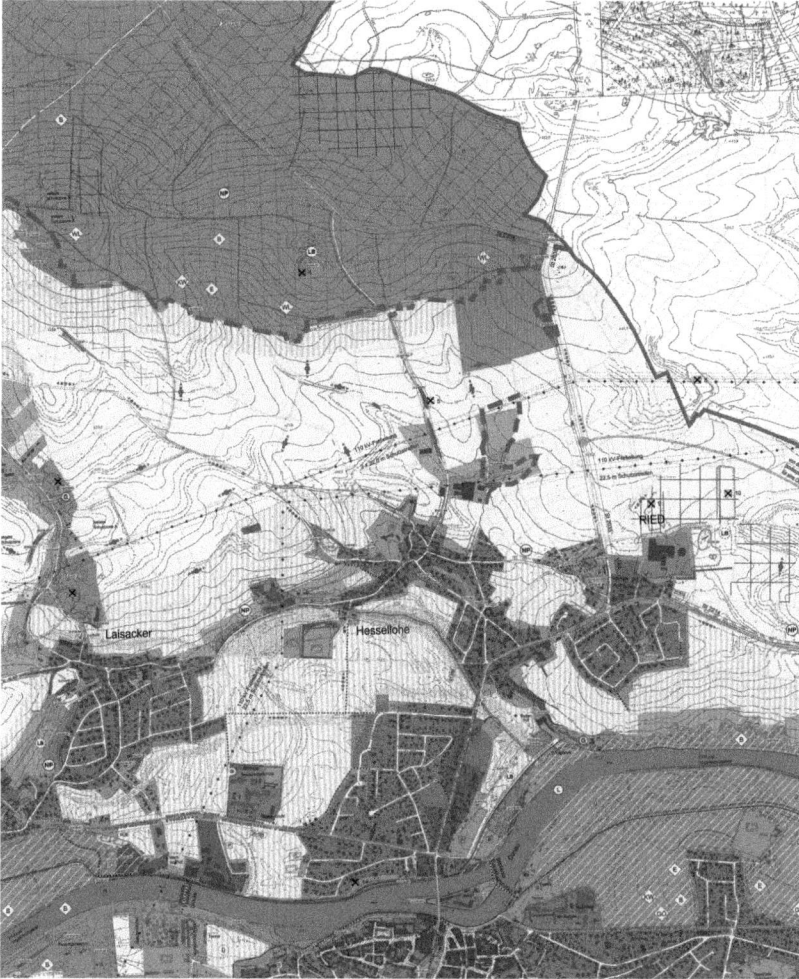

Source: Große Kreisstadt Neuburg an der Donau

finances, municipalities could no longer afford to prepare speculative land-use plans, reducing the problem of fallow building land somewhat. Most developments require a binding land-use plan given the fact that they are unlikely to blend in, and very few municipalities will prepare a binding land-use plan without an investor lined up due to the costly and lengthy procedure in light of the uncertainty over demand. In fact, it has become common practice that the developer approaches the municipality with a land-use plan (project and infrastructure plan), which is also time limited if approved by the municipality, or that the municipality recovers the costs of the land-use plan via an urban development contract. The preparatory

Figure 7.2: Binding land-use plan 'Bullbug'

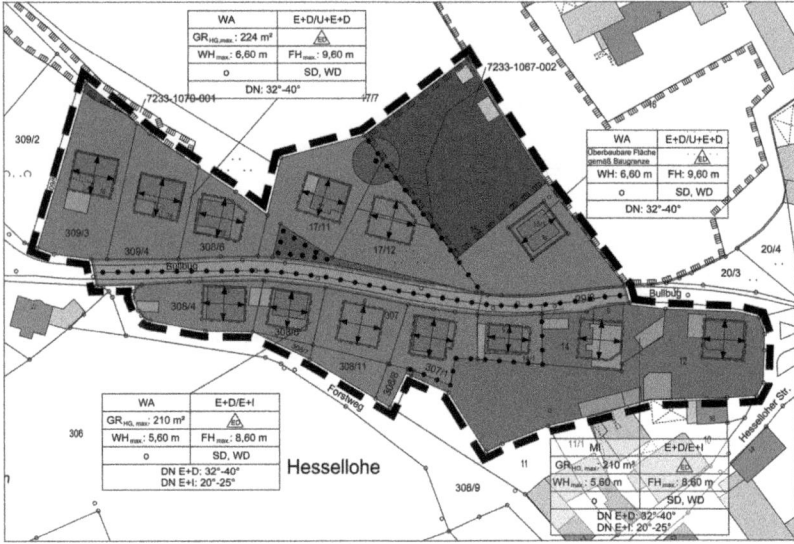

Bebauungs- und Grünordnungsplan Nr. 8-13   M 1 : 1.000

Source: Große Kreisstadt Neuburg an der Donau

Figure 7.3: Overview of approved binding land-use plans in Ried subdistrict

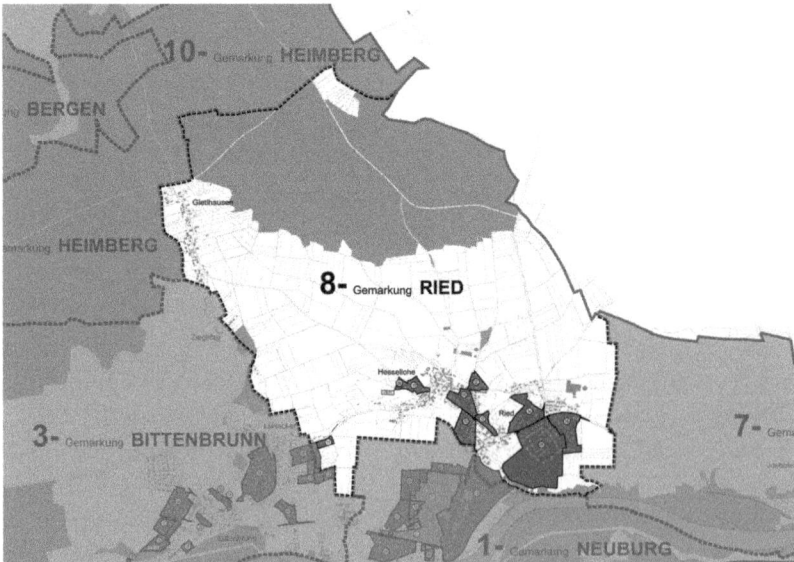

Source: Große Kreisstadt Neuburg an der Donau

land-use plan is frequently amended (Feiertag and Schoppengerd, 2023). There is no entitlement for a binding land-use plan to be drafted. This places the municipality in a strong position, at least in theory, to shape the outcomes of the development.

The Dutch planning system is held in high esteem internationally. The 2008 reform of the Dutch Spatial Planning Act established a clear separation between indicative policy and binding rules. The *structuurvisie* ('structure vision') sets outs the long-term development of a municipality and is indicative, whereas the *bestemmingsplan* ('land-use plan') outlines the rules against which development will be tested. The Spatial Planning Act requires municipalities to zone their whole territory, granting direct development rights for landowners. Although it is possible to draft a single land-use plan, the municipal territory is usually a patchwork of plans of variable size and approved at different times (see Figures 7.4 and 7.5). The municipality determines the use of land, with land-use rules attached. These include, at the very least, a definition of the use classes and building rules, for example, massing, building lines and so on. It can even prescribe the percentage of social or affordable housing. All plans can be consulted in a national database, and together, they cover every square inch of the Netherlands.[1]

Figure 7.4: Land-use plan Anna's Hoeve, Hilversum, including revisions

Source: www.ruimtelijkeplannen.nl

Figure 7.5: Land-use plan boundaries East Hilversum

Source: www.ruimtelijkeplannen.nl

Dutch planning has been described as 'development led', and the land-use plan has been described as being more akin to a contract following a long process of negotiations (Buitelaar et al, 2011; Tennekes, 2018). Although the importance of the private sector has grown significantly since the 1990s, municipalities continue to play a key role in the planning process, including land assembly (Van der Krabben and Jacobs, 2013). It is unlikely that prevailing land-use plans will grant the development rights needed for the landowner to realise their plans, so the developer and the municipality usually work together on the realisation of a project of which the land-use plan is the final piece in the jigsaw, often preceded by private contracts about public cost recovery. Attempts to reinvigorate the steering function of the land-use plan and incorporate more flexibility through less prescriptive rules have failed (Buitelaar et al, 2011; Dembski, 2020). There has been a long-standing tradition of large-scale development (Tennekes et al, 2015), which was only briefly interrupted by the Global Financial Crisis, whereas in all other cases, municipalities have reverted to small-scale land-use plans not dissimilar to a planning application.

Switzerland has recently amended its Spatial Planning Act, with the aim to significantly reduce urban sprawl, in response to a popular initiative. Despite strong population growth over the past two decades, similar to that of the UK, it opted to limit building land supply for at most 15 years and reduce building land reserves where this is exceeded. There is substantial divergence in planning instruments, as each of the 26 cantons has its own building decrees, though the Spatial Planning Act provides a general framework. A key feature of Swiss planning at the regional and local levels is the division of land into building zones, agricultural zones and protection zones. The local land-use plan outlines the planned development in combination with the municipal building code and grants direct development rights to landowners. It distinguishes categories of land uses, with generic rules on building height, massing and so on attached to each. In particular for residential areas, the building height is often expressed in the number of floors. Although the plan is binding on landowners and grants development rights, proposals still require a building permit and undergo scrutiny by a local expert committee advising on design matters.

So far, the Swiss planning system appears to be a textbook example of a zoning system that defines development rights for the entire territory. However, municipalities are likely to designate complex site as zones requiring a special land-use plan (see Figures 7.6 and 7.7). This allows them to define land-use rules that differ from the local building code, usually with the intention of allowing not only higher densities but also additional requirements for place making. This usually involves (commissioned) design competitions to improve the quality of the project. Municipalities can even retrospectively demand a special land-use plan within three months of a building application (for example, in Canton Bern). Furthermore, these plans are subject to direct democracy and need to be approved in a local referendum, which ensures that public consultation is very thorough.

In summary, all three zoning systems exercise a high degree of control over development while, at the same time, being development led to a considerable degree. This does not mean that local spatial development frameworks have no function in guiding development; rather, it emphasises that development rights are usually granted in response to proposed development. The German and Swiss planning systems tend to grant development rights for small-scale development within the built-up area in principle through the 'blend-in' rule and the municipal zoning plan, respectively. The Netherlands, where small-scale development is relatively less important (Tennekes et al, 2015), also has mechanisms for deviating from the land-use plan. However, all three countries retain full control over large-scale development. The only

Figure 7.6: Land-use plan with designated areas for special land-use plan (numbered)

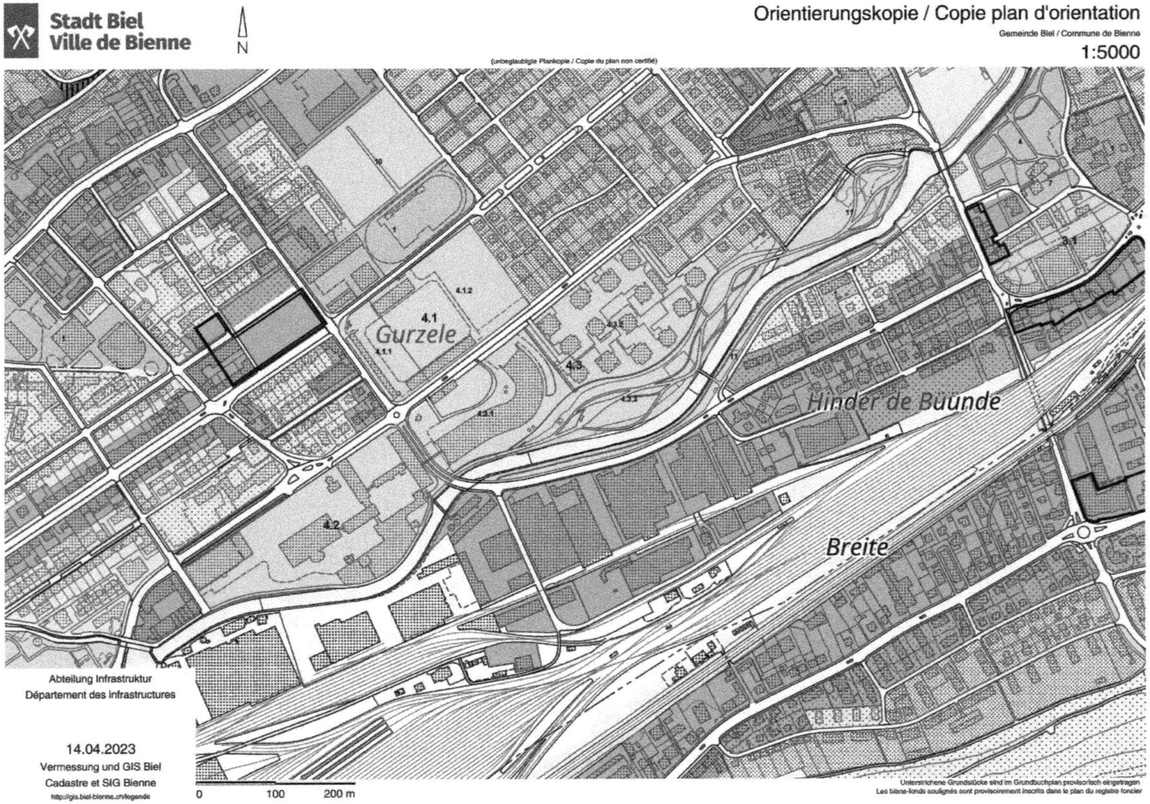

Source: Stadt Biel/Ville de Bienne

Figure 7.7: Special land-use plan Gygax East (No. 4.3.2)

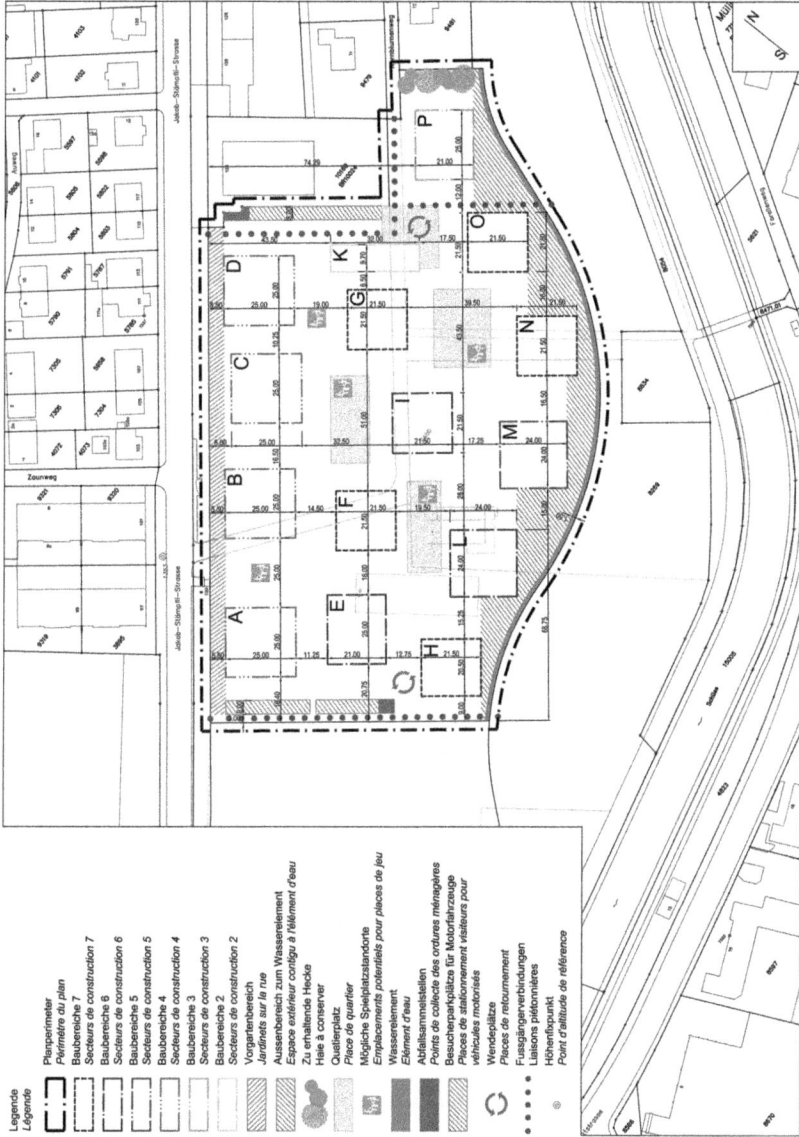

Legende
Légende

	Planperimeter *Périmètre du plan*
	Baubereiche 7 *Secteurs de construction 7*
	Baubereiche 6 *Secteurs de construction 6*
	Baubereiche 5 *Secteurs de construction 5*
	Baubereiche 4 *Secteurs de construction 4*
	Baubereiche 3 *Secteurs de construction 3*
	Baubereiche 2 *Secteurs de construction 2*
	Vorgartenbereich *Jardinets sur la rue*
	Aussenbereich zum Wasserelement *Espace extérieur contigu à l'élément d'eau*
	Zu erhaltende Hecke *Haie à conserver*
	Quartierplatz *Place de quartier*
	Mögliche Spielplatzstandorte *Emplacements potentiels pour places de jeu*
	Wasserelement *Elément d'eau*
	Abfallsammelstellen *Points de collecte des ordures ménagères*
	Besucherparkplätze für Motorfahrzeuge *Places de stationnement visiteurs pour véhicules motorisés*
	Wendeplätze *Places de retournement*
	Fussgängerverbindungen *Liaisons piétonnières*
	Höhenfixpunkt *Point d'altitude de référence*

Source: Stadt Biel/Ville de Bienne

115

risk for the municipality is that a plan is not implemented or is overturned by the administrative courts due to procedural errors given that the right to prepare a land-use plan and determine its content is not questioned as long as it respects environmental norms and generic legal principles of good administration.

Conclusion

The chapter began with the question of whether rule-based planning systems would be better able to deliver affordable housing and place making than the discretionary system currently in place. Recent planning reforms in England have clearly pushed for more certainty for developers while, at the same time, promoting design quality. This tension between the two will be difficult to reconcile, and the brief analysis of a select number of European zoning systems shows that they value control, and thus the potential for beauty, over speed. Although zoning has all but disappeared from the reform agenda, the lessons remain relevant in light of the ongoing debates on the performance of the English planning system.

One of the key assumptions is that regulatory planning systems are directly providing development rights. However, looking at planning systems in Europe, this is only true to some degree. In all three countries reviewed earlier, land-use plans will provide development rights, but these rarely suit the needs of developers. What could be regarded as a design flaw of these systems is actually intended. While land-use plans can be legally challenged, landowners/developers will be unable to force their own vision for an area upon the local planning authority as is the case with the planning appeals process in England. The developer needs the local planning authority to create development rights by approving a land-use plan that accommodates the proposed development.

In practice, therefore, planning systems with a zoning approach are almost equally flexible. Most land-use plans are comparable to planning applications for a larger site and involve a similar range of reports. These are often prepared directly by the developer in collaboration with the municipality. The land-use plan is the legal document that seals a long process of negotiation about design standards and land-value capture. It is not the beginning of the process but the end.

The debate in the UK should not be whether a regulatory or a zonal planning system is better but how the relationship between the state and market is defined and how the existing instruments deliver place making. This would mean reflecting on factors that undermine the role of the local planning authority, such as: chronic underfunding, which undermines both the speed and the quality of decision making; the presumption in favour of sustainable development, which often pushes local planning authorities to accept development in suboptimal sites; and the risk-rewarding nature of the appeals system when planning permission is refused. The debate about regulatory or discretionary systems is less important than addressing these issues in delivering a planning reform that results in a less adversarial planning culture and thus increases certainty.

Note

[1] See: www.ruimtelijkeplannen.nl

References

Airey, J. and Doughty, C. (2020) *Rethinking the Planning System for the 21st Century*, London: Policy Exchange.

Berisha, E., Cotella, G., Janin Rivolin, U. and Solly, A. (2021) 'Spatial governance and planning systems and the public control of spatial development: a European typology', *European Planning Studies*, 29(1): 181–200.

Booth, P. (1995) 'Zoning or discretionary action: certainty and responsiveness in implementing planning policy', *Journal of Planning Education and Research*, 14(2): 103–12.

Booth, P. (2003) *Planning by Consent: The Origins and Nature of British Development Control*, London: Routledge.

Booth, P. (2007) 'The control of discretion: planning and the common-law tradition', *Planning Theory*, 6(2): 127–45.

Breach, A. (2019) *Capital Cities: How the Planning System Creates Housing Shortages and Drives Wealth Inequality*, London: Centre for Cities.

Buitelaar, E., Galle, M. and Sorel, N. (2011) 'Plan-led planning systems in development-led practices: an empirical analysis of the (lack of) institutionalisation of planning law', *Environment and Planning A*, 43(4): 928–41.

Carmona, M., Alwarea, A., Giordano, V., Gusseinova, A. and Olaleye, F. (2020) *A Housing Design Audit for England*, London: Place Alliance.

Cheshire, P., Nathan, M. and Overman, H. (2014) *Urban Economics and Urban Policy: Challenging Conventional Policy Wisdom*, Cheltenham: Edward Elgar.

Crow, S. (1996) 'Development control: the child that grew up in the cold', *Planning Perspectives*, 11(4): 399–411.

Davies, H.W.E. (1998) 'Continuity and change: the evolution of the British planning system, 1947–97', *Town Planning Review*, 69(2): 135–52.

Davy, B. (1996) 'Baulandsicherung: Ursache oder Lösung eines raumordnungspolitischen Paradoxons [Building land management: cause or solution of a planning policy paradox]', *Zeitschrift für Verwaltung*, 21(2): 193–208.

Dembski, S. (2020) '"Organic" approaches to planning as densification strategy? The challenge of legal contextualisation in Buiksloterham, Amsterdam', *Town Planning Review*, 91(3): 283–303.

Feiertag, P. and Schoppengerd, J. (2023) 'Flexibility by frequent amendments. The practice of land use planning in Germany', *Planning Practice and Research*, 38(1): 105–22.

Gallent, N., de Magalhaes, C. and Freire Trigo, S. (2021) 'Is zoning the solution to the UK housing crisis?', *Planning Practice and Research*, 36(1): 1–19.

Hilber, C. and Vermeulen, W. (2016) 'The impact of supply constraints on house prices in England', *The Economic Journal*, 126(591): 358–405.

Janin Rivolin, U. (2008) 'Conforming and performing planning systems in Europe: an unbearable cohabitation', *Planning, Practice and Research*, 23(2): 167–86.

Lord, A.D. and Tewdwr-Jones, M. (2014) 'Is planning under attack? Chronicling the deregulation of urban and environmental planning in England', *European Planning Studies*, 22(2): 345–361.

MHCLG (Ministry of Housing, Communities and Local Government) (2020a) *Planning for the Future*, London: MHCLG.

MHCLG (2020b) *Changes to the Current Planning System: Consultation on Changes to Planning Policy and Regulations*, London: MHCLG.

MHCLG (2021) *National Model Design Code*, London: MHCLG.

Moroni, S., Buitelaar, E., Sorel, N. and Cozzolino, S. (2020) 'Simple planning rules for complex urban problems: towards legal certainty for spatial flexibility', *Journal of Planning Education and Research*, 40(3): 320–31.

Muñoz Gielen, D. and Taşan-Kok, T. (2010) 'Flexibility in planning and the consequences for public-value capturing in UK, Spain and the Netherlands', *European Planning Studies*, 18(7): 1097–131.

Sutcliffe, A. (1988) 'Britain's first Town Planning Act: a review of the 1909 achievement', *Town Planning Review*, 59(3): 289–303.

Tennekes, J. (2018) 'Negotiated land use plans in the Netherlands: a central instrument in Dutch "active" and "passive" land policy', in J.-D. Gerber, T. Hartmann and A. Hengstermann (eds) *Instruments of Land Policy: Dealing with Scarcity of Land*, Abingdon: Routledge, pp 101–13.

Tennekes, J., Harbers, A. and Buitelaar, E. (2015) 'Institutional arrangements and the morphology of residential development in the Netherlands, Flanders and North Rhine-Westphalia', *European Planning Studies*, 23(11): 2165–83.

Van der Krabben, E. and Jacobs, H. (2013) 'Public land development as a strategic tool for redevelopment: reflections on the Dutch experience', *Land Use Policy*, 30: 774–83.

Ward, S.V. (2010) 'What did the Germans ever do for us? A century of British learning about and imagining modern town planning', *Planning Perspectives*, 25(2): 117–140.

Ward, S.V. (2020) 'Why did Britain reject zoning first time around?', *Town and Country Planning*, 89(9–10): 312–19.

Wetzstein, S. (2017) 'The global urban housing affordability crisis', *Urban Studies*, 54(14): 3159–77.

Planning and the environment in England, 2010–22: cutting 'green crap', Brexit and environmental crises

Richard Cowell, Thomas B. Fischer and Urmila Jha Thakur

Introduction

As a substantive field, the environment casts an important but distinctive light on the notion of 'planning failure' and its relationship with wider 'state failure'. For a start, one must acknowledge that countries throughout the world have underachieved when it comes to adequately addressing major environmental problems. Analysts in many states, the UK included, have observed a tendency for national state environmental institutions to lose power and capacity since the late 1990s, leading this period to be labelled as 'one of stagnation and decline in the environmental nation state' (Mol, 2016: 52). Momentum was also knocked by the 2008 financial crash. Performance deficits have been particularly acute for cross-national environmental problems like climate change and biodiversity loss that have complex causes in patterns of production, consumption and mobility. The question that arises, then, is whether planning systems have evolved in ways that serve to ameliorate deficiencies in national environmental governance systems or exhibit tendencies that reflect and exacerbate wider failings.

Certainly, the evolution of planning in the UK can be seen as leading and then broadening the front of state environmental governance. From its birth in public health concerns in the 19th-century city, the planning system has provided mechanisms for enabling environmental factors to be considered in decisions about land use, development and infrastructure, and for protecting valued landscapes, buildings and wildlife habitats from damaging development. Since the 1980s, the environmental role of planning has expanded to embrace wider, more systemic issues, including pollution, air and water quality, biodiversity loss, and climate change. Beliefs about how planning might achieve positive environmental outcomes have extended from relatively straightforward protective actions to orchestrating urban forms that might better support multiple environmental and social goals, and reduce demands for car-based travel and energy, water and other resources. Indeed, planning was one of the first policy subsystems to be charged with delivering sustainable development (Owens and Cowell, 2011).

Broadening remits, however, tell us relatively little about environmental performance. Adding ever-more issues to the 'to-do' list of planning may overburden the system with expectations and perhaps even exemplify 'local scalar dumping', that is, passing responsibilities to local agencies with limited powers and resources in lieu of more effective national action. Moreover, planning has never just been about environmental 'delivery'; rather, it involves the balancing of multiple economic, social and environmental objectives. Given this multifaceted, goal-balancing challenge, the environmental 'outcomes' of planning depend greatly on how trade-offs are struck and which objectives are prioritised. Charging planning with achieving 'sustainable development', itself a fluid 'figure of resolution' between multiple goals (Myerson and Rydin, 1996), arguably adds to the ambiguity. It also risks disguising the dominant reality in England that it is development goals – especially for housing and infrastructure – that have been most firmly institutionalised within the planning system, with environmental factors often just providing caveats to how growth objectives are achieved.

One cannot examine whether planning or the state has failed 'the environment' without recognising that 'the environment' can itself be (re)interpreted in diverse ways. This matters, as this chapter will show, because pro-growth and deregulatory challenges have rarely been accompanied with overt attacks on the importance of environmental goals. Nevertheless, efforts to render environmental concerns compatible with dominant developmental objectives have often either selectively elevated certain environmental concerns while marginalising others or constructed 'the environment' as something that can be managed and moulded in ways that do not limit development, in line with weak sustainability thinking (Fischer, 2022). Such interpretative issues have substantive material implications for the kinds of environments delivered, and dealing with them places planning on the front line.

Focusing on the environmental role of planning as a linear, instrumental function also neglects the important political effects of planning. Planning has had a vital role in promoting sustainability by providing arenas in which the environmental impacts of development become visible and contested. Over time, the resulting debates and resistance have contributed to the questioning of business-as-usual development trajectories, reframing policy priorities, and to the formation of lower-impact alternatives (as observed with roads and minerals policies in the 1990s [see Owens and Cowell, 2011]). Thus, the extent to which planning provides opportunities for projects, plans and policies to be scrutinised and challenged is vital in understanding its environmental effects and provides a key link between planning and wider policy systems.

From this discussion, it is clear that care is required in evaluating the relationship between planning and wider notions of state 'failure' in the environmental field, and this has informed our approach in this chapter. There is a need to give close attention to the detail of planning policies and regulations, how they affect the weight given to environmental goals and risks, and the opportunity structures available to challenge unsustainable development. It is also necessary to examine shifts in wider systems of environmental governance, as the planning system has often been enrolled as an implementing agent for environmental policies determined outside planning, notably, those emanating from the European Union (EU). A longitudinal perspective is also valuable, both to encompass the ceaseless reform proposals and to track the extent to which radical-sounding intentions translate into substantive change (Haughton and Allmendinger, 2016). One can point to various moments where pro-market, growth-promoting planning reforms have been modified and (partially) reversed in the face of pressure to deal with environmental problems (Lowe and Flynn, 1989; Owens and Cowell, 2011; Lord and Tewdwr-Jones, 2014).

In this chapter, we analyse changes to the relationship between planning and the environment from 2010 to 2022. We focus on the situation in England, as both planning and environmental policy has evolved in rather different ways in the devolved governments of Northern Ireland, Scotland and Wales (Cowell et al, 2020). We also focus primarily on the actions of central government to adjust the legislative, policy and regulatory framework of planning, including reform proposals, rather than offering a detailed analysis of local implementation. From an environmental perspective, it is useful to analyse this period in two eras, divided by the 2016 EU referendum. First, we examine 2010–16, a period characterised by the erosion of the capacity of the planning system to support environmental protection, though partly contained by the requirement to comply with EU environmental regulations. The second era, from 2016 onwards, is characterised by the complex interplay between two situations: one is Brexit, which potentially allowed the Conservative government's deregulatory impulses freer rein in the environmental sphere; the other is the mounting urgency and political salience of environmental problems, especially the 'climate' and 'nature' crises. An important unfolding question is how far addressing environmental crises will serve to temper the continued reflex for pro-development planning reforms or, potentially, lead to planning gaining a more durable and effective role in the UK's wider environmental governance system.

The 2010–16 era: from 'get rid of all the green crap' to 'take back control'

While the Conservative Party heralded its 2010 administration as 'the Greenest Government Ever', its performance in office is arguably better characterised by Prime Minister David Cameron's call to 'get rid of all the green crap' (Sparrow, 2013; Carter and Clements, 2015). Pro-growth measures introduced in response to economic recession, austerity measures and growing partisanship in the Conservative Party over environmental issues led to policy vacillation and to swingeing reductions in the capacity of the main planning and environmental ministries (the Department for Communities and Local Government [DCLG] and the Department for Environment, Food and Rural Affairs [DEFRA]), environmental agencies (Mol, 2016) and local planning authorities. In response, two thirds of local authorities scaled back work on climate change in the face of cost-cutting pressures (Green Alliance, 2011). National government strategy making on the environment largely ceased, and in planning, the system was subjected to a whole number of changes, many of them taken forward in the Localism Act 2011.

The planning reforms that unfolded in the years after 2010 share many characteristics with previous reforms in their treatment of environmental issues. In key justifications for the reforms, planning is scapegoated as a barrier to investment and growth (see Chapter 1). However, reform documents made little overt criticism of the role of planning in promoting environmental goals; indeed, in *Open Source Planning* (Conservative Party, 2010), we see environmental concerns selectively co-opted as one of the many goals harmed by the previous Labour government's centralising tendencies. The environment was also represented as a beneficiary of the Conservatives' 'localism' agenda, because it would 'allow' planning 'to focus on promoting the sustainable development that local communities want' (Conservative Party, 2010: 5), which would thus, apparently, dissolve potential growth–environment tensions. There was a characteristic reaffirmation of support for protecting certain land-use categories (national parks, sites of special scientific interest [SSSIs] and high-quality agricultural land) (see DoE, 1980) and an equally characteristic sidelining of wider, 'non-local' environmental issues (Cowell and Owens, 2006). Nevertheless, beyond the emollient discourse of localism, in a whole number of ways, the changes wrought to planning after 2010 served to diminish its capacity to address environmental challenges.

National planning policy was tilted in a more firmly pro-growth direction. The government's goal of simplifying national planning policy guidance led to the library of advice inherited from the previous Labour government being condensed into a single, 60-page document: the *National Planning Policy Framework* (NPPF) (DCLG, 2012). The new NPPF also introduced 'a presumption in favour of sustainable development' as a core goal of planning. However, any environmental sheen to this move was vitiated by the simultaneous mobilisation of interpretations of sustainable development that largely eroded any distinction between sustainable development and economic growth. In the ministerial foreword, the 2012 NPPF made it clear that 'development means growth' and that 'significant weight should be placed on the need to support economic growth through the planning system' (DCLG, 2012: para 19).

Political desires to reduce regulatory burdens on developers and position house building as a tool to grow the economy led to numerous environmental principles, policies and standards being diluted or abolished. Policies underpinning 'compact settlement' models of sustainable development were removed, notably, minimum housing densities and the prioritisation of brownfield sites; additionally, policies encouraging less car-dependent urban forms were weakened. Environmental impact assessments (EIA) screening thresholds were raised in 2015 by the government for housing and other types of developments from 0.5 to 5 ha (Fischer, 2023). Policies for promoting zero-carbon homes were progressively dismantled through replacing targets and standards with pro-market, voluntaristic and industry-led approaches (O'Neill and Gibbs, 2020).

As well as weakening national-level environmental planning policies, the scope for local agency on environmental problems was circumscribed, as the NPPF made it clear that any local regulatory innovation around the energy and environmental performance of buildings should be 'consistent with the Government's zero carbon buildings policy and adopt nationally described standards' (DCLG, 2012: para 95). While neighbourhood plans are regarded as a key tool of 'localism', government guidance made it clear that neighbourhood plans could not provide for less growth than was allocated in the overarching local authority plans (see Chapter 3). Furthermore, neighbourhood planning has only used sustainability appraisal when under pressure to do so (Fischer and Yu, 2018).

These various changes to the system had the effect of diminishing the legitimate scope within planning for challenging unsustainable development or pursuing better environmental outcomes. These tendencies were reinforced by other key developments. At an overarching governance level, the government abolished important environmental bodies, in particular, the Sustainable Development Commission and the Royal Commission on Environmental Pollution, both sources of independent analysis on environmental policy issues. Within planning specifically, the 2010–15 Coalition government maintained and extended Labour's fast-track decision-making process for 'nationally significant infrastructure'. This process not only centralised determinations of 'need', insulating them from challenge as individual projects come forward, but also provided rationalisations for allowing infrastructure projects to trump environmental goals (Lee et al, 2013). The government also resisted calls for allowing the consent regime to 'test' proposed energy-generating infrastructure against the stringent emissions reductions required to meet the carbon budgets prescribed by the Climate Change Act 2008 (DECC, 2011; Cowell, 2013).

Alongside these policy changes, ideas were advancing across planning and environmental domains that would come to have lasting implications for conceptions of the environment and what it meant to sustain it. The government began piloting forms of 'biodiversity offsetting' (HM Government, 2011), a mechanism designed to recompense the adverse biodiversity impacts of development with measurable biodiversity benefits. While there were aspirations that the measures would deliver 'more, better, bigger and joined up networks of habitat' (HM Government, 2011: para 2.50), there are long-standing questions as to whether focusing on compensatory 'environmental gains' as a by-product of development impacts diminishes the efforts given to impact avoidance and risks jeopardising environmental qualities and species assemblages that cannot easily be restored (Boucher and Whatmore, 1993; zu Ermgassen et al, 2019). How far such mechanisms deliver dividends for biodiversity depends greatly on the extent to which governments see them primarily as a means of making managing development impacts 'simple', 'straightforward' and 'cost effective' for developers (HM Government, 2011: para 2.39).

In sum, the 2010–16 period saw both planning and environmental policy subjected to diminishing capacity, legitimacy and efficacy, driven by pro-growth agendas and hostile ideologies of 'state shrinkage' in the Conservative Party (Cowell, 2013). Two things acted as a brake. One was resistance from environmental non-governmental organisations (NGOs), which, among other things, conducted a high-profile campaign to reduce the growth emphasis of the 2012 NPPF (Shepherd, 2021). However, NGO successes were modest, being limited to some light softening of the pro-development wording but without much changing the overall thrust. The second brake was EU membership and the requirement on the UK government to implement EU environmental legislation. There are numerous areas where this legislation interfaces with planning – on wildlife habitats, birds, waste, air quality and requirements for impact assessment – and examination of the formulation of the NPPF shows how these environmental policy areas tended to experience less rollback than those rooted mostly in domestic legislation, as is the case with planning. Indeed, in the UK, as in other member states, the EU's environmental governance regime came to be regarded as a valuable corrective to the frailties of national-level action (Burns et al, 2016). Its environmental directives often provided a set of stringent, harder-edged standards and implementation time frames that contrasted with the more flexible, discretionary character of UK planning and environmental law. EU laws also came backed by arrangements for oversight, monitoring and enforcement, which diminished the scope for domestic political or economic convenience to trump environmental concerns. The EU environmental governance system is also relatively durable, operating within a set of environmental principles and a commitment to ongoing environmental improvement that insulate it from short-term political calculation. While not perfect, the contrast between EU environmental policy and the constant policy churn in UK planning could not be more stark (Fischer et al, 2018).

If EU membership offered a bulwark against efforts to weaken the environmental role of planning, this effect was often unwelcome to government ministers. EU legislation was subject to successive regulatory reviews to assess whether implementation was needlessly 'gold-plated' and 'for reducing the burdens on business' (Department for Business, Innovation and Skills, 2010; HM Government, 2012). Ministers also criticised what they perceived as EU 'regulatory creep ... imposing additional and expensive requirements on the planning system', all the worse for being 'over and above long-standing, domestic environmental safeguards in planning law'.[1]

Given this wider atmosphere, the UK's referendum decision to leave the EU in June 2016 – so-called 'Brexit' – was potentially highly momentous for the UK's system of environmental governance and, within that, the environmental role of planning. Environmental issues were largely sidelined during the Brexit referendum debates, featuring mainly in the coded criticism of 'EU red tape'. Nevertheless, wrangling over Brexit did generate an uptick in swipes at environmental policy, usually as a means of illustrating the potential benefits of 'taking back control' from the EU. Boris Johnson, then foreign secretary and subsequently prime minister, gives a classic example of such rhetorical linkage between sovereignty, deregulation and the belittling of environmental regulation:

> We can simplify planning ... and perhaps we would then be faster in building the homes young people need; and we might decide that it was indeed absolutely necessary for every environmental impact assessment to monitor two life cycles of the snail and build special swimming pools for newts – not all of which they use – but it would at least be our decision.[2]

After four years of political turmoil, the UK government left the EU with a Brexit deal (the 2020 2,555-page-long 'EU and UK Trade and Cooperation Agreement') that, outside the particular circumstances of Northern Ireland, did relatively little to tie its hands on environmental issues (Moore, 2019). In effect, Brexit gave UK ministers a level of legislative autonomy on the environment that they have always enjoyed in the context of planning. Given the anti-'red tape' rhetoric of Brexit-supporting politicians and the impetus for pro-growth policies in planning, one can see why environmental interests were concerned that Brexit would herald similar deregulation in the environmental sphere. What has happened so far is more nuanced than this, as we review in the next section.

The 2016–22 era: navigating Brexit, nature and climate crises, and so on

Within the planning system, the signal reform proposals of the 2016–22 period centred on the *Planning for the Future* White Paper (MHCLG, 2020). This repeated familiar discourses of planning failure: slating the system for being 'outdated', 'ineffective', 'too complex' and 'unpredictable' (MHCLG, 2020: 6, 10, 14), and as hindering the delivery of sufficient, high-quality development. The proposals' most eye-catching idea was to supplant the discretionary qualities of development plans and development control with a rules-based, three-tier zoning-style planning system, involving: 'growth areas', which automatically confer outline planning approval for land allocated to them; 'renewal areas', covering existing built areas where smaller-scale development is appropriate; and 'protected areas', where development is restricted (MHCLG, 2020: 20; see also Chapter 7). Local plans would thus 'set clear rules rather than general policies', with less detail, consisting mainly of 'a core set of standards and requirements for development', or setting out site- or area-specific parameters and opportunities' (MHCLG, 2020: 20). The intended result was to establish 'a clear and predictable basis for the pattern and form of development in an area' (MHCLG, 2020: 26).

In a further echo of previous Conservative planning reform proposals, the White Paper was thin, slippery or silent on how environmental goals fitted in. Specific types of environmental areas were offered relative insulation from the pro-development thrust and largely allocated to 'protected areas', including National Parks (MHCLG, 2020: 32), areas of outstanding natural beauty (AONBs), 'Local wildlife sites' (MHCLG, 2020: 29) and green belts (MHCLG, 2020: 23, 32), as well as many areas of flood risk (MHCLG, 2020: 28, 32). The main environmental issue to receive detailed attention was design, with proposals for extending the use of design codes and officer support. However, one gets the sense that 'the environment' was being rendered manageable by representing it primarily as a local, aesthetic concern, somewhat separate from the environment as a series of vital, life-supporting processes – a tendency observed in previous planning reforms (Cowell and Owens, 2006; Cowell, 2013). Although the White Paper name-checked wider environmental concerns, including 'environmentally friendly homes' and reducing 'our reliance on carbon-intensive modes of development' (MHCLG, 2020: 8, 25), precise proposals on these issues fell beyond the White Paper itself.

The prime minister sought to align boosting development with environmental protection in his call to 'build back better, build back greener, build back faster' (Johnson, 2020), but this rhetorical elision points to the yawning environmental contradiction in *Planning for the Future*. On the one hand, the proposals placed greater emphasis on up-front rules and planning zones in development plans: with fewer checks or consultation to take place with individual planning applications, such plans would become pivotal mechanisms for ensuring that development is environmentally sustainable. On the other hand, there was the expectation that these much more important plans could be produced quickly, with a suggested statutory timetable of 'no more than 30 months' (MHCLG, 2020: 20; see also MHCLG, 2020: 40–1). Speed was to be achieved by proposals to reduce the examination of plans (MHCLG, 2020: 41) and to greatly scale back 'unnecessary assessments and requirements that cause delay and challenge in the current system' (MHCLG, 2020: 20). The perceived 'burden' of environmental assessment had long been an object of government concern, and this is an area where the new legislative freedoms created by Brexit were to be taken forward in planning reforms. *Planning for the Future* touted the development of 'a quicker, simpler framework for assessing environmental impacts and enhancement opportunities' (MHCLG, 2020: 22) but offered little in the way of detail. Evidence that less comprehensive, less participatory forms of assessment can effectively lead to high-environmental-quality outcomes is currently lacking (Fischer et al, 2021).

Overall, the mantra of speed and predictability in the service of development that dominated *Planning for the Future* is hard to reconcile with a need for a planning system that deals carefully and justly with environmental risks, and works assiduously to maintain and enhance vital environmental assets. However, such contradictions can serve to stall or derail pro-market reforms, especially where environmental challenges acquire institutional, societal and political salience. We detail three such challenges here: creating a new, post-Brexit environmental governance regime; biodiversity loss and the nature crisis; and net-zero climate change legislation.

A post-Brexit environmental governance regime

An unexpected outcome of the Brexit vote was a considerable upturn in the UK government's attention to the environment, propelled by darkening scientific messages of environmental crises, increased public concern and the environmental 'governance gaps' created by Brexit (Burns et al, 2016). On the latter, there was the need to recreate domestically the environmental functions previously provided by EU membership, notably, the monitoring, oversight and enforcement functions provided by the European Commission and European courts. This led to the creation of a new watchdog body, the Office for Environmental Protection (OEP), which is tasked with holding the government to account for its environmental performance by scrutinising policy, fielding complaints, monitoring progress and taking enforcement action on breaches in environmental law (DEFRA, 2019). Further impetus was generated by the actions of Michael Gove, Secretary of State for the Environment from 2017 to 2019. Gove was keen to present leaving the EU as an opportunity for 'competitive emulation' in UK environmental policy, captured in the slogan 'Green Brexit'. These pressures undoubtedly injected more strategic action (and staffing capacity) into DEFRA, yielding, among other things, the 25 Year Environment Plan and commitments to a system of legally binding environmental targets.

Many of these steps were finally institutionalised in the Environment Act 2021, but what are the implications for planning? Much will depend on the strength of the new environmental governance regime itself, where there is much disquiet that the UK government has taken steps to limit the powers of the OEP and its independence from government.[3] Much will also depend on whether the remit of the new machinery is narrowly confined to specific aspects of environmental law or empowered to scrutinise the environmental performance of the state in general, including the planning system. In a positive early move, the OEP criticised the lack of inter-ministerial integration around the environment, highlighting the disconnection between planning policy (the levelling-up strategy and national policy statements for infrastructure) and the goals of the 25 Year Environment Plan (OEP, 2022).

This begs the significant question of how planning might be refashioned to help deliver statutory environmental targets. *Planning for the Future* (MHCLG, 2020: 56) made a general reference to wanting the planning system to 'play a pro-active role' in supporting 'the ambitions of our 25 Year Environment Plan' by 'promoting environmental recovery and long-term sustainability' but went no further. Taking the planning system beyond 'considering' environmental targets within a 'balancing' approach to making decisions towards charging the system with actively helping to deliver environmental targets is highly novel governance territory in which few states around the world can offer any insight (Cowell et al, 2021).

Biodiversity loss and the nature crisis

The last couple of decades have been characterised by growing global-level warnings about the precipitous decline in biodiversity, the potential for ecosystem collapse and the need for states to ramp up efforts to reverse this trend (see, for example, Mortel, 2021). The agenda has been recognised by the UK government – chastened perhaps by the presentation of the UK as one of the most nature-depleted countries in the world (Natural History Museum, 2021) – which has responded with some important measures, notably, the institution of a statutory nature recovery target in the 2021 act. At the time of writing (December 2022), it was unclear how precisely this target would be framed and how this new target will get translated into implementation measures. Systems of agricultural support are obviously a major area for delivery, but so too is the planning system. Here, a key question is whether biodiversity target delivery will prove subservient to well-institutionalised planning policy reflexes or prompt more fundamental questioning of planning's role in promoting biodiversity.

Policy development to date has been highly contradictory. Concern for the 'nature crisis' has not deflected the current government's interest in reforming the robust legal systems of protection offered by the EU Habitats and Birds Directives (Branson, 2021; Stroud et al, 2021) – another area, like EIAs, where Brexit had been presented as an opportunity for creating new domestic approaches that offer more 'flexible' and 'creative' ways of achieving environmental protection. This has stoked environmental NGO concerns that this is 'walking out on the basic principles of conservation from sites and species' in favour of 'aggregate national improvement' (Branson, 2021). The present vehicle for achieving these reforms is the Retained EU Law (Revocation and Reform) Bill, a potentially far-reaching law that 'sunsets' large swathes of retained EU law and grants ministers considerable powers to decide whether to revoke, restate or replace them, though debars them from making any replacements that would 'increase the regulatory burden' (under Clause 15[5]) (see Lee, 2022). Should it come to pass, such legislation not only threatens biodiversity protection but also, to the extent that EU-derived law is replaced with more flexible, discretionary provisions, erodes a whole series of checks on ministerial power (Lee, 2022).

Fears that development may be rendered compatible with biodiversity goals by stripping the latter of inconvenient, spatially embedded qualities also haunt the agenda of biodiversity net gain. Previous work on biodiversity offsetting, discussed earlier, has been given impetus by a statutory 'net gain' requirement being placed on developers in the Environment Act 2021. There is little question that, for England, addressing biodiversity decline requires significant efforts to restore and recreate habitats, beyond conserving what presently exists. The government has also taken some steps to tackle the frailties of offset systems, notably, the difficulty of maintaining gains in the long term, by instituting a guarantee in the 2021 act that biodiversity enhancements need to be secured for at least 30 years, with the help of planning obligations or conservation covenants. However, long-standing problems with extracting environmental gains from developers remain. Thus far, developers' tendency to secure on-site gains, that is, within land that they control, has caused ecologically problematic trade-offs and significant diminution of green space, highlighting risks of the system being manipulated (Fair, 2021). It remains unclear at present who or what will benefit from biodiversity net gain: biodiversity, as the new measures treat any net loss as a trigger for action; or developers, as the process serves primarily to make impact management responsibilities predictable, affordable and replicable. Outcomes may be greatly shaped by technical minutiae, such as the 'biodiversity metrics' for calculating gains and losses, and local authority oversight capacities to effectively scrutinise net-gain provisions.

Net zero on climate change

A key part of the environmental backdrop to the post-2010 government's activities has been climate change. Here, a gradual ramping up of policy attention was precipitated by the Climate Change Act 2008, which committed UK governments to reducing greenhouse gas emissions by 80 per cent by 2050 from a 1990 baseline. The act instigated governance machinery for preparing five-yearly carbon budgets, monitoring progress on emission reductions and holding the government to account (by the Climate Change Committee). In their emphasis on outcome targets and independent oversight, these arrangements had stylistic echoes of EU environmental governance and have been widely credited with driving policies to support emissions reductions (Averchenkova et al, 2020). Despite (or perhaps because of) its efficacy, the 2008 act has been a bête noire for sections of the Tory Right, which have sought its removal. For most of the 2010–16 period, planning-related action was notable mostly for insulating key development decisions from emissions reduction requirements, as with housing and major infrastructure, but this insulation has been increasingly eroded. First, the 2015 Paris Agreement on Climate Change underscored the 80 per cent by 2050 emissions-reduction target; then, amid the political turmoil of Brexit, the Theresa May government passed an amendment to the Climate Change Act committing to bring all greenhouse gas emissions to net zero by 2050 (Climate Change Act 2008 (2050 Target Amendment) Order 2019). This move was galvanised by the proliferation of declarations of 'climate emergencies' across all levels of government, including the UK Parliament.

These moves have had widespread and potentially significant effects on planning, but many are unfolding largely outside the conventional policy-making machinery – a good example of how the opportunity structures created by the planning system can exert leverage on business as usual. Environmental NGOs and activist legal groups have used the policy resources of climate change legislation to mount legal challenges to various aspects of government policy, including: whole programmes, such as the roads programme, which has been legally challenged on the grounds of its incompatibility with climate change policy[4]; systems of planning policy, notably, the national policy statements for major energy infrastructure; and controversial pet government projects, such as the new runway at London Heathrow Airport. At the same time, local planning authorities across the country have wielded their climate emergency declarations to challenge growth allocations (as in Oxfordshire) and a host of development projects, from bypasses (for example, in Hereford) to airports (for example, in Bristol). There have been some notable wins, for example, ministerial rejection of the Tulip Tower project in London – a significant case because grounds for rejection included embodied emissions from the 'unsustainable scale' of reinforced concrete use (Colley, 2021).

The need to align development trajectories with net zero – with its exacting substantive goal and time frame – has undercut the government's ability to construct planning primarily as a stable, predictable framework for development. There are clear signs that the government would wish to 'tame' net zero by emphasising marketable solutions and technical fixes – electric vehicles, hydrogen, and carbon capture and storage – satisfying the 'climate sceptics' and 'climate go-slowers' in the Conservative Party that are resistant to regulation (Carter and Clements, 2015). Nevertheless, the instability is perpetuated by the need to retrospectively reconsider inadequate and unsustainable policy agendas (many of them inheriting their environmental deficiencies from the 2010–16 period), as well as unresolved dilemmas around decarbonising domestic heating or the role of nature-based solutions, where the balance between markets, state action, techno-fixes and behavioural change has yet to settle. The *Planning for the Future* White Paper did little more than issue a loose intention to amend the NPPF in order to address 'those areas where a reformed planning system can most effectively address climate change mitigation and adaptation' (MHCLG, 2020: 21). Meanwhile, coalitions of NGOs, the Climate Change Committee and cross-party groups of members of parliament have all pressed the government to make climate change central to planning policy (Donnelly, 2021).

Outlook

By the end of 2022, it was highly unclear how far and in what ways these various environmental challenges would affect the planning system, especially given the host of contradictory forces. On the capacity front, new proposals were made to reduce the civil service to pre-Brexit levels, despite the increased domestic workload that Brexit created, both in the environmental arena and elsewhere (Donnelly, 2022). This initiative fell by the wayside, but the economic crises precipitated by COVID-19 and the war in Ukraine, and exacerbated by the Liz Truss prime ministerial debacle, have triggered a second wave of public sector austerity across national and local government. Discretionary, creative long-term environmental responses could be a casualty.

On the policy front, most of the proposals of the *Planning for the Future* White Paper were dropped, as the public unpopularity of the implications were exploited by the government's political opponents (see Chapter 1). In the June 2021 by-election, the Conservatives lost the safe seat of Chesham and Amersham on a massive swing to the Liberal Democrats, with the following being a key plank of the successful candidate's platform: 'I will campaign tirelessly against the government's new planning law, which is set to rip power away from local communities and see the Chilterns' distinctive beauty lost forever.'[5] Once more, pro-market planning reforms have been stymied by environmental concerns, though it is notable that yet again – for the Conservatives – it is the electoral salience of amenity and countryside protection that is the more influential factor rather than the reforms' failure to adequately respond to urgent, systemic environmental problems. Indeed, the successor to the White Paper, the 2022 Levelling-up and Regeneration Bill, says little about the environment at all, beyond a plan to replace EIA and strategic environmental assessment with new 'environmental outcomes reports'. This emphasis on outcomes could provide a mechanism to align the planning system with the environmental outcomes of net zero, biodiversity net gain and the targets provided for in the Environment Act 2021. Equally, they could demote environmental assessment from a tool of project and policy development to a low-cost, post hoc checklist. Characteristically, the proposals are too vague to judge, having been preceded by neither trials nor analysis (Fischer, 2023).

Conclusion

In conclusion, we return to our opening question and ask whether policy developments in planning helped to mitigate or exacerbate the problematic environmental performance of the UK state in England. Across the period since 2010, the environmental performance of planning has suffered collateral damage from periods of funding austerity, as well as being subjected to waves of policy changes that undermine its environmental role. Arguably, these are less matters of 'state failure' than deliberate, ideologically driven regulatory rollback. Until Brexit, however, there remained the stabilising framework of EU environmental policy, which – though rarely perfectly implemented – offered a system of bedrock protections. Since the Brexit vote, more starkly opposing forces have been in play. Leaving the EU created new uncertainties for environmental governance, which has begun to experience the kind of instability familiar to observers of planning policy. Uncertainties have arisen from the struggle to create new domestic environmental institutions and from ministers exploring the new freedoms Brexit has given them, including pursuing opportunities for regulatory flexibility and streamlining. Set against these uncertainties, the implications of climate change, the nature crisis and the emergence of a new domestic environmental governance regime all push in the direction of firmer, long-term, goal-driven frameworks for planning.

How this situation will settle is now more subject to the vicissitudes of national domestic politics, and what new institutional compromises may emerge is fundamentally unclear. One can observe a partial redistribution of the governance language of 'targets', 'delivery' and 'urgency' towards the environment and away from being the exclusive preserve of growth and development lobbies. One might hope that the societal need for powerful, effective long-term frameworks to deal with existential environmental crises brings with it a robust, durable framework for planning as a vital tool for enabling necessary and just sustainability transitions – in effect, that the need to address 'state failure' on the environment helps to curb and reverse policy failures in planning. Equally, however, the factionalised approach to the environment within the Conservative Party may lead to inaction or further policy contradictions, or the pursuit of policies that serve to tame, remould and prioritise environmental objectives in ways that facilitate incumbent development interests and perpetuate present problems. Much will depend on the outcomes of disputes in diverse arenas: some of them are visible and electorally salient, such as where the development impacts of deregulation meet the amenity concerns of the Cheshams and Amershams; while others are lower in profile and technical, as with the debates around the construction of 'biodiversity net gain' metrics, the fate of retained EU law and the efficacy of the OEP. The environmental role of planning is likely to be further buffeted by all of these developments.

Notes

[1] Quotes from Eric Pickles MP, *Hansard*, 6 December 2012, written ministerial statements, DCLG, planning administration, Columns 71–72WS.
[2] Quote from Boris Johnson, speech, 14 February 2018, 'The road to Brexit: a United Kingdom'.
[3] See, for example, the discussion at: https://hansard.parliament.uk/lords/2021-09-08/debates/962D384A-3300-47A2-A2C3-9A9CFFD84050/EnvironmentBill#contribution-94A7AB71-587A-49CF-9C0D-83D499983966
[4] See: www.crowdjustice.com/case/stop-largest-ever-roads-programme/
[5] Sarah Green, successful Liberal Democrat candidate, quoted in 'Chesham and Amersham candidates share by-election priorities'. Available at: www.bbc.co.uk/news/uk-england-beds-bucks-herts-57203281

References

Averchenkova, A., Fankhauser, S. and Finnegan, J. (2020) 'The impact of strategic climate legislation: evidence from expert interviews on the UK Climate Change Act', *Climate Policy*, 21(2): 251–63.

Boucher, S. and Whatmore, S. (1993) 'Green gains? Planning by agreement and nature conservation', *Journal of Environmental Planning and Management*, 36(1): 33–49.

Branson, A. (2021) 'Habitats Regulations: what plans to "refocus" nature rules could mean for EU-derived case law', ENDS Report, 29 July. Available at: https://www.endsreport.com/article/1720383/habitats-regulations-plans-refocus-nature-rules-mean-eu-derived-case-law

Burns, C.A., Jordan, A., Gravey, V., Berny, N., Bulmer, S., Carter, N. et al (2016) 'The EU referendum and the UK environment: an expert review'. Available at: https://ukandeu.ac.uk/partner-reports/the-eu-referendum-and-uk-environment-expert-review/

Carter, N. and Clements, B. (2015) 'From "greenest government ever" to "get rid of all the green crap": David Cameron, the Conservatives and the environment', *British Politics*, 10(2): 204–25.

Colley, T. (2021) 'Plans for "unsustainable" Tulip Tower thrown out by Minister', ENDS Report, 12 November. Available at: https://www.end sreport.com/article/1733079/plans-unsustainable-tulip-tower-thrown-minister

Conservative Party (2010) *Open Source Planning. Policy Green Paper No. 14*, London: Conservative Party.

Cowell, R. (2013) 'The greenest government ever? Planning and sustainability in England after the May 2010 elections', *Planning Practice and Research*, 28(1): 27–44.

Cowell, R. and Owens, S. (2006) 'Governing space: planning reform and the politics of sustainability', *Environment and Planning C: Government and Policy*, 24(3): 403–21.

Cowell, R., Ellis, G., Fischer, T., Jackson, A., Muinzer, T. and Sykes, O. (2020) 'Integrating planning and environmental protection: an analysis of post-Brexit regulatory styles and practitioner attitudes in the UK', *Planning Theory and Practice*, 21(4): 570–90.

Cowell, R., Fischer, T.B. and Jackson, T. (2021) 'Instituting space for the environment. How might we give the spatial demands of environmental policy goals a firm presence in the planning system? A think piece', April, Cardiff University, University of Dundee and University of Liverpool. Available at: www.researchgate.net/publication/352120535

DCLG (Department for Communities and Local Government) (2012) *National Planning Policy Framework*, London: DCLG.

DECC (Department for Energy and Climate Change) (2011) *Overarching National Policy Statement for Energy* (EN-1), London: The Stationery Office.

DEFRA (Department for Environment, Food and Rural Affairs) (2019) 'New Office for Environmental Protection will ensure governments maintain green credentials'. Available at: https://deframedia.blog.gov.uk/2019/10/16/new-office-for-environmental-protection-will-ensure-gove rnments-maintain-green-credentials/

Department for Business, Innovation and Skills (2010) 'Government ends goldplating of European regulations'. Available at: www.gov.uk/governm ent/news/government-ends-goldplating-of-european-regulations

DoE (Department of the Environment) (1980) *Development Control: Policy and Practice*, Circular 22/80, London: HMSO.

Donnelly, M. (2021) 'Campaigners demand urgent ministerial statement requiring planning decisions to comply with climate goals', ENDS Report, 17 December. Available at: https://www.endsreport.com/article/1736 133/campaigners-demand-urgent-ministerial-statement-requiring-plann ing-decisions-comply-climate-goals

Donnelly, M. (2022) 'Civil service jobs reduction plan "will require frontline public service cuts", government review finds', ENDS Report, 8 August. Available at: https://www.endsreport.com/article/1795355/civil-service-jobs-reduction-plan-will-require-frontline-public-service-cuts-government-review-finds

Fair, J. (2021) ' "Ecologically disastrous": the lessons from "early adopters" that have pioneered net gains', ENDS Report, 14 September. Available at: https://www.endsreport.com/article/1726222/ecologically-disastrous-lessons-early-adopters-pioneered-net-gain

Fischer, T.B. (2022) 'Taxonomies of sustainable investment and the application of EIA and SEA: a silver bullet for sustainable development? A response to Dusík and Bond', Impact Assessment and Project Appraisal, 40(2): 118–22

Fischer, T.B. (2023) 'Simplification and potential replacement of EA in the UK: is it fit for purpose?', Impact Assessment and Project Appraisal, 41(3): 233-237.

Fischer, T.B. and Yu, X. (2018) 'Sustainability appraisal in neighbourhood planning in England', Journal of Environmental Planning and Management, 6: 939–59.

Fischer, T.B., Glasson, J., Jha Thakur, U., Therivel, R., Howard, R. and Fothergill, J. (2018) 'Implications of Brexit for environmental assessment in the UK: results from a one-day workshop at the University of Liverpool', Impact Assessment and Project Appraisal, 36(4): 371–7.

Fischer, T.B., Muthoora, T., Chang, M. and Sharpe, C. (2021) 'Health impact assessment in spatial planning in England: types of application and quality of documentation', Environmental Impact Assessment Review, 90: 106631.

Green Alliance (2011) Is Localism Delivering for Climate Change?, London: Green Alliance.

Haughton, G. and Allmendinger, P. (2016) 'Think tanks and the pressures for planning reform in England', Environment and Planning C: Government and Policy, 34(8): 1676–92.

HM Government (Her majesty's Government) (2011) The Natural Choice: Securing the Value of Nature, London: DEFRA.

HM Government (2012) Report of the Habitats and Wild Birds Directive Implementation Review, London: DEFRA.

Johnson, B. (2020) 'Economy speech', Dudley, 30 June. Available at: www.gov.uk/government/speeches/pm-economy-speech-30-june-2020

Lee, M. (2022) 'The future of environmental protection: law, process and the Retained EU Law (Revocation and Reform) Bill', Brexit and Environment Network. Available at: www.brexitenvironment.co.uk/2022/09/29/retained-eu-law-revocation-and-reform-bill/

Lee, M., Armeni, C., de Cendra, J., Chaytor, S., Lock, S., Maslin, M. et al (2013) 'Public participation and climate change infrastructure', *Journal of Environmental Law*, 25(1): 33–62.

Lord, A. and Tewdwr-Jones, M. (2014) 'Is planning "under attack"? Chronicling the deregulation of urban and environmental planning in England', *European Planning Studies*, 22(2): 345–61.

Lowe, P. and Flynn, A. (1989) 'Environmental politics and policy in the 1980s', in J. Mohan (ed) *The Political Geography of Contemporary Britain*, Basingstoke: Macmillan, pp 255–79.

MHCLG (Ministry for Housing, Communities and Local Government) (2020) *Planning for the Future*, London: MHCLG.

Mol, A.P.J. (2016) 'The environmental nation state in decline', *Environmental Politics*, 25(1): 48–68.

Moore, B. (2019) 'Loosening the constraints: the environment in the revised Brexit deal', Brexit and Environment Network. Available at: www.brexit environment.co.uk/2019/10/17/revised-brexit-deal/

Mortel, M.J. (2021) 'IPCC–IPBES scientific outcome'. Available at: https:// ipbes.net/sites/default/files/2021-06/2021_IPCC-IPBES_scientific_outco me_20210612.pdf

Myerson, G. and Rydin, Y. (1996) *The Language of the Environment: A New Rhetoric*, London: UCL Press.

Natural History Museum (2021) 'Biodiversity trends explorer, biodiversity indicators'.

O'Neill, K. and Gibbs, D. (2020) 'Sustainability transitions and policy dismantling: zero carbon housing in the UK', *Geoforum*, 108: 119–29.

OEP (Office for Environmental Protection) (2022) *Taking Stock: Protecting, Restoring and Improving the Environment in England*, Worcester: OEP.

Owens, S. and Cowell, R. (2011) *Land and Limits: Interpreting Sustainability in the Planning Process*, 2nd edn, London: Routledge.

Shepherd, E. (2021) 'Ideology and institutional change: the case of the English National Planning Policy Framework', *Planning Theory and Practice*, 22(4): 519–36.

Sparrow, A. (2013) 'Did David Cameron tell aides to "get rid of all the green crap"?', *The Guardian*, 21 November.

Stroud, D.A., Cromie, R., Finlayson, M., Mundkur, T., Pritchard, D., Spray, C. et al (2021) *International Treaties in Nature Conservation: A UK Perspective*, Totnes: Biodiversity Press.

Zu Ermgassen, S.O.S.E., Baker, J., Griffiths, R.A., Strange, N., Struebig, M.J. and Bull, J.W. (2019) 'The ecological outcomes of biodiversity offsets under "no net loss" policies: a global review', *Conservation Letters*. Available at: https://conbio.onlinelibrary.wiley.com/doi/full/10.1111/conl.12664

Stuck on infrastructure? Planning for the transformative effects of transport infrastructure

Chia-Lin Chen

Introduction

Transport infrastructure is essential for sustaining and facilitating everyday activities. As an agent of change, transport shapes territorial development, as illustrated by two economists writing half a century apart. Colin Clark's (1958) path-breaking piece, 'Transport: maker and breaker of cities', reviews the role of transport over two centuries up to the mid-1950s and embraces the arrival of the 20th-century road/car era, when cars began to revolutionise travel and personal freedom. Similarly, Edward Glaeser's (2020) recent review, 'Infrastructure and urban form', captures technological advances and geographical changes in transport over three major stages: the emergence of new transport technology; the expansion of transport networks around the new technology; and the restructuring of existing networks.

However, mega-transport investments have long been a subject of fierce debate and controversy. In his classic work *Great Planning Disasters*, Hall (1980) applied Friend and Jessop's (1969) uncertainty models to analyse the planning processes of mega-transport project sagas, including London's third airport, London's motorways and San Francisco's Bay Area Rapid Transit (BART) systems. He challenged the mainstream rational model approach for its failure to consider imperfect information, the conflicting values and interests of actors, and unquantifiable or unremunerative objectives.

Proposals for mega-infrastructure projects are inevitably controversial due to competing interests and demands, increasingly expansive networks, complex human settlements, high costs, and potential environmental disturbance. Since the 2008 financial crisis, an economic narrative has suggested that transport investment creates, sustains or unblocks jobs (Masden and McDonald, 2019). Providing persistent inequalities, England has been criticised for its lack of transport infrastructure investment, making it one of the most polarised countries among advanced economies. The policy objective for investing in mega-transport infrastructure, such as High Speed

Two (HS2), has widened its conventional impacts beyond increasing network capacity, unblocking congestion and travel time savings to embrace further transformative effects, including addressing regional inequalities.

Over the past decade, the phrase 'Rebalancing Britain', which first appeared in a consultation document (DFT, 2011), has been used as the primary justification for HS2. Since the election of the Conservative–Liberal Democrat Coalition government in 2010, followed by subsequent Conservative administrations after 2015, various reforms, funding programmes and policy documents on rail infrastructure have been produced, aiming to address inequality at different institutional levels. The most recent of these documents, the Levelling-up and Regeneration Bill, was introduced in February 2022. This chapter aims to answer a key question: given the strategic role that HS2 plays in supporting long-term regional growth and addressing Britain's polarised economic geography, are planning reforms or newly developed policies, amid existing planning systems/tools, conducive to supporting this goal?

This chapter will focus on the planning challenges associated with addressing regional inequalities in response to the transformative effects of future high-speed rail (HSR) in England. To begin, I will review the evidence of the regional impacts of existing mainline rail upgrading and the newly built High Speed One (HS1) investment, as well as key arguments for HS2 in 'Rebalancing Britain'. The evidence highlights the relevance of inadequately addressed intra-regional inequality. Next, the planning policy reforms and changes occurring over the past decade, from 2010 to the latest development in 2022, will be examined. The status quo of planning contexts for expected transformative effects from three perspectives will be considered: national commitment to rail infrastructure; intra-regional inequality and spatial equity; and institutional reform and spatial governance. Finally, I will suggest an outlook for the future based on what has unfolded over the recent decade.

Rail improvements and transformative effects in England

High-speed travel is seen as a symbol of a modern society. According to Directive 96/48, HSR is defined by the European Commission as having a minimum speed of 250 kph on specially built lines and 200 kph on upgraded high-speed lines. The International Union of Railways (UIC, 2008) also adopts this definition, recognising that the development of modern HSR is shaped by varied contextual conditions. Campos and De Rus (2009), who analysed data on 166 high-speed train (HST) projects in 20 countries, distinguished four HST models: the exclusive exploitation model, the mixed high-speed model, the mixed conventional model and the fully mixed model.

Upgrading inter-city rail lines

England holds a significant place in the history of rail transportation, having established the world's first inter-city railway between Liverpool and Manchester in 1830, and the Stockport and Darlington Railway in 1825. However, from the 1960s onward, as other nations, such as Japan and France, began to invest in HSR development, England faced a challenging situation in which building new rail lines appeared unjustifiable given the serious deficit of the rail operation and the obsolescence of its facilities. However, there remained a growing demand for inter-city rail services, which seemed at odds with the general decline of the rail industry.

To address the issue of railway modernisation, the British Rail Board commissioned the Beeching Report in 1963 (British Rail Board, 1963). This report called for the closure of unprofitable routes and investment in growing markets where rail transportation held obvious advantages, such as rail freight containers and longer-distance inter-city rail services. Consequently, the rail network was cut from 28,000 km to 17,000 km between 1963 and 1975.

In response to the growing demand for faster inter-city rail services, two British HSR technological approaches were developed to upgrade inter-city rail travel to achieve a maximum speed of 200 km per hour. These approaches included the advanced passenger train (APT), a tilting train, and the HST, which used diesel traction and was faster and less expensive. The APT was authorised in 1968 but abandoned in the early 1980s after a trial event. However, in Sweden and Italy, the tilting technology later proved feasible, and, ironically, the APT train, the Pendolino, was imported from Italy at a later stage. As a result, the first upgraded rail services in the UK were the InterCity 125, inaugurated in 1976 on the Great Western Main Line between London and Swansea, followed by the InterCity 225 on the East Coast Main Line (in 1982), the InterCity 125 on the Midland Main Line (in 1990) and APT Pendolino trains on the West Coast Main Line (in 2008).

During a period of widespread deindustrialisation and a difficult transition to a new knowledge-based service economy, the arrival of the InterCity 125/225 (Barnett, 1993) had a significant impact. Chen and Hall (2011, cited in Chen, 2013) conducted a longitudinal study to investigate the influence of the British InterCity 125/225 on the space economy. They found that on a national scale, HSR had varied and demonstrable effects on cities located within one to two hours from London, resulting in renewed economic activity. However, this effect was neither automatic nor universal. HSR towns situated within an hour could benefit from exploiting both commuting and intrinsic economic strengths in knowledge-intensive activities. On the other hand, two-hour HST accessibility could benefit mainly from exploiting knowledge-intensive economic functions. Beyond the two-hour mark, the effect of HSR appeared weak.

At the intra-regional level, Chen and Hall's (2012, cited in Chen, 2013) study revealed that major regional cities had been strengthened by their positioning as HSR hubs; however, this has not necessarily translated into economic benefits for surrounding hinterlands. A widening gap has been observed between core cities with favourable HSR services and places with weaker economic performance and limited access to major HSR hubs, particularly in Northern England. Clearly, HSR cannot be expected to serve all locations, and there is a strategic imperative to enhance the intra-regional network between HSR hubs and regional transport networks. This would foster a spatial-economic relationship between regional centres and their hinterlands, generating and amplifying wider economic benefits. For instance, Burnley, a town as equidistant from Manchester as Reading is from London, has no direct rail connection, resulting in weak economic performance (Lucci and Hildreth, 2008). In such cases, improved intra-regional services to regional centres are essential, though not sufficient, to improve economic prospects for urban centres that have lost their traditional industrial roles and are struggling to transition to the knowledge economy.

Overall, upgrading has been the predominant approach adopted in the English context to address inter-city rail demand from the 1970s until the opening of the Channel Tunnel Rail Link (CTRL) by Queen Elizabeth on 6 November 2007. *The Right Line: The Politics, the Planning and the against-the-Odds Gamble behind Britain's First High-Speed Railway* (Faith, 2007) recounts the dramatic story of this achievement. However, it remains unclear whether upgrading alone, without building new lines, is the most effective approach. During the years of upgrading engineering work, rail services have frequently been subject to severe delays or cancellations. The difficulties are attributed to the formidable challenges posed by the extent to which upgrading conventional rail lines could accommodate long-haul inter-city, short-haul intra-regional and freight services. For example, experiences from the West Coast Main Line have shown that upgraded inter-city rail services exclusively benefit towns and cities with relatively superior economic performances. Prioritised inter-city passenger services also result in limited capacity for other services, creating bottlenecks in intra-regional commuting services. As demonstrated earlier, the limited capacity of upgraded approaches restricts opportunities to extend benefits to wider intra-regional transformation (Chen and Hall, 2012).

The first newly built HSR: HS1

A golden opportunity arose for planning the first newly built HSR link when the British and French governments signed the Channel Tunnel Treaty in 1986. Unlike demand-led approaches, the rationale for constructing the 109 km CTRL (later referred to as HS1) is closely associated with territorial transformation. First, this was to facilitate the development of the Thames Gateway[1] in order to address the persistent spatial imbalance of a conventionally affluent west and a less developed east within Greater London and the South East. The saga of planning the correct line into Central London via the north of the Thames significantly contributed to this goal (Faith, 2007). Notably, major urban transformations have occurred in the East London Central Business District (CBD) around Stratford, where the London Olympic Games took place in 2012, and Central London regeneration around Kings Cross/St Pancras stations and their surroundings.

Second, with government subsidy, CTRL was expected to provide regeneration benefits for East Kent (Norman and Vickerman, 1999). Since 2009, seaside resorts like Margate and Ramsgate within the district of Thanet where the economy is fragile have been connected to London with faster services, including the UK's first domestic high-speed commuter service (British Rail Class 395 Javelin) operated by Southeastern on HS1. However, findings from an ex post study of HS1 could not provide clear-cut evidence showing immediate economic benefits for fragile places in developing knowledge economies when their rail accessibility improved (Chen and Vickerman, 2017, 2020). In addition to facilitating regeneration benefits in East Kent with better rail links, the Turner Contemporary Art Gallery, opened in 2011, has contributed to generating positive social and economic impacts that address local challenges – an essential catalyst for local transformation through the arts.

However, the territorial dynamism brought about by HS1 does not tackle the persistent North–South divide. Instead, since the newly built HS1 serves mainly Greater London and the South East, two regions with the strongest economic performance in England, this rail improvement could strengthen connectivity around the South and worsen regional disparity between Southern and Northern England.

Urgency of HS2 development

Since the turn of the millennium, a number of policy documents have raised awareness of the increasing demand for inter-city long-distance rail and the requirement for a substantial increase in rail capacity. A strategic document entitled *Everyone's Railway: The Wider Case for Rail* was published in 2003 by the now-defunct Strategic Rail Authority (2003). This document called for a long-term investment agenda to tackle capacity constraints on the principal North–South routes (Strategic Rail Authority, 2003). *The Eddington Transport Study* (Eddington, 2006) provided evidence of an unprecedented increase in rail travel demand over the previous decade. The 2007 White Paper *Delivering a Sustainable Railway* (DfT, 2007a) estimated that by 2030, high demand for long-distance passenger travel would result in severe overcrowding on commuter services into London and on longer-distance inter-city business networks

(DfT, 2007a, 2007b). While a new North–South HSR line was considered, it was not yet the chosen solution. As the Department for Transport (DfT, 2007a: 67) stated: 'On the basis of the present carbon footprint of electricity generation, the balance of advantage would appear to favour services running at conventional speeds on reopened alignments.' Following the modernisation of the West Coast Main Line in December 2008, the government initiated planning for HS2, which triggered a new wave of political engagement.

It is important to note that the idea of continually planning new HSR lines had been actively advocated by the foresighted figure of Jim Steer, even before the CTRL was officially completed in 2007 and the national government had explicitly embraced the White Paper of the HS2 plan in 2010. In 2006, Steer founded the not-for-profit company Greengauge 21, which has become one of the UK's leading transport sector specialists committed to providing evidence for a full and open debate on HSR (Harman, 2006; SDG, 2008). Anecdotally, Steer is also said to have been the mastermind behind urging the renaming of the CTRL as HS1, as it was logical to start with HS1 and then move on to a visionary HSR network, namely, HS2, HS3 and so on.

Planning for a new HSR network began during the tenure of the Labour government with a policy document titled *Britain's Transport Infrastructure, High-Speed Two* in 2009 (DfT, 2009). This document announced the establishment of a separate company called High Speed Two Limited, which was tasked with advising ministers on relevant issues. This approach was modelled after the successful creation of separate companies for the CTRL and Crossrail. The feasibility and credibility of HS2 were studied, with a focus on addressing the demand for future long-haul inter-city rail. In the White Paper titled *High Speed Rail*, published in March 2010 (DfT, 2010), a strategic case for HS2 was considered from the perspective of conventional transport economics, including rail capacity, efficient connectivity, productivity and urban economies. The White Paper emphasised the spatial focus on towns in London and the South East, demonstrating how HS2 could alleviate London's commuting problems and enhance its long-term competitiveness. While regions outside London were referenced, the White Paper emphasised city-led regional development through improved connections between major cities in the Midlands and the North. The following section focuses on the evolution of planning policy environments from 2010 to 2022 to understand the extent to which policy and tools underlying the planning environment support or discourage transformative effects.

Examining the planning policy environment for expected transformative effects

Wavering national commitment to HS2: the changing plans

Since 2010, the need to improve rail infrastructure at the national level has been recognised, resulting in renewed commitment to rail investment following years of underinvestment and infrastructure fragmentation. Pledging to address these failures, the Treasury has stated that 'Infrastructure networks form the backbone of a modern economy and are a major determinant of growth and productivity' (HM Treasury, 2011: 5).

Under the Coalition government, Labour's HS2 policy remained a key focus, emphasising the strategic role of HS2 in bridging the North–South divide. In February 2011, a national consultation was held for Phase 1 of HSR, *Investing in Britain's Future Project* (DfT, 2011)', during which then Secretary of State for Transport Philip Hammond stated:

> I believe that a national high-speed rail network from London to Birmingham, with onward legs to Leeds and Manchester, could transform Britain's competitiveness as profoundly as the coming of the railways in the 19th century. It would reshape Britain's economic geography, helping bridge the north–south divide though massive improvements in journey times and better connections between cities – slashing almost an hour off the trip from London to Manchester.

Yet, the commitment of the Coalition government to HS2 was questionable in light of its pursuit of a fiscal austerity programme at the time of the project's announcement. The resulting perception of HS2 as a 'jam tomorrow' project was due to the central government's reluctance to allocate significant funding towards its implementation. Moreover, austerity measures limited the resources available to local governments, which were responsible for planning and investing in preparation for the arrival of HSR in their cities. This restricted the opportunities available to local governments to maximise the benefits of HSR in their respective regions.

Second, a series of government reports stressed the need for rail reform to improve the efficiency of conventional rail lines. The *Rail Value for Money Studies* (DfT and ORR, 2011) highlighted that cost reduction should be 20 to 30 per cent, identifying inefficiencies costing £2.5–£3.5 billion, funded by passengers and taxpayers. Furthermore, *Reforming Railways: Putting the Customers First* (DfT, 2012a) advocated affordability as well as efficiency. In March 2012, a consultation took place to consider rail decentralisation, but nothing materialised. More positively, the *Great British Railways: Williams–Shapps Plan for Rail* (DfT, 2021b) recently announced the overhaul of rail reform, perceiving rail from a comprehensive network perspective rather than individual lines. However, it is worrisome that the government's reliance on private finance results in development interests driven by private promoters rather than planning merit. For instance, when encountering rail inefficiency, the government seeks private involvement and aims to reduce dependency on government subsidies. Then Secretary of State for Transport

Justine Greening MP stated that 'the industry, as a whole, needs to become less dependent on government subsidies and should aim to fully close the efficiency gap identified by Sir Roy [McNulty] by 2019' (DfT, 2012b). A similar concern had been expressed by Norman and Vickerman (1999) regarding the development at Ebbsfleet.

Persistent objections to HS2 have been raised since its inception. Despite all-party support, HS2 has encountered several obstacles. With escalating costs and limited resources, the HS2 plan was returned to the drawing board. The Oakervee Review (DfT, 2020: 13), commissioned to advise on the 'Notice to Proceed' decision for HS2 Phase 1, emphasised that modifications to the HS2 plan were necessary, highlighting that 'HS2 can be part of a transformational economic change, but only if it is properly integrated with other transport strategies, especially those seeking to improve inter-city and intra-regional transport'. This resulted in the latest policy, *Integrated Rail Plan for the North and Midlands* (DfT, 2021a), which consequently cancelled the eastern leg to Sheffield and Leeds. The East Midlands Parkway would be the final stop of the new HS2 line. The government argued that this change was due to an escalation of the cost to an unaffordable level of £185 billion following COVID-19, among various competing rail capital commitments, claiming that the new plan of £96 billion would improve rail services to Leeds in the 2030s rather than 2043. Figure 9.1 compares the rail network in the initial HS2 plan and the latest integrated rail plan.

Central government's wavering commitments raise questions about the extent to which planning for the transformative effects of transport infrastructure can be met given the constantly changing plans. The latest integrated rail plan, with major cutbacks, such as the cancelling of new HSR lines to Sheffield and Leeds, further illustrates the inconsistent commitments from central government. This cancellation means that conventional upgrading approaches must be adopted to provide additional capacity that may be required in the future. Meanwhile, potential regeneration opportunities for both cities around HS2 stations have been missed given the strategic gateway for regional and national connectivity. This has left local governments struggling to keep pace with the lingering uncertainty, which is unfavourable to any long-term strategic planning. The decisions resulting from these changes, such as capacity, location and routing, may result in suboptimal options and discounted effects. Similar lessons from HS1 could be learnt in this regard. Norman and Vickerman (1999) highlighted the importance of the station strategy in the East Thames Corridor, with an intermediate station at Ebbsfleet having potentially regenerative benefits. However, they noted that some of these benefits would come at the expense of commitments made at Ashford back in 1986–87.

Figure 9.1: A juxtaposition of the HS2 routes and stations in 2010 and 2021

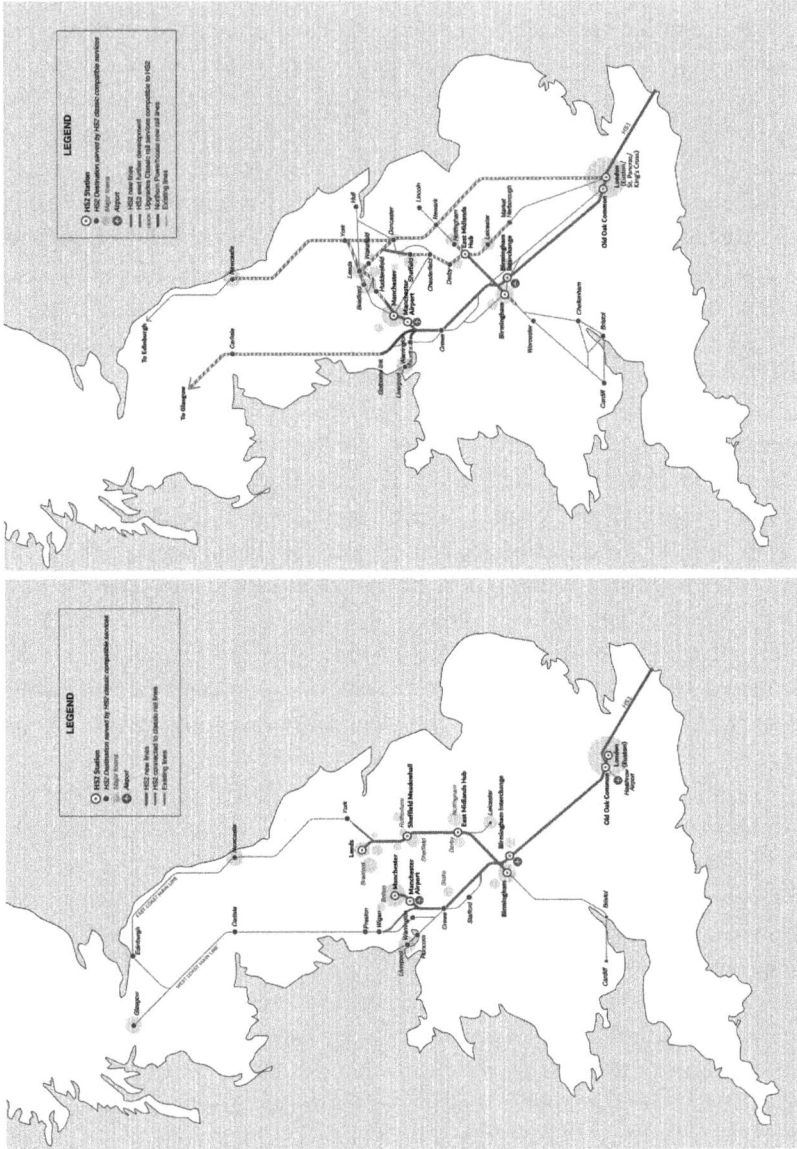

Source: Adapted from Department for Transport (2013, 2021a)

Intra-regional inequality and spatial equity

Given that 'Rebalancing Britain' is a core objective of HS2, it is widely agreed that HSR alone is insufficient for rebalancing regional disparity and that it is difficult to disseminate the benefits beyond the city centres served by HST connections to help the more deprived areas within a wider region. Northern Powerhouse Rail (NPR) is a strategic rail network plan for the North of England (featuring new and upgraded rail lines), which aims to improve and invest in intra-regional rail infrastructure, and to transform the rail services to make it easier to move between towns and cities in the north (TfN, 2019a). A similarly ambitious plan was previously presented under the umbrella of The Northern Way (2007), which could be regarded as a key foundation of the later Northern Powerhouse. The new development is the first statutory sub-national transport authority in England outside Greater London. Transport for the North (TfN) was created to support investment needs for East–West connections among major cities and towns in the North, regarded as equally important as the North–South HS2 connection, if not more so. The strategic transport plan demonstrates a strategic vision at the trans-regional level in the North to combat the dominance of Greater London and the South East.

The potential wider impacts of strategic infrastructure projects have been clearly highlighted, and as illustrated by the following quote, this is a view shared by local key players. The Greater Manchester HS2 NPR growth strategy, entitled *The Stops Are Just the Start* (GMCA, 2021a), for example, provides a key framework integrating place making, employment and sustainability with the 2040 Greater Manchester transport strategy:

> It is much more than an infrastructure project – it has the potential to be a social and economic catalyst for the region and the people and businesses of the North. It is an investment in infrastructure that will deliver benefits to the economy, quality of life, education and the environment. (TfN, 2019b: 4)

Although NPR aims to improve connectivity between key centres and their city regions in the North, it largely overlooks more deprived areas outside these city regions, exacerbating their marginalisation. Figure 9.2 provides a comparison between two rail improvement plans for Northern England. The Hall Plan of 2014 (Hall et al, 2014; illustrated in the top panel) displays how the HS2 rail infrastructure could be utilised to serve the region more extensively. In contrast, the vision of the NPR network (depicted in the bottom panel) prioritises major cities and towns in the TfN plan, leaving certain rail lines, often in more deprived areas, with inadequate transport services. For example, the South Fylde Line between Blackpool and Preston,

Figure 9.2: A juxtaposition of the SYNAPTIC S-Map 2030 North West proposal (top panel) and the vision for the Northern Powerhouse Rail network (bottom panel)

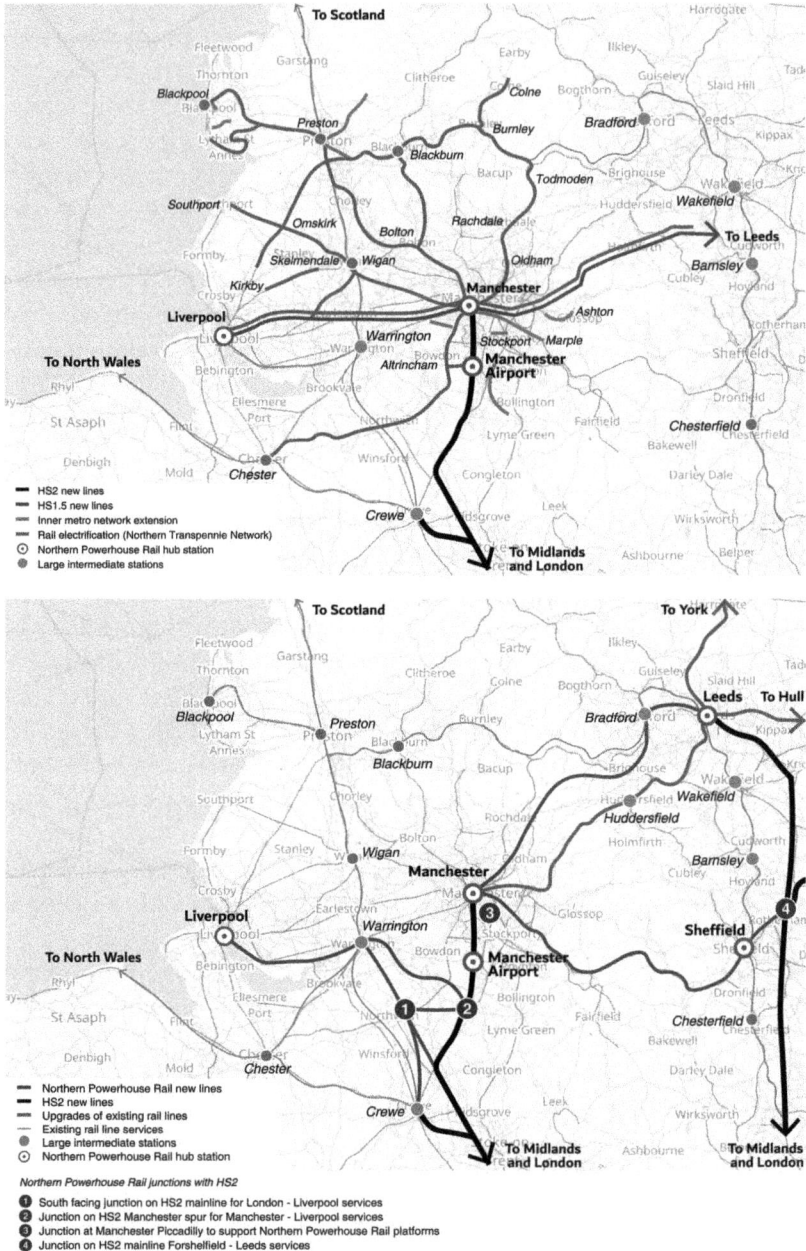

Source: Top panel adapted from Chen and Hall (2013); bottom panel adapted from Transport for the North (TfN, 2019a)

as well as the line between Blackburn and Manchester, are neglected in the NPR plan. Thus, the intra-regional rail network primarily serves major cities and towns, excluding peripheral areas with limited accessibility, thereby further entrenching the unequal distribution of resources in the region.

Neglected rail improvements are associated with weaker economic performance and social problems, as also reflected in deteriorated rail accessibility within the region. Such rail capacity issues have persisted over time and pose threats of worsening regional inequality. For instance, while London and major regional cities like Manchester have been connected with frequent inter-city train services, three trains per hour and a clock-face schedule, the rail link between Manchester and its hinterlands has deteriorated. Table 9.1 compares train times and frequencies in 2008 and 2022 between London Euston and Manchester Piccadilly with those between London Euston and Oldham Mumps Metrolink, one of Manchester's hinterlands. In 2022, the transit time between Manchester and Oldham is 20 minutes longer, while the time between London and Manchester is slightly shorter or unchanged. Again, 'Transport investment alone will not "rebalance" the UK economy (conclusion 4 in section 5)' (DfT, 2020: 36). If inter-city connectivity through HSR has been enhanced while intra-regional connectivity remains unimproved, this inequality may lead to increasing intra-regional inequality.

Table 9.1: Inequality of rail accessibility in Greater Manchester: core versus periphery

	September 2008			May 2022		
From	EUS	EUS	EUS	EUS	EUS	EUS
To	MAN	MAN	MAN	MAN	MAN	MAN
Departs (time)	06:55	07:20	07:35	06:16	06:36	07:20
Arrives (time)	09:07	09:28	09:49	08:27	08:46	09:27
Total train time (hour: min)	02:12	02:08	02:14	02:11	02:10	02:07
Changes	0	0	0	0	0	0
Inter-city and further into regional hinterland (London Euston–Oldham Mumps Metrolink)						
	September 2008			May 2022		
From	EUS	EUS	EUS	EUS	EUS	EUS
To	OLM	OLM	OLM	OLM	OLM	OLM
Departs (time)	06:55	07:20	07:35	06:16	06:36	07:20
Arrives (time)	10:07	10:28	10:57	10:01	10:14	11:14
Total train time (hour: min)	03:12	03:08	03:22	03:45	03:38	03:39
Changes	3	2	2	3	3	3

Source: Adapted from Lucci and Hildreth (2008) and National Rail Enquiries (2022)

As indicated, spatial equity in England should extend beyond a simplistic North–South division and take into account existing intricate and persistent intra-regional inequality, particularly in intermediate and peripheral areas outside core city regions. These areas are impacted by 'archipelago economies' (Rodríguez-Pose and Fitjar, 2013) and necessitate urgent attention. However, under the dominant evidence-based resource-allocation regime, such as the UK's transport analysis guidance (TAG), there have been difficulties in justifying investments in transport infrastructure in deprived areas. TAG has progressed in recent years by acknowledging non-user benefits, including agglomeration economies, productivities and so on (DfT, 2014), and a new *Levelling Up Toolkit* (DfT, 2022) has replaced the *Rebalancing Toolkit* (DfT, 2017). However, these toolkits offer technical guidance with steps and templates for analyses rather than providing targeted support for the requirements of deprived areas. Due to limited funding resources, it is difficult to prove the claimed impact of transport on spatial equity because transport in deprived areas is a necessary but insufficient condition.

Additionally, competition for resource allocation can arise from other modes of transportation, such as car use, due to data misinterpretation. Therefore, proactive and steadfast intra-regional public transport improvement with excellent access to HSR hubs is necessary to restrict further increases in car use. For example, a recent survey of 2,637 people residing in English towns indicated that only 6 per cent were satisfied with car travel, whereas 27 and 22 per cent were satisfied with train and bus travel, respectively (NIC, 2021a). Nevertheless, without detailed information on sample sizes or the percentage of survey participants, these findings indicate higher satisfaction with public transport, which is likely being utilised to justify investment and resource allocation in car travel and road transport instead of improving public transport.

The evolution of institutional reforms of spatial governance and capacity building

In addition to HS2 and intra-regional transport improvement (including deprived hinterlands), another key element to attain the objective of HS2 in curbing the UK's polarised economies and yielding wider developmental effects is conducive and integrated spatial developmental strategies at local, city and regional levels. These spatial strategies are influenced by institutional reforms over the past decade, which determined the mechanism/power, capacity and resources for planning intervention and governance. Since 2010, substantial institutional transformations in three domains (spatial, governance and capacity building) have curtailed local authorities' ability to engage in strategic deliberations around HS2's potential for effecting change at the regional level, despite progress at city-regional levels.

Fragmented spatial governance

The cessation of regional government tiers following the ascension of the Coalition government to power is concerning (see Chapter 4). Local enterprise partnerships (LEPs) were established for wider spatial collaboration beyond individual local authorities to develop local priorities (HM Government, 2010). The result is the absence of a legally mandated regional framework to facilitate the dispersion of agglomeration economies around HSR hubs from metropolitan areas to surrounding regions.

This preference for smaller governments via LEPs has resulted in growing tensions between local authorities and business groups; indeed, whether LEPs are effective in addressing spatial inequality is increasingly questionable. Devolution deals (Sandford, 2023), initially introduced in 2015 under the Cameron administration and later in 2019 under the Johnson administration, reflected a move from a business-led to combined-authorities-led approach for spatial governance, with devolved power and allocated resources in such areas as transport, skills, employment, health, land and housing, public services, and finance. Devolution details vary with the deal made between each local democratic institution and Whitehall, but they may offer a means to address tensions around inequality issues. Gradually, LEPs have also been required to be integrated[2] with the new devolved democratic institutions.

Under the devolution agenda, local authorities were encouraged to form (mayoral) combined authorities or combined county authorities. Initially, the government required a directly elected mayor for combined authorities; however, disagreement resulted in the decision that both mayoral and non-mayoral combined authorities should be formed, with the latter having limited powers, for example, a 'Level 2' deal, including local transport and adult education functions, but excluding certain powers and funding, such as control of new investment funds and the ability to introduce a council tax precept. Hampshire County Council stated in 2016, for instance, that it did 'not see [a mayor] as the right model for a large, diverse and extensively rural area such as Hampshire and the Isle of Wight' (Paine, 2016). Conversely, some combined authorities managed to elect their own mayor and negotiate with Whitehall for maximum power and resources to implement their local spatial strategies, which integrated with HS2. For instance, Greater Manchester Combined Authority (GMCA) has envisaged regeneration around stations and along the route, as set out in the Manchester Piccadilly Strategic Regeneration Framework (SRF) and local growth strategies (GMCA, 2021b). This seems to reflect an essentially laissez faire approach taken by central government. As such, the devolution deals largely depend on the collective decision of local politics: the stronger the local leadership, the stronger the collaboration, the more power and resources can be secured. That said, without a strategic regional framework, no regional intervention could be made to address issues of deprived areas, which tend to attract fewer resources and power because of weak local leadership.

David Cameron's 'Big Society' agenda was put forward in the context of a worsening unbalanced Britain, in the belief that businesses know both how to innovate and grow economies, and how to address the geographical disparity prevailing in this uneven development. Devolving power away from bureaucratic governments is part and parcel of a localism agenda promoted by the Cameron administration, where greater levels of individual autonomy and responsibility could be reached by reducing the deficit and rebalancing the economy for a better Britain. The HS2 plan was clearly regarded as a key policy area that could contribute to the transformation. Yet, a critical question arises: can a rebalanced economic model be achieved by the private sector? As noted earlier, the LEPs are now intended to be integrated with local democratic institutions. This hints at the ineffectiveness of reliance on LEPs and the need for public intervention to address the deprived situations that the private sector is not willing to tackle.

Capacity building

Apart from the fragmented planning power derived from institutional reform, weak capacity building at the local level is also a barrier to transformative effects. First, would Northern productivity be achieved in the austerity period with major public spending cuts? The recent 'Levelling Up' White Paper, as an overarching framework setting out a 'moral, social and economic programme', is the latest epitome of the government's claimed commitment to be overcoming inequality by spreading opportunity more equally across the UK (HM Government, 2022). The government believes that by 'extending opportunities across the UK we can relieve pressures on public services, housing and green fields in the southeast. And well-being in the southeast by improving productivity in the north and Midlands' (HM Government, 2022). However, the period of austerity public spending cuts between 2010 and 2020 has been described as 'a lost decade' (Toynbee and Walker, 2020), eroding resilience in the North with serious consequences for the most vulnerable.

Second, with limited resources and funding support through competitive grant schemes, deprived places were likely to be incapable of producing convincing applications in time. The dominance of major regional centres and city regions boosted by HSR somehow overshadowed the capacity building and needs of hinterlands, for example, smaller or weaker places within conurbations or wider regions. Is there any awareness of this key barrier? In a recent online workshop linked to a National Infrastructure Commission (NIC, 2021a) report entitled *Infrastructure, Towns and Regeneration*, a participant from the Local Government Association (LGA) Economic

Environment, Housing and Transport Board expressed frustration, asking how the conversation between central government and local government officers could be refocused to produce more community-based/place-based decision making, that is, how local voices could be heard more easily (NIC, 2021b). The event host admitted:

> every place is different, and the goal is to abandon the term 'shovel ready' and make expert advice available.... There isn't one size fits all that different towns in different connections and outside conurbations have different sorts of relationships, and so it is very much about allowing that capacity building to take place. (NIC, 2021b)

Third, the reality of frequent central dramatic reshuffling has influenced local stability via the changing priority and degree of devolution. At the same NIC launch event, a representative from the Midlands reflected on his observations over the past 30 years, claiming that in comparison with the relatively stable local level:

> central government changes with bewildering regularity at both ministerial level but particularly civil servant level ... having that kind of ongoing dialogue with central government is really challenging from a local perspective.... I just wonder whether your report addressing that issue recognises that issue and how it wants to put that sort of relationship between the centre and the local on a more consistent footing. (NIC, 2021b)

As a result, considering the traditionally separated relationship between the central and local state, a general inconsistency and fragmentation of urban and regional development is unfortunately taking place, which leads to local intervention exploiting wider HS2 impacts, with difficulties caused by changing plans, problematic spatial governance and weak capacity building.

Future outlook

By examining three key themes in relation to planning contexts and policy reforms over the past decade, this chapter reflects a long-term process of muddling through – an incremental and pragmatic approach to planning the future of the HSR network (HS2) for transformative effects, that is, 'Rebalancing Britain', which the Conservative Party promised to address before claiming power. First, unlike market-led approaches and an unawareness of missed opportunities for addressing regional imbalances or reducing widening regional inequalities during the upgrade of the West Coast Main Line, the aim for HS2 in 'Rebalancing Britain' is specifically manifest.

Although the planning decision of HS2 received cross-party support, implementation has been shaped by uncertainties, such as the changing nature of travel and commuting patterns brought about by COVID-19 and cost escalation, alongside the interwoven relationship with other relevant policy areas, such as rail reform. From the rail infrastructure perspective, England's path dependency (its extensive rail network and conditions), national commitment and appraisal guidance play an important role in the planning process. Clearly, transport investment alone will not rebalance the UK economy. Strategic integrated planning for such effects is key, yet the economic and strategic cases are unaligned.

Second, the planning challenges to transformative effects are enormous when institutional reform and spatial governance are fragmented and counterproductive. Decentralisation reform was supposed to address the centralised state. However, the abolition of regional government when the Coalition government came to power posed a serious question: how would 'regional development' operate in the absence of a regional government? Also, before a real devolution is functioning, the constant change of key transport decisions and ad hoc funding streams announced at the central level generate consequent correspondingly ad hoc local reactions and campaigns. Consequently, the transformative effects of mega-rail transport projects for addressing regional inequality are in peril of failing, as no long-term, integrated approaches are taken to deliver this objective. Emphasising the transformative effects of HS2 appears empty rhetoric without allocated resources and integrated interventions to enable institutional arrangements to spread the benefits to disadvantaged places within a region. Both transport (for 'thick' high-speed and 'thin' intra-regional rail lines and other modes) and non-transport interventions are required to deliver over a long-term time frame.

The third aspect is especially critical because intra-regional inequality has been overshadowed and ignored by inter-regional competition. Over the last decade, policy development in planning and related fields has illustrated that history has repeated itself; however, this time, instead of purely missing opportunities, the claimed effects have been made without meaningful content. Wray et al (2020) reminds us that muddling through and incrementalism is the nature of Britain's approach to planning transport infrastructure. The outlook for the future depends on strong policy coordination at the central and local levels, as well as local consensus, coping with unexpected changes by sharing visions at the local level. We need to look at learning good practice for capacity building at the local level.

Although HS2 offers a major opportunity to reshape uneven spatial-economic development, transport is widely regarded as a necessary but insufficient condition (Fogel, 1964). To achieve positive territorial transformation, strategic planning with a package of planning interventions that includes both transport and non-transport elements over the long term is essential. HSR can transform regional economies, but this transformation is neither automatic nor guaranteed. HSR alone cannot achieve regional development. HSR should be seen as one element in a comprehensive policy of regeneration and transformation. Both thick (high-speed) and thin (intra-regional) lines are essential. Beyond HSR cities, could benefits to the core and periphery be shared more equally? Nothing is guaranteed, but it is certain to fail if no efforts are made. Two reforms are especially highlighted here to address overlooked core–periphery inequality:

- Institutional reform: decentralisation and devolution are welcome, but fragmentation challenges must be overcome to avoid silo planning and disintegrated policies resulting from long-term austerity and devolution in grabbing power and funding sources.
- Appraisal reform: is it possible to advance appraisal framework beyond agglomeration economies around key regional centres, that is, from user benefits (cost benefit analysis; CBA) to agglomeration effects (wider economic benefits; WEBs) to transformative benefits? How can the transformation appraisal of declining places best be evaluated? Perhaps the answers warrant a debate on the value judgement. The potential achievement lies in when an equity-led planning concern could be prioritised over the efficiency-led spending scrutiny.

New forms of development may emerge that further complicate matters. For instance, changing work and travel patterns, such as pervasive work from home resulting from the COVID-19 pandemic, as well as new transport technology, such as shared mobilities and driverless/electric cars, would bring about uncertainty in transport demand. In addition, recent events like the 2022 cost-of-living crisis following the war in Ukraine, compounded by inadequate national policies and international geopolitical tensions, have added new challenges to the already-complex landscape. Considering the enormous scale of construction cost in rail improvement, the current HS2 cost is likely to rise further in the future. In conclusion, while uncertainties and potential challenges remain in the future of HS2 and related policies, adopting equity planning and strategic governance could help overcome these obstacles and achieve transformative effects. Let us remain optimistic about the future and work towards creating a more equitable and sustainable transportation system for all.

Acknowledgements

The author would like to express gratitude to Wenkang Tian for her help in reproducing four comparable maps (Figures 9.1 and 9.2) based on the existing policy documents and proposals, which were produced with different styles.

Notes

[1] The Thames Gateway refers to an area stretching 70 km from inner East and South-east London on both sides of the River Thames and the Thames Estuary.

[2] With more devolution deals granted at the local level, new conflicts between LEPs and combined authorities emerged. On this issue, government guidance categorises three pathways regarding the process for integrating LEPs into these democratic institutions (DLUHC and DBEIS, 2022). The first two pathways are straightforward: either Pathway 1 – integrating the LEP into local democratic institutions; or Pathway 2 – maintaining the LEP until a devolution deal is agreed. The most challenging, Pathway 3, refers to areas where the devolution deal and boundary does not fully match the LEP area and, consequentially, a local solution must be found.

References

Barnett, R. (1993) 'British Rail's InterCity 125 and 225', *Built Environment*, 19(3–4): 163–82.

British Rail Board (1963) *The Reshaping of British Railways*, London: Her Majesty's Stationery Office.

Campos, J. and De Rus, G. (2009) 'Some stylized facts about high-speed rail: a review of HSR experiences around the world', *Transport Policy*, 16(1): 19–28.

Chen, C.-L. (2013) 'The spatial-economic impact of high-speed trains: nationally (the UK IC125) and regionally (a British–French comparison)', PhD thesis, University College London, UK.

Chen, C.-L. and Hall, P. (2011) 'The impacts of high-speed trains on British economic geography: a study of the UK's InterCity 125/225 and its effects', *Journal of Transport Geography*, 19: 689–704.

Chen, C.-L. and Hall, P. (2012) 'The wider spatial-economic impacts of high-speed trains: a comparative case study of Manchester and Lille sub-regions', *Journal of Transport Geography*, 24: 89–110.

Chen, C.-L. and Hall, P. (2013) 'Using High Speed Two to irrigate the regions', *Built Environment*, 39(3): 355–68.

Chen, C.-L. and Vickerman, R. (2017) 'Can transport infrastructure change regions' economic fortunes? Some evidence from Europe and China', *Regional Studies*, 51(1): 144–60.

Chen, C.-L. and Vickerman, R. (2020) 'Quantifying the economic and social impacts of high-speed rail: some evidence from Europe and the People's Republic of China', in Y. Hayashi, K.E. Seetha Ram and S. Bharule (eds) *Handbook on High-speed Rail and Quality of Life*, Tokyo: Asian Development Bank Institute, pp 283–303.

Clark, C. (1958) 'Transport: maker and breaker of cities', *Town Planning Review*, 28(4): 237–50.

DfT (Department for Transport) (2007a) *Delivering a Sustainable Railway*, London: Department for Transport.

DfT (2007b) *Towards a Sustainable Transport System*, London: The Stationery Office.

DfT (2009) *Britain's Transport Infrastructure High Speed Two*, London: Department for Transport.

DfT (2010) *High Speed Rail*, London: The Stationery Office.

DfT (2011) *High Speed Rail: Investing in Britain's Future Consultation*, London: Department for Transport.

DfT (2012a) *Reforming our Railways: Putting the Customer First*, London: The Stationery Office.

DfT (2012b) 'Rail reform command paper: oral statement about modernising and investing in the infrastructure of the railway network', 8 March. Available at: https://www.gov.uk/government/speeches/rail-reform-command-paper-oral-statement

DfT (2013) *High Speed Rail: Investing in Britain's Future – Phase Two: The Route to Leeds, Manchester and Beyond*, London: The Stationary Office.

DfT (2014) *Rebalancing Britain: From HS2 towards a National Transport Strategy*, London: Department for Transport.

DfT (2017) *Strategic Case Supplementary Guidance. Rebalancing Toolkit: Moving Britain Ahead*, London: Department for Transport. Available at: https://greenertransportsolutions.com/wp-content/uploads/2018/02/supplementary-guidance-rebalancing-toolkit.pdf

DfT (2020) *The Oakervee Review of HS2*, London: HM Government.

DfT (2021a) *Integrated Rail Plan for the North and Midlands*, London: Department for Transport.

DfT (2021b) *Great British Railways: Williams–Shapps Plan for Rail*, London: Department for Transport.

DfT (2022) *Transport Business Cases: The Levelling Up Toolkit*, London: Department for Transport. Available at: https://assets.publishing.service.gov.uk/government/uploads/system/uploads/attachment_data/file/1054072/transport-business-cases-levelling-up-toolkit.pdf

DfT and ORR (Office of Rail Regulation) (2011) *Realising the Potential of GB Rail: Final Independent Report of the Rail Value for Money Study*, London: Department for Transport and Office of Rail Regulation.

DLUHC (Department for Levelling UP, Housing and Communities) and DBEIS (Department for Business, Energy & Industrial Strategy) (2022) 'Local enterprise partnerships: integration guidance'. Available at: www.gov.uk/government/publications/local-enterprise-partnerships-integration-guidance

Eddington, R. (2006) *The Eddington Transport Study: Understanding the Relationship: How Transport Can Contribute to Economic Success*, London: HMSO.

Faith, N. (2007) *The Right Line: The Politics, the Planning and the Against-the-Odds Gamble behind Britain's First High-Speed Railway*, London: Segrave Foulkes.

Fogel, R.W. (1964) *Railroads and American Economic Growth*, Baltimore: Johns Hopkins University Press.

Friend, J.K. and Jessop, W.N. (1969) *Local Government and Strategic Choice*, London: Tavistock Publications.

Glaeser, E. (2020) 'Infrastructure and urban form', National Bureau of Economic Research Working Paper Series, No. 28287. Available at: www.nber.org/papers/w28287.pdf

GMCA (Great Manchester Combined Authority) (2021a) *HS2 and Northern Powerhouse Rail Growth Strategy: The Stops Are Just the Start*, Manchester: Great Manchester Combined Authority.

GMCA (2021b) 'Update on HS2 and Northern Powerhouse Rail', 10 September. Available at: https://democracy.greatermanchester-ca.gov.uk/documents/s16466/16%20GMCA%2020210910%20HS2%20and%20Northern%20Powerhouse%20Rail.pdf

Hall, P. (1980) *Great Planning Disasters*, London: Weidenfeld and Nicolson.

Hall, P., Thrower, D. and Wray, I. (2014) 'High-Speed North: building a trans-Pennine mega-city', *Town & Country Planning*, 83(4): 160–7.

Harman, R. (2006) *High Speed Trains and the Development and Regeneration of Cities*, London: Greengauge21.

HM Government (Her Majesty's Government) (2010) *Local Growth: Realising Every Place's Potential*, London: The Stationery Office.

HM Government (2022) *Levelling up the United Kingdom*, London: HM Government. Available at: https://assets.publishing.service.gov.uk/government/uploads/system/uploads/attachment_data/file/1052706/Levelling_Up_WP_HRES.pdf

HM Treasury (Her Majesty's Treasury) (2011) *National Infrastructure Plan 2011*, London: The Stationery Office.

Lucci, P. and Hildreth, P. (2008) *City Links: Integration and Isolation*, London: Centre for Cities.

Masden, G. and McDonald, N.C. (2019) 'Institutional issues in planning for more uncertain futures', *Transportation*, 46: 1075–92.

National Rail Enquiries (2022) 'Plan your Journey'. Available at: www.nationalrail.co.uk

NIC (National Infrastructure Commission) (2021a) *Infrastructure, Towns and Regeneration*, London: NIC. Available at: https://nic.org.uk/app/uploads/NIC-Infrastructure-Towns-and-Regeneration-Report.pdf

NIC (2021b) 'Infrastructure, towns and regeneration launch event', 23 September. Available at: www.youtube.com/watch?v=QyilU0hln8c

Norman, C. and Vickerman, R. (1999) 'Local and regional implications of trans-European transport networks: the Channel Tunnel Rail Link', *Environment and Planning A*, 31: 705–18.

Paine, D. (2016) 'Failure to resolve mayors question lead to two-tier devo stalemate', *Local Government Chronicle*, 17 February. Available at: https://www.lgcplus.com/politics/devolution-and-economic-growth/failure-to-resolve-mayors-question-leads-to-two-tier-devo-stalemate-17-02-2016/

Rodríguez-Pose, A. and Fitjar, R.D. (2013) 'Buzz, archipelago economies and the future of intermediate and peripheral areas in a spiky world', *European Planning Studies*, 21(3): 355–72.

Sandford, M. (2023) 'Devolution to local government in England', Research Briefing 07029, House of Commons Library. Available at: https://researchbriefings.files.parliament.uk/documents/SN07029/SN07029.pdf

SDG (Steer Davies Gleave) (2008) *High Speed 2: Economic and Regeneration Impacts for Birmingham Final Report*, London: Greengauge 21 and Birmingham City Council.

Strategic Rail Authority (2003) *Everyone's Railway: The Wider Case for Rail*, London: Strategic Rail Authority.

TfN (Transport for the North) (2019a) 'Strategic transport plan', February. Available at: https://transportforthenorth.com/wp-content/uploads/TfN-final-strategic-transport-plan-2019.pdf

TfN (2019b) 'The potential of Northern Powerhouse Rail'. Available at: https://transportforthenorth.com/wp-content/uploads/Potential-of-NPR_TfN-web.pdf

The Northern Way (2007) *Strategic Direction for Transport*, Newcastle upon Tyne: The Northern Way.

Toynbee, P. and Walker, D. (2020) *The Lost Decade 2010–2020 and What Lies Ahead for Britain*, London: Guardian Faber Publishing.

UIC (International Union of Railways) (2008) *General Definitions of Highspeed*, Paris: UIC.

Wray, I., Thrower, D. and Steer, J. (2020) 'High speed rail in Northern England: tactics and policies for implementing mega plans by modular incrementalism', *Built Environment*, 46(3): 466–84.

Conclusion

John Sturzaker and Olivier Sykes

Introduction

As we discussed in Chapter 1, this book was prompted by the publication of the Planning White Paper in August 2020 and the 'radical' reform it proposed. That White Paper had forewords written by then Prime Minister Boris Johnson and then Secretary of State for Housing, Communities & Local Government Robert Jenrick. To say that the landscape has shifted somewhat since then would be an understatement. The White Paper has now largely been abandoned, with some of its contents included in a new Levelling-up and Regeneration Bill. The department of the UK government responsible for planning has been renamed as the Department for Levelling Up, Housing and Communities. At the time of writing in February 2023, the secretary of state in place at the head of that department is Michael Gove, who, precedent suggests, is unlikely to be in place when you read this, and there have been an astonishing six different planning ministers in the last 12 months. However, most significantly, the UK has had three different prime ministers during this period, with Liz Truss replacing Boris Johnson on 6 September 2022, leading to a record-breaking short period of office before being replaced by Rishi Sunak on 25 October 2022. All of this means that the proposals in the Planning White Paper are of little relevance to the future of planning in England. That does not mean, however, that this book is of no relevance; the opposite, in fact, is true, as its central 'thesis' that constant cycles of often ill-conceived central government reform and tinkering have failed to establish consistency and stability around planning seems more salient than ever.

The controversy generated by the Planning White Paper and the consequent loss of a by-election in Chesham and Amersham were arguably the beginning of the end for Boris Johnson's premiership. While he was ultimately dethroned by his party due to other factors too numerous to detail here, the inability of his government to successfully introduce changes to the planning system illustrates neatly our argument that the 'failure' of this book's title is not that of planning but that of the state within which planning operates, as well as the political party that has led that state for much of the last 50 years. The period since 2020 illustrates too how the symbolic and rhetorical power of planning in the UK goes far beyond what its legislative framework might suggest – it is variously seen as the cause of, and solution to, an enormous range of society's problems, from poverty to obesity (Sturzaker and Lord, 2018).

More specifically, this book has provided a powerful critique of the period since 2010, in which the UK has been led by the Conservative Party, and the often-chaotic approach to planning that characterised this time. There is little to suggest that the current prime minster will introduce any more coherent thinking to the system, with Sunak 'caving in' (Allegretti, 2022) in an early battle with his backbenchers over housing targets in local plans. We can therefore expect the chaos to continue, but if an alternative is sought, this volume offers a clear view of what might need to change.

In the rest of this chapter, we first summarise the findings of Chapters 2–9, identifying the key messages that the authors of those chapters have drawn out. We then go on to look across those chapters and identify commonalities and differences around four key themes: rhetoric (of ministers and other politicians, and others); rapidity (of reform and counter-reform of planning systems and processes); resourcing (reflecting upon the gap between what is proposed or set down in legislation and reality, often due to systemic and systematic underfunding of planning); and regressive outcomes (often as a consequence of one or all of the preceding three).

From housing to infrastructure: the story of 12 years of planning in a failed state

Chapter 2: 'The (housing) numbers game'

Since the latter decades of the 20th century, there has been an annual shortfall in the number of new homes constructed relative to housing demand. The planning system has often been accused of being the primary cause of this by governments of different political complexions. Chapter 2 examined the evidence that exists to back or refute this claim.

The chapter began with a stark reminder of the statistics around housing (un)affordability in England: whether owner occupation, private renting or social renting, the proportion of a household's income required to be spent on housing has increased since 2010, in some cases, dramatically. There are, of course, various contributory factors for this. The planning system can only really influence supply, so this chapter focused upon the numbers of housing delivered by the planning system relative to need/demand and explored the extent to which it is fair to blame the planning system for any undersupply, returning to 1979 as a starting point for analysis. The analysis shows that house price and housing unaffordability grew fairly consistently between the 1970s and 1990s, with a sharper increase since that time, ameliorated slightly by the slump following the 2008 financial crash. Housing supply in England, meanwhile, has rarely exceeded 150,000 per annum since the 1980s, when the last remnants of local authority building died away after Margaret Thatcher's anti-state reforms.

A significant factor in recent times has been the standard method for calculating the need for housing in each local authority – the regional planning system that used to undertake this task was abolished in 2010 after being described as a 'failed Soviet tractor style top-down' system (DCLG, 2010). After finding that local authorities were insufficiently compliant, the government introduced the standard method in 2018 to enforce a centralised target – this, in turn, decried by Liz Truss, short-lived prime minister, as a 'top-down, Whitehall-inspired Stalinist' approach (Malnick, 2022). As noted earlier, Rishi Sunak is to make the targets produced by the standard method advisory, allowing rural local authorities, where pressure for new homes is often highest, to deliver fewer homes if the target would 'significantly change the character of an area' (Allegretti, 2022). This highlights the tension between centralism and localism explored in Chapter 3. Chapter 2 concluded by reflecting upon the hollowness of housing targets in terms of considering housing as more than merely bricks and mortar, with the importance of a safe, secure and spacious home being emphasised by the COVID-19 pandemic.

Chapter 3: 'Localism: the peccadillos of a panacea'

Launched with much fanfare as a new scale and alternative to the regional planning structures established in England under the New Labour governments of the 1990s and 2000s, localism's most tangible effect on planning has been the rights conferred on local communities and businesses to prepare neighbourhood plans. With the government agenda for planning attempting to balance localism and centralism, Chapter 3 reflected on the legacies and lessons of almost a decade of experience of neighbourhood planning, as well as its future, which, though as uncertain as every other aspect of planning reform under the current 'administration', appears broadly secure.

The chapter started by reflecting on the green shoots of localism, the 'sick-inducing' (Merrick, 2014) press conference between the prime minister and deputy prime minister of the 2010–15 Coalition government. The 'programme for government' of that Coalition expounded upon the need to distribute power to people, and the Localism Act 2011 was a key component of converting that rhetoric into law. The introduction of neighbourhood planning, along with the abolition of regional planning, was, in turn, the most important part of that legislation for planning. These changes were intended to free communities from what was described as an intensely top-down and bureaucratic approach to planning (for housing) and empower them to create imaginative and context-specific plans for the places in which they lived and worked, with the end result of permitting more (housing) development than under the previous system. As Chapter 3, and many others, have demonstrated, this latter ambition was not realised, with the number of houses permitted and constructed showing no noticeable increase as a result of neighbourhood planning.

Chapter 3 went on to explore what neighbourhood planning has actually achieved, drawing on updated quantitative evidence on the scale and demographic spread of neighbourhood plans. It shows that while there have now been a fairly large number of neighbourhood plans begun and, indeed, completed (2,700 and 1,200, respectively), there are serious grounds for concern about the types of communities who are making most effective use of the powers in the Localism Act. Poorer communities are much less likely to begin the process of producing a neighbourhood plan and equally unlikely to then progress that plan to completion. Reasons for this include the long-established tendency for wealthier individuals and communities to be more likely to engage in planning activity of any sort (Matthews and Hastings, 2012) and the pre-existing systems of governance in rural (generally wealthier) parts of England that give them a 'head start' with neighbourhood planning. However, Chapter 3 also discussed other factors, such as the unequal impact of state spending due to 'austerity' (Sturzaker and Nurse, 2020) and, drawing on our own recent work, the apparent tendency for local politicians in some places to impose additional barriers on attempts by deprived communities to prepare neighbourhood plans (Sturzaker et al, 2022).

Chapter 3 suggested that this inequity in neighbourhood plan coverage is problematic in itself, as it excludes some communities from full participation in their government (Arnstein, 1969), but is more troubling because it entrenches and exacerbates spatial inequality. The chapter concludes by suggesting that the latest proposed reforms to planning will do little to address this issue.

Chapter 4: 'Planning at the "larger than local" scale: where next?'

Since 2010 and the abolition of the regional scale of planning in England, there have been different initiatives that have sought to address the 'larger than local' scale. Initially, under the 2010–15 Coalition government, an economically focused and partnership-governance model was privileged through the establishment of local enterprise partnerships (LEPs) with an economic development remit and weak ties to statutory planning (arrangements in other parts of the present UK remained more or less the same). In England, however, the 2010s saw a gradual 'hardening' of sub-regional governance arrangements in some places with the emergence of combined authorities (CAs), most focused on city-regional areas. In some instances, these have embarked on strategic planning processes under different powers and models, seen by some commentators as heralding a return to strategic planning reflection and capacity. However, the Planning White Paper and subsequent Levelling-up and Regeneration Bill have little further to say on the strategic scale of planning. Chapter 4 explored some of these issues based on the experience of the past decade and the current prospects for planning at the 'larger than local' scale.

Chapter 4 first set these changes to strategic planning within the broader context of the North–South divide, that is, the persistent economic gap between South East England and Northern England, and the recurring attempts to address that gap. Perhaps curiously, one of the first acts of the 2010–15 Coalition government was to abolish regional planning, long seen as a tool to assist in addressing regional inequalities. Regional planning was, however, seen as undemocratic, so it is equally curious that the LEPs that partially replaced it were arguably even less accountable (Bentley et al, 2010; Pugalis, 2011). LEPs were followed by a series of experiments with different forms of sub-regional governance across England, including so-called 'metro mayors', city deals and CAs. A key theme that unifies these experiments is their framing by, and reliance on, central government. None of them brought the tax-raising powers that some argue are essential for more effective sub-national governance.

There remains no sign of such powers in more recent changes, badged as part of the 'levelling up' agenda. Instead, levelling up has involved numerous schemes of grants and other funds to towns and local authorities across England. As we go on to discuss, the transparency and equity of these funding allocations leaves a great deal to be desired, and it seems that, for now, the 'pendulum' of British regionalism discussed in Chapter 4 has yet to swing back in the direction of more substantive changes to systems of governance. Critical voices even argue that the Levelling-up and Regeneration Bill will make matters much worse when it comes to planning at the 'larger than local' scale 'by abolishing the duty to co-operate and replacing it with a much weaker policy compliance test' (Ellis, 2022: 247), and continuing the voluntary basis on which instruments like joint spatial development strategies may be taken up.

Chapter 5: 'PD games: death comes to planning'

The extension of permitted development rights to make the conversion of buildings to residential use easier presents a typical example of the faith in deregulation as a pathway towards aligning development with demand. But what have been the impacts of this experimentation? Has it resulted in good-quality housing? And what might be the impacts of any extension of such rights on residential quality? These issues were explored in Chapter 5 through a case study focusing on health.

Chapter 5 explored how, beyond the bold claims for reform issued periodically by ministers over the last 12 years, fundamental changes to the secondary legislation that sets out much of the detail underpinning planning processes have made it much easier to convert buildings of varying types into housing. The General Permitted Development Order and Use Classes Order are examples of such secondary legislation. Introduced in 1948 to permit small-scale development and allow local authorities to focus their attentions on more substantive issues, through a series of amendments in 2010, 2012, 2013, 2015 and 2016, the scope of the legislation has been significantly broadened. As with many of the other changes to planning analysed in this book, the extension of permitted development has been justified as a means of reducing bureaucracy and increasing housing supply. However, as Chapter 5 made clear, in this context, 'bureaucracy' is vitally important in regulating the location and quality of homes, and much of the housing permitted by the recent changes is poor against both measures.

The chapter looked in particular at the implications for health of this example of deregulation in relation to three factors that planning, and planners, have lost control over as a result of development not requiring planning permission. The first of these is location, and evidence is drawn upon to show that many permitted development homes are poorly located in relation to green space, health services, shops or air quality. The second is space standards and the consequence of the decision to exempt permitted development homes from such standards until 2021. Much of the housing built was therefore of a size that many consider to be inappropriately small. The third is the loss of the ability to use land-value capture mechanisms, commonly used for 'standard' developments in England, to pay for facilities to mitigate some of these problems. The extension of permitted development, then, has manifestly reduced the quality of new homes built in England over the last decade and meant that many of the poorest in society are forced to live in conditions that those with more choices would consider appalling.

Chapter 6: 'Building beauty? Place and housing quality in the planning agenda'

Place and housing quality are a perennial debate in England. Periodic commissions and research studies have highlighted the failings of governance and production systems, which appear to consistently underperform in their roles as regards facilitating and delivering good design. However, this failure is arguably rooted in the ebb and flow in design interest and focus at the government level. The design debate has a cyclical character, forever shifting from a position of strong governance oversight to the view that the market will find its own quality threshold, and back again. Chapter 6 examined the 'failure' to deliver a consistent approach to place and housing quality over the last ten years. This period is one in which a legacy of design oversight by the Commission for Architecture and the Built Environment (CABE) was jettisoned in favour of 'market mechanisms'. Released from planning strictures, the market has been allowed to deliver the 'slums of the future' though the exercise of permitted development rights. However, elsewhere in the general market, the conservative 'beauty' aesthetic has been re-rooted in the form of the Office for Place, set up by the UK government in 2021, which marks the normal cyclical return to design oversight, though one that leans heavily on classical urbanism delivered through design coding. The return of this oversight has been welcomed by many, who view the Office for Place structure as something that can be evolved to correct at least some of the failings of design governance that have become apparent in the last decade.

The chapter started and ended by reflecting upon the new Office for Place for England and the increased use of codification in relation to the design of new development. As with some other topics discussed in this book, these ideas are not new and reflect another 'pendulum' of changing attitudes and structures of planning. From Ancient China, through Ancient Rome, the Renaissance and the Great Fire of London, to the garden cities of the early 20th century, design coding has been used to guide the development of urban form. Likewise, CABE was a precursor of the Office for Place, seeking to improve the quality of development in England.

CABE was one victim of the 'bonfire of the quangos' (Siddique, 2010) of the 2010–15 Coalition government, seen as being part of the bureaucracy that the incoming administration was determined to slim down. Of course, as noted earlier, without such 'bureaucracy', it is hard to control or guide the quality of development, and the emphasis on increasing the quantity of (housing) development since 2010 has seen a diminution of quality of design. The abolition of regional government, discussed at more length in other chapters, was also deleterious for design, as the regional development agencies had promoted and invested in design. Various studies, including those undertaken by Carmona et al (2020), have highlighted the impacts of these changes and the poor quality of much new development. Chapter 6 referred to another recurring trend, that is, the blaming of local authorities for problems caused by national government, but by 2018, the pendulum had swung back in favour of more control over design. The Building Better, Building Beautiful Commission (2018–20) led to the creation of the Office for Place and the creation of a National Model Design Code. How this centralisation and codification can be squared with localism and the ongoing emphasis on communities being involved in planning decision making has yet to become clear, as is the conflict between permitted development (discussed in Chapter 5) and design quality.

Chapter 7: 'Zoning in or zoning out? Lessons from Europe'

The critique of planning and new proposals to reform the planning system and 'rethink planning from first principles' led in 2020 to proposals for the introduction of a regulatory zonal planning system, which it was claimed would create a faster and better planning system than the existing discretionary approach. But are these proposals based on an oversimplified understanding of the differences between discretionary and regulatory models, neglecting, for example, the negotiation between stakeholders and the flexibility that also exists in regulatory planning systems?

Chapter 7 placed proposals for a zoning approach within the broader context of an increase in the use of rule-based instruments in the otherwise discretionary English planning system. These include the permitted development rights covered in Chapter 5 and the design codes discussed in Chapter 6. As Chapter 7 noted, the increasing prevalence of such instruments reflects a belief that they will result in quicker, more certain decisions for developers and better-quality outcomes. The chapter explores this belief by comparing the English experience with the zoning systems more common in other parts of Europe, starting by understanding how 'exceptional' the English approach actually is. Ostensibly, the discretion offered by the English system, with most decisions taken on a case-by-case basis, is starkly different from a zoning approach. However, in practice, zoning plans are heavily reliant on the ability of decision makers to grant exemptions in order to respond to inevitable changes in conditions. The extensive use of such exemptions, argued Chapter 7, may give local planning authorities more discretion than in the English system.

The key argument, therefore, is not a question of discretionary versus zoning planning in principle but how the system is used and whether the aim is one of ensuring development quality at sufficient quantity in the right place. Through detailed exploration of how planning works in Germany, the Netherlands and Switzerland, Chapter 7 revealed that these systems do deliver on this aim, in contrast to the English system (the housing outcomes of which are discussed in Chapter 2). Rather than the type of system in place, the bigger difference between those countries and England is that in the former, local authorities retain more power over development: until and unless they approve a land-use plan that accommodates the proposals of developers, development cannot take place. While development rights are usually granted where there is a demand for development, there is significantly less scope for developers to ignore the plans of local authorities by appealing to the government (in the form of the Planning Inspectorate in England).

Chapter 8: 'Planning and the environment in England, 2010–22: cutting "green crap", Brexit and environmental crises'

The 2020 proposed reforms of planning were launched with a critique of the impacts of environmental regulation on the speed of development – the idea of 'counting newts' as a constraint on development has been a popular trope in this recurring critique, used again by ex-Prime Minister Boris Johnson. Challenges to environmental protection have been partly allied with the decision to leave the European Union (EU). Claims that this would result in a 'Green Brexit' have always been met with caution by environmental planners and campaigners. Now it seems that the same narrative of 'constraint' warranting deregulation will be deployed domestically as the focus changes from the effects of EU environmental legislation on planning.

Chapter 8 began by acknowledging that it is not only the UK that has failed to adequately address major environmental problems; rather, this is a problem in many countries, with state environmental institutions reduced in power and capacity since the late 1990s – a trend exacerbated by the 2008 financial crash. Planning, both in the UK and elsewhere, emerged from public health and environmental concerns, and planning now has a wide environmental role. In England, developmental objectives have become the focus of planning systems, with environmental factors reduced to caveats in relation to those objectives – development can take place subject to certain environmental constraints. The broader transparency and openness of planning to participation and engagement is also critical to how well it considers environmental issues. The substantive analysis of Chapter 8 is divided into two chronological sections: 2010–16 and 2016–22.

The first period can be characterised by Prime Minister David Cameron's (2010–16) call to 'get rid of all the green crap'. Through this period, planning was scapegoated as a barrier to growth, with, as we have discussed in other chapters, deregulation and cuts to budgets being seen as ways to reduce bureaucracy. Local authorities and other state actors had their ability to deal with climate change and other environmental issues cut – decisions that seem staggeringly foolhardy at the time of writing as summer temperatures in the UK break records. The dismantling of policies for promoting zero-carbon homes, as well as the better insulation that involved, seems likewise profoundly unwise. Chapter 8 argues that one of the few brakes on the UK government going yet further was the EU and the requirements of the UK's membership thereof to adhere to various standards on habitats, air quality and impact assessment.

The second period, since the UK's decision to leave the EU, is therefore characterised by the extent of change possible since the brake of EU membership has no longer been in place. The *Planning for the Future* White Paper of 2020, the prompt for this book, presents environmental issues as primarily a local, aesthetic concern rather than concerning the life-supporting processes that are vital for human health and happiness. It is as yet unclear how strong, post-Brexit, wider processes of environmental governance will be – and, of course, how these will interact with whatever planning system emerges from the ongoing planning reform process. The chapter identified critical issues, such as biodiversity loss, the nature crisis and net zero, as being central to these questions.

Chapter 9: 'Stuck on infrastructure? Planning for the transformative effects of transport infrastructure'

A strong sub-theme of the debate on planning is that relating to infrastructure, with comparisons being made in the press with the time it takes to build projects in other jurisdictions. The infrastructure planning regime has been reformed in response. But is planning the real reason for long timeframes in project development and implementation? The High Speed Two (HS2) project is due to be complete in 2040, which will be some 76 years after the Shinkansen system started operating in Japan; 76 years before that was 1888, the year of the first 'Race to the North' as operators of the West and East Coast Main Lines in Britain accelerated their services between London and Edinburgh; and 76 years before that was 1812, when the Middleton Railway, serving coal pits at Leeds in England, became the first to use steam locomotives successfully in regular service. These are long timescales. Chapter 9 questions whether planning is really the cause of this?

Chapter 9 reviewed the evidence underpinning claims that investment in infrastructure like high-speed rail can help address regional inequalities. There is unquestionably some evidence that it can, though this is dependent on factors including the adaptability of regional economies. The chapter concludes that *intra*-regional inequality is perhaps as important as *inter*-regional, yet it is rarely a focus of discussions on infrastructure. Chapter 9 then traced the evolution of HS2, noting the absence of strategic regional government (discussed in more depth in Chapter 4), which would otherwise be a key factor in the extent to which infrastructure delivers regional economic benefits. The wider context of rail infrastructure, specifically, the poor and worsening quality of existing rail lines, and the lack of any coherent plan to address this, is highlighted as a major issue. While the chapter acknowledges that transport investment alone will not rebalance the UK economy, such 'boring' spending on local infrastructure is argued to be essential. Similarly, although decentralisation and devolution are welcome, fragmentation challenges must be overcome to avoid uncoordinated policies between national-level infrastructure planning decisions like HS2 and territorial planning and place making at intra-regional scale. Transport, and HS2, must be seen as one element of a comprehensive approach – it is safe to say that there is little evidence of such an approach among the policy announcements and interventions of the last 12 years.

Cross-cutting themes and recurring findings

In the previous section, we summarised the findings of Chapters 2–9 of this book. Now, we look across those chapters to identify cross-cutting themes and recurring findings. We organise these into four sections:

- Rhetoric: the use by government ministers and others of powerful language, often critical of the planning system and/or the planners who work within it, to justify the changes they wish to make to how planning operates. The use of discourse to justify the actions of politicians is, of course, *de rigueur* – politicians who did not make bombastic claims would be extremely unusual. We highlight the use of language here because it reinforces a clear pattern of 'attack' (Lord and Tewdwr-Jones, 2014) upon planners and planning, which we have suggested elsewhere contributes to poorer planning outcomes (Sturzaker and Lord, 2018). It is therefore far from harmless.
- Rapidity: the speed with which changes to legislation and policy have been introduced since 2010, often replicated by the speed of further changes to remedy ill-thought-through or executed reforms. This characteristic can be seen from the earliest days of the 2010–15 Coalition government, when the wide-ranging Localism & Decentralisation Bill (later the Localism Act 2011) was introduced with no preceding White or Green Paper, something that was unusual at the time. This pattern has continued, with real impacts on planning – changes to planning that are then amended or withdrawn have significant implications for local authorities trying to implement national policy, who may waste many months on drafting local plans, for example.
- Resourcing: across the chapters in this book, we have heard about ambitious plans from the UK government for planning in England. The same is true, of course, for many other policy sectors over the last 12 years, from education to health. In nearly all instances, however, the parallel programme of 'austerity' that has been implemented has severely limited the opportunities for the delivery of these plans. Cuts to local government budgets of 86 per cent over this period have meant that the grand promises have not yielded results on anywhere near the scale promised.
- Regressive outcomes: from the recent claims made around 'levelling up', back through the preceding decade's talk of rebalancing the UK, ministers have claimed that the changes they are making will improve lives and outcomes for all across diverse places. This is unsurprising: explicitly stating that things would get worse for many people, particularly the

poor, is an unlikely vote winner. However, the previous three recurring factors, along with other drivers, including seemingly ideology and electoral tactics, have, in fact, had this result. Challenges like Brexit have exacerbated this, notably, impacting hardest places and communities that were already 'left behind' with higher food price inflation (Bakker, et al, 2023) and the loss of multiannual EU structural funds. But, even notwithstanding that decision, there is evidence from multiple policy areas that the consequence of many of the changes to planning since 2010 has been to make the poor poorer.

We now expand upon each of these points.

Rhetoric

The first thing to note here is the striking similarity between the language being used in 2010 with that deployed today. The Conservative Party's *Open Source Planning Green Paper*, published in February 2010, referred to the planning system as being 'almost wholly negative and adversarial ... [creating] bureaucratic barriers rather than enabling communities to formulate a positive vision of their future development' (Conservative Party, 2010: 1). It said that there would be 'Radical change' in order that 'Communities should be given the greatest possible opportunity to have their say' (Conservative Party, 2010: 1). Ten years later, Boris Johnson's foreword to the Planning White Paper, presumably unconsciously, included uncanny echoes of that language. He described the planning system as 'outdated and ineffective', delivering 'nowhere near enough homes in the right places' (MHCLG, 2020: 6). He too promised 'radical reform' to 'give you a greater say over what gets built in your community', and a planning system that, by removing discretion, would be 'simpler, clearer and quicker' (MHCLG, 2020: 6).

The secretaries of state in charge of planning in 2010 and 2020 were also saying very similar things. In 2010, Eric Pickles was effusive about how the government were freeing people from the constraints of the previous planning system: 'Communities will no longer have to endure the previous government's failed Soviet tractor style top-down planning targets ... regional plans ... were a national disaster that robbed local people of their democratic voice, alienating them and entrenching opposition against new development' (DCLG, 2010). In 2020, Robert Jenrick, in his own foreword to the White Paper, likewise promised that the government's reforms would ensure that 'Communities will be reconnected to a planning process that is supposed to serve them, with residents more engaged over what happens in their areas' (MHCLG, 2020: 8).

Specific elements of critique have included that 'Planning "isn't brain surgery"' (Carpenter, 2011) and so should be opened up to the public; yet, nine years later, the White Paper concluded that the planning system 'is too complex' (MHCLG, 2020: 10). As we have discussed throughout this book, housing is seemingly an obsession with the Conservative Party, with Pickles in 2010 proclaiming that the reforms promoted at that time would increase house building. The White Paper, however, identified the fact that 'planning simply does not lead to enough homes being built' (MHCLG, 2020: 20). Another obsession is bureaucracy, with: Pickles advocating 'unshackling developers from a legacy of bureaucratic planning' in 2011 (DCLG, 2011); CABE being accused of operating as a 'design police' (Sharro, 2010); and Johnson decrying the 'newt-counting delays in our system' and promising to 'scythe through red tape' (Johnson, 2020).

At the same time, aware of the enormous symbolic power of the environment, ministers are enduringly keen to emphasise their protection thereof. David Cameron claimed that his was 'the greenest government ever' (quoted in Carter and Clements, 2015: 210). In 2015, the extension of permitted development was promoted because it would help in 'protecting our precious green belt' (MHCLG, 2015), and the 2020 White Paper stated that reforms would protect 'our unmatchable architectural heritage and natural environment' (MHCLG, 2020: 10).

A neutral observer might wonder how it is possible for planning to be simultaneously faster, more inclusive, less bureaucratic, more certain, greener and yet deliver more housing. As we have seen throughout this book, despite their grand claims, ministers have yet to devise a planning system that does indeed deliver on all those fronts.

Rapidity

As noted earlier, a pattern of quick, and perhaps ill-thought-out, changes to planning and governance was set in 2010, when the Localism & Decentralisation Bill was published without a preceding White Paper. This was criticised implicitly by the Communities and Local Government Committee (House of Commons, 2011: 18) and explicitly by others, including Friends of the Earth (Parliament.UK, 2011). This resulted in a lack of broad consultation on the overall approach sought by the government, and there was a similar lack of debate on the bill itself.[1] A great deal of the detail on aspects of planning reform, including neighbourhood planning, was contained in 'secondary' legislation that was published later and/or amendments to previous legislation. This meant that the neighbourhood planning process was 'complex' (Sturzaker and Gordon, 2017: 1329) – ironic given the claim mentioned earlier by a minister that planning is not 'brain surgery'.

This complexity is echoed in other aspects of planning. Permitted development rights, as discussed in Chapter 5, have been expanded in each of the years of 2010, 2012, 2013, 2015, 2016, 2020 and 2021. Keeping up with this pace of change is not just a problem for planners like us who have to teach our students about the constantly changing landscape of planning law! Needless to say, this does not make planning any easier to engage with for the public, and planning practitioners themselves have found it increasingly difficult to navigate the system. Commenting on the frequency of amendments even to the primary legislation establishing the planning system, Pritchard (2022: 244) thus notes that it is 'very difficult for a non-lawyer to understand exactly what is being amended by any particular clause and to what effect'. The standard method for establishing housing need is another area that has seen considerable change since it was introduced in 2018 – with a 'clarification' in 2019, changes proposed in 2020 and further suggestions that it would be amended again, perhaps in response to political pressure from Conservative members of parliament (MPs) (Donnelly, 2020). As noted earlier, the current UK prime minister has made the targets emerging from the standard method optional, which evidence suggests will see many local authorities seeking to reduce the number of homes they build.

The context within which planning takes place, particularly at the 'larger than local' scale, has also been subject to waves of change. The regional scale favoured by the Labour government of 1997–2010 was rapidly de-prioritised and de-funded by the abolition of, among other things, regional spatial strategies, government offices for the regions, regional development agencies and regional assemblies. LEPs were a partial replacement for these, intended to be led by the private sector and with boundaries determined by the places involved, ostensibly reflecting 'functional geographies', not imposed from above. 'Regional' remains a word scarcely seen in policy or rhetoric, but the anomaly of England being the only country in Europe without any form of required, as opposed to voluntary, strategic planning, and the problems this causes, was quite quickly remedied. An amendment to the Localism Act 2011 allowed for the creation of 'city deals' between city-regions and the government, which could involve strategic planning. City deals were signed from 2012 onwards. As noted in Chapter 4, the relationship between City Deals and elected police and crime commissioners (from 2012 onwards) has never been clear, with the elected 'metro mayors' (from 2017 onwards) adding to the complexity. At the inter-regional level, initiatives like the Northern Powerhouse, Transport for the North and the Midlands Engine, promoted from around 2014 onwards, have briefly sparkled but lacked proper financial support and, certainly in the case of Transport for the North, have been 'de-fanged' if they became too influential. The latest proposed legislation, the Levelling-up and Regeneration Bill also leaves strategic planning at the 'larger than local' scale as a 'purely voluntary pursuit outside of London' (Pritchard, 2022: 245), meaning that 'the question of how to effectively manage the key strands of strategic geography in England, let alone the development of a national strategy have been ignored' (Ellis, 2022: 246).

Resourcing

'Non ringfenced government grants to local authorities have fallen from £32.2 billion in 2009/10 to £4.5 billion in 2019/20' (Arnold and Stirling, 2019: 1). This has fallen further since then, despite the 'levelling up' funds discussed in Chapter 4. Arnold and Stirling predicted a funding gap of over £25 billion by 2024/25. While state spending has fallen across the board in the period since 2010, the cuts to local authority budgets have been particularly severe: between 2009/10 and 2018/19, government departmental spending was cut by 11 per cent, but the budget for the Ministry of Housing, Communities & Local Government (now Department for Levelling Up, Housing and Communities) was cut by an astonishing 86 per cent (Arnold and Stirling, 2019). These cuts were not spread equally across the country, as we return to later, and nor were they spread equally across local authority departments. Unsurprisingly, local government has sought to protect the most vulnerable, seeking to limit the cuts to social care, education and so on. Planning, conversely, has seen more significant cuts in spending, with one study estimating a reduction of 42 per cent between 2009/10 and 2017/18 (Kenny, 2019). Some changes to planning law and policy have reduced local authority budgets further: by removing some development from planning control, permitted development legislation also removes the requirement to pay a fee for consideration of a planning application. At the same time as the cuts noted here, local authorities are being asked to do more, in all these areas and more – Arnold and Stirling (2019) highlight additional duties in relation to public health, social care and homelessness, all of which are likely to receive a higher priority than planning.

These reductions in budgets and increased workload have, of course, impacted upon different aspects of planning. In Chapter 2, we read about the constraints placed on local authorities to plan properly for the optimum type, quality and location of housing. In Chapter 3, the limited spread of neighbourhood planning was partly ascribed to an under-resourcing of the system since its inception. At the strategic scale, Mayor of Greater Manchester Andy Burnham was eloquent about the reliance of CAs on central funding and their lack of capacity to generate revenue. Diminished local authority planning teams, perhaps now without any form of specialist design expertise, means that local scrutiny of design is impaired; likewise, in the absence of a body like CABE, this gap cannot be filled through other means. An alarming two thirds of local authorities have cut back on their climate-change activity according to Chapter 8, and, again, the abolition of such oversight bodies as the Sustainable Development Commission exacerbates the issue. Overall, the picture is not encouraging in general and is particularly gloomy for those living in more deprived communities.

Regressive outcomes

The significant cuts to central and local government spending discussed in the preceding section have not been evenly distributed across the country – indeed, far from it. Hastings et al (2015) and Lowndes and Gardner (2016) are among those who have plotted the regressive nature of cuts, with more deprived local authorities seeing sharper reductions in budgets. This has had the effect of reducing the 'premium' on expenditure per capita once enjoyed by the most deprived quintile of local authorities from 46 to 19 per cent (Arnold and Stirling, 2019: 3). When he was Chancellor of the Exchequer, present Prime Minister Rishi Sunak was recorded boasting about this in Tunbridge Wells, one of the more affluent parts of England,[2] making explicit what has seemingly been an implicit aim of government policy since 2010. What have been the impacts of this approach in relation to planning and development?

Poor-quality housing is a characteristic of England, with inadequate insulation, small rooms and lack of access to high-quality outdoor space problems that afflict many of us. As with many other parts of life, these problems are worse if you are poor. The poorest have less choice about where they live and appear to be the main target for some of the worse permitted development conversions of offices and so on. In turn, they are the most exposed to such problems as the impacts of climate change or COVID-19, having homes that are less resilient and smaller, and in locations like industrial estates. This leads to worse health outcomes, in turn, bringing, alongside the obvious problems for those individuals affected, more pressure on local authority budgets.

The cuts to those budgets discussed earlier were intended to be eased by new sources of funding, such as the Towns Fund or the Levelling Up Fund. However, as discussed in Chapter 4, these funds have, to an almost ludicrous degree, been allocated to areas suffering less from extant budget cuts. A total of 87 per cent of Towns Fund allocations have gone to areas with Conservative MPs, seemingly in direct conflict with advice from civil servants. The Levelling Up Fund, likewise, has seen funding going to Conservative seats, including that of the current prime minister, one of the least deprived places in England. As Chapter 4 concluded, this approach gives the lie to any notion of true levelling up, inevitably meaning that some places will remain 'left behind'.

As a consequence of all that has been discussed in this chapter – indeed, this book – there are limited tools available to planners to try and redress the balance. Neighbourhood planning, one of the flagship planning policies of the Localism Act 2011, has been shown to benefit those who are wealthier in various ways. The lack of any statutory strategic planning across most of England means that the tools that may historically have been available to allocate development across local authority boundaries are likewise absent. The net result of all this is that the disadvantaged are losing out, and not only is planning not helping, but in some instances, due to the centrally determined resource constraints and policy contradictions that planners have to labour under, it is actively making things worse.

Conclusion

The *Open Source Planning Green Paper* of 2010 (Conservative Party, 2010) contained ambitious proposals for radical changes to planning at every scale, from national to community. This was accompanied by rhetoric advocating a move to a 'post-bureaucratic age' in relation to planning and other functions of government (Cameron, 2009). Perhaps inevitably, upon collision with the weight of that bureaucracy and the history of planning legislation stretching back more than 100 years, those proposals were watered down. Nevertheless, the Localism Act 2011 and many subsequent pieces of primary and secondary legislation did enact significant changes to the structures and processes of planning. Therefore, the planning system in place at the time of writing at the end of 2022 is quite different from that of May 2010, when the Conservative-dominated Coalition government came to power.

This, in itself, is as it should be – we agree with the following, expressed so cogently by the Uthwatt Committee of 1942:

> Town and country planning is not an end in itself; it is the instrument by which to secure that the best use is made of the available land in the interests of the community as a whole. By nature it cannot be static. It must advance with the condition of society it is designed to serve. (Uthwatt, 1942: 12)

Neither ourselves nor any of the authors of the contributions to this book are zealous defenders of some previous configuration of planning laws and policies; rather, we firmly believe that planning must change as society changes. We do, however, hold that certain principles must be at the core of whatever approach to planning society determines is appropriate. These include: that planning must consider both strategic and tactical matters (that is, that there should be some form of larger-than-local or strategic planning); that local communities must be given a strong voice but that there should be checks and balances to avoid the 'tyranny of the majority'; that progressive outcomes that balance different interests and policy objectives should be the aim of every planning decision made; and that all of this must be appropriately resourced by the state. These principles are, we suggest, widely understood and agreed upon by planning scholars around the world.

It is our view, supported by the evidence in this book and studies of planning, local government and related fields, that the last 12 years represent an unprecedented failure of the UK government to design and implement a functioning planning system. In relation to the first three of the 'Four Rs' we have discussed in this chapter – rhetoric, rapidity of reform and resourcing – ministers have repeatedly made poor decisions and made the jobs of planners harder than they already were. This has, in turn, greatly exacerbated the 'Fourth R': regressive outcomes.

Whether by accident or design, the Conservative-led UK governments of 2010–15, 2015–17, 2017–19 and 2019 onwards have consistently undermined principles of effective planning, to the extent that some have argued that the planning settlement of the Town & Country Planning Act 1947 has effectively been destroyed (Ellis, 2021). In that context, optimistic souls might have hoped that the radical nature of the 2020 Planning White Paper might have led to an exciting re-imagining of planning in England. However, as others have pointed out, the White Paper sought 'the wrong answers to the wrong questions' (Booth et al, 2020). As we have shown in this book, zoning and the other proposed, and instituted, reforms to planning in England seem unlikely to address the long term issues the nation faces.

We do not wish to finish this book on an entirely gloomy note; despite the catalogue of failings we have outlined in this text, there is room for optimism. There are many ideas out there that could contribute to a re-imagining of planning – from the Town & Country Planning Association's Raynsford Review[3] to the Royal Town Planning Institute's Plan the World we Need campaign.[4] What is needed is a successful, not failing, state that can devote the time and energy needed to reinvigorating the planning project. We can only hope that, at some point soon, this becomes the reality. In the meantime, we will continue to work within the cracks of the system we have and make the case for a better alternative.

Epilogue: after 2022 …

It would be hard to sign off a volume like this without commenting on events since the first draft of the text was completed in August 2022. In this time, the UK has seen the fleeting premiership of Liz Truss and the economic turmoil and fallout from the 'mini-budget' of her Chancellor of the Exchequer, Kwasi Kwarteng. Meanwhile, her replacement, Rishi Sunak, has vaunted the benefits of a new agreement with the EU on Northern Ireland as it places the region in an 'unbelievably special position' with access to both the UK and EU markets, making it the 'world's most exciting economic zone' (cited in Walker, 2023) – a privilege the whole UK enjoyed before the 'Brexit' he campaigned for! As regards the

Kwarteng 'mini-budget', many commentators have linked this to the 'hard' application of the economic prescriptions of some of the same think tanks that have helped to construct and sustain the narrative of planning failure introduced in the first chapter. Commenting on the Kwarteng mini-budget, Mark Littlewood of the free-market think tank the Institute of Economic Affairs, for example, excitedly gushed that 'This isn't a trickle-down budget, it's a boost-up budget. The government has announced a radical set of policies to increase Britain's prosperity' (IEA, 2022). Back in the real world, it was subsequently reported that between the date of the 'boost-up' mini-budget announcement on 23 September 2022 and Friday 14 October, the Bank of England spent around £65 billion to try and restore some stability to Britain's bond market. However, within weeks of this reputation-shredding, internationally humiliating fiasco, in response to a speech to the Confederation of British Industry (CBI) by new Prime Minister Rishi Sunak, Matthew Lesh (2022: emphases added), Head of Public Policy at the Institute of Economic Affairs, was opining that 'Sunak entirely failed to discuss the *single biggest handbrake on our prosperity*: Britain's broken planning system', which 'hampers the construction of infrastructure, factories, lab space and housing, which are all essential to innovation and growth'. It seems that one cannot keep an opaquely funded free-marketeering think tank down and that planning in particular is always kept on stand-by to be wheeled out as and when needed for any 'Look at that guy!' moments designed to distract attention from deeper and more egregious failures of government policy. This example also serves to finally remind us that while the preceding chapters have been critical of the record of governments since 2010, the seemingly perennial narrative of planning failure is not solely promulgated by a given administration or by one party. Wolf (2023), in reporting on two recent reports on the state of the UK's regional economy/ies – 'Tackling the UK's regional economic inequality', co-authored by former Labour Party Shadow Chancellor Ed Balls (Stansbury et al, 2023), and 'Capital losses: the role of London in the UK's productivity puzzle' from the Centre for Cities (Rodrigues and Bridgett, 2023) – notes that their 'analyses do come up with one common conclusion: the country needs a radical liberalisation of controls on land use'. Meanwhile, the Labour Party's '5 missions for a better Britain' (Labour Party, 2023) refers to 'Updating our planning system to remove barriers to investment in new industries.' It seems clear that regardless of what the future days hold, the themes explored in this book will retain their relevance. While needing to remain positive about well-considered proposals for change, planners will also need to be on their guard against taking the fall for any failings for which they are not responsible and that not infrequently arise from ill-conceived centrally directed planning policies whose impacts they have warned about.

Notes

1   See: www.theguardian.com/law/2011/aug/02/localism-bill-debate-rush
2   See: www.theguardian.com/politics/2022/aug/05/video-emerges-of-rishi-sunak-admitt ing-to-taking-money-from-deprived-areas
3   See: https://tcpa.org.uk/resources/the-raynsford-review-of-planning/
4   See: www.rtpi.org.uk/new/our-campaigns/plan-the-world-we-need/

References

Allegretti, A. (2022) 'Sunak to scrap housebuilding targets after pressure from Tory MPs', *The Guardian*, 5 December. Available at: www.theguard ian.com/politics/2022/dec/05/sunak-backs-down-on-housebuilding-targ ets-after-pressure-from-tory-mps

Arnold, S. and Stirling, A. (2019) *Councils in Crisis: Local Government Austerity 2009/10–2024/25*, London: New Economics Foundation.

Arnstein, S.R. (1969) 'A ladder of citizen participation', *Journal of the American Planning Association*, 35(4): 216–24.

Bakker, J.D., Datta, N., Davies, R. and De Lyon, J. (2023) 'Brexit and consumer food prices: 2023 update – CEP BREXIT ANALYSIS NO. 18, London: Centre for Economic Performance, London School of Economics and Political Science. Available at: https://cep.lse.ac.uk/pubs/download/ brexit18.pdf

Bentley, G., Bailey, D. and Shutt, J. (2010) 'From RDAs to LEPs: a new localism? Case examples of West Midlands and Yorkshire', *Local Economy*, 25: 535–57.

Booth, P., Bradley, Q., Brownill, S., Chapman, K., Clifford, B., Colenutt, B. et al (2020) 'The wrong answers to the wrong questions', The Town & Country Planning Association. Available at: www.tcpa.org.uk/the-wrong-answers-to-the-wrong-questions

Cameron, D. (2009) 'A new politics: the post-bureaucratic age', *The Guardian*, 25 May. Available at: www.theguardian.com/commentisfree/ 2009/may/25/david-cameron-a-new-politics3

Carmona, M., Alwarea, A., Giordano, V., Gusseinova, A. and Olaleye, F. (2020) 'A housing design audit for England'. Available at: https://indd. adobe.com/view/23366ae1-8f97-455d-896a-1a9934689cd8

Carpenter, J. (2011) 'Planning "isn't brain surgery", says communities minister', Planning Resource. Available at: https://www.planningresou rce.co.uk/article/1093322/planning-isnt-brain-surgery-says-communit ies-minister

Carter, N. and Clements, B. (2015) 'From "greenest government ever" to "get rid of all the green crap": David Cameron, the Conservatives and the environment', *British Politics*, 10(2): 204–25.

Conservative Party (2010) *Open Source Planning Green Paper*, London: The Conservative Party.

DCLG (Department for Communities and Local Government) (2010) 'Eric Pickles puts stop to flawed regional strategies: revoking the regional strategies'. Available at: https://www.gov.uk/government/news/eric-pick les-puts-stop-to-flawed-regional-strategies-today

DCLG (2011) 'Growth plan to transform empty offices into new homes'. Available at: https://www.gov.uk/government/news/growth-plan-to-transform-empty-offices-into-new-homes

Donnelly, M. (2020) 'MHCLG confirms that proposed new standard housing need method will be "rebalanced" to focus on urban areas', Planning Resource. Available at: www.planningresource.co.uk/article/1700151/ mhclg-confirms-proposed-new-standard-housing-need-method-will-reb alanced-focus-urban-areas

Ellis, H. (2021) 'The spirit of '47', Town and Country Planning, May/June: 155–6.

Ellis, H. (2022) 'The Levelling-up and Regeneration Bill: fiddling while England Burns?', Town and Country Planning, July/August: 246–9.

Hastings, A., Bailey, N., Bramley, G., Gannon, M. and Watkins, D. (2015) The Cost of the Cuts: The Impact on Local Government and Poorer Communities, York: Joseph Rowntree Foundation.

House of Commons (2011) Communities and Local Government Committee: Localism – Third Report of Session 2010–12, London: The Stationery Office.

IEA (Institute of Economic Affairs) (2022) 'IEA responds to mini budget statement'. Available at: https://iea.org.uk/media/iea-responds-to-mini-budget-statement/

Johnson, B. (2020) PM economy speech, 30 June. Available at: https://www.gov.uk/government/speeches/pm-economy-speech-30-june-2020

Kenny, T. (2019) Resourcing Public Planning: Five Stories about Local Authority Planning in England and Recommendations for the Next Chapter, London: Royal Town Planning Institute.

Labour Party (2023) '5 missions for a better Britain: secure the highest sustained growth in the G7'. Available at: https://labour.org.uk/missions/growing-the-economy/

Lesh, M. (2022) 'The prime minister's words are no substitute for bold action to turbocharge innovation', Institute of Economic Affairs, 21 November. Available at: https://iea.org.uk/media/the-prime-ministers-words-are-no-substitute-for-bold-action-to-turbocharge-innovation/

Lord, A. and Tewdwr-Jones, M. (2014) 'Is planning "under attack"? Chronicling the deregulation of urban and environmental planning in England', European Planning Studies, 22(2): 345–61.

Lowndes, V. and Gardner, A. (2016) 'Local governance under the Conservatives: super-austerity, devolution and the "smarter state"', Local Government Studies, 42(3): 357–75.

MHCLG (Ministry of Housing, Communities and Local Government) (2015) 'Thousands more homes to be developed in planning shake up'. Available at: www.gov.uk/government/news/thousands-more-homes-to-be-developed-in-planning-shake-up

MHCLG (2020) *Planning for the Future: White Paper August 2020*, London: MHCLG.

Malnick, E. (2022) 'Liz Truss: I'll put an end to "Stalinist" housing targets', *The Telegraph*, 16 July. Available at: www.telegraph.co.uk/politics/2022/07/16/liz-truss-put-end-stalinist-housing-targets/

Matthews, P. and Hastings, A. (2012) 'Middle-class political activism and middle-class advantage in relation to public services: a realist synthesis of the evidence base', *Social Policy and Administration*, 47(1): 72–92.

Merrick, J. (2014) 'Cameron/Clegg Rose Garden love-in was "sickening", says Lib Dem adviser Julia Goldsworthy', *The Independent*, 16 March. Available at: www.independent.co.uk/news/uk/politics/cameron-clegg-rose-garden-lovein-was-sickening-says-lib-dem-adviser-julia-goldswor thy-9194832.html

Parliament.UK (2011) 'Localism Bill: memorandum submitted by Friends of the Earth'. Available at: https://publications.parliament.uk/pa/cm201 011/cmpublic/localism/memo/loc111.htm

Pritchard, A. (2022) 'A planning bill in all but name', *Town and Country Planning*, July/August: 244–5.

Pugalis, L. (2011) 'Look before you LEP', *Journal of Urban Regeneration and Renewal*, 5: 7–22.

Rodrigues, G. and Bridgett, S. (2023) 'Capital losses: the role of London in the UK's productivity puzzle', Centre for Cities, March. Available at: www.centreforcities.org/wp-content/uploads/2023/03/London-produ ctivity-March-2023.pdf

Sharro, K. (2010) 'Why not abolish CABE altogether?', *Design Curial*, 14 September. Available at: www.designcurial.com/news/why-not-abol ish-cabe-altogether-

Siddique, H. (2010) 'Ministers plan to axe 177 quangos, according to leaked list', *The Guardian*, 24 September. Available at: www.theguardian.com/politics/2010/sep/24/bonfire-of-quangos-177-abolished

Stansbury, A., Turner, D. and Balls E. (2023) 'Tackling the UK's regional economic inequality: binding constraints and avenues for policy intervention', M-RCBG Associate Working Paper No. 198. Available at: https://dash.harvard.edu/bitstream/handle/1/37374470/198_AWP_ final.pdf?sequence=1&isAllowed=y

Sturzaker, J. and Gordon, M. (2017) 'Democratic tensions in decentralised planning: rhetoric, legislation and reality in England', *Environment and Planning C: Politics and Space*, 35(7): 1324–39. Available at: https://doi.org/doi:10.1177/2399654417697316

Sturzaker, J. and Lord, A. (2018) 'Fear: an underexplored motivation for planners' behaviour?', *Planning Practice & Research*, 33(4): 359–71.

Sturzaker, J. and Nurse, A. (2020) *Rescaling Urban Governance: Planning, Localism and Institutional Change*, Bristol: Policy Press.

Sturzaker, J., Sykes, O. and Dockerill, B. (2022) 'Disruptive localism: how far does clientelism shape the prospects of neighbourhood planning in deprived urban communities?', *Planning Theory & Practice*, 23(1): 43–59.

Uthwatt, A.A. (1942) *Final Report (of the) Expert Committee on Compensation and Betterment*, London: HMSO.

Walker, P. (2023) 'Sunak draws ire after hailing Northern Ireland's access to UK and EU markets', *The Guardian*, 28 February. Available at: https://www.theguardian.com/politics/2023/feb/28/sunak–northern–ireland–access–uk–eu–markets–trade–deal

Wolf, M. (2023) 'The UK economy has two regional problems, not one', *Financial Times*, 5 March. Available at: www.ft.com/content/5b1c5cc4–6961–4bbc–9132–ac6472796395

Index